FIELD GUIDE TO DINOSAURS

STEVE BRUSATTE

Quercus

FIELD GUIDE TO DINOSAURS

STEVE BRUSATTE

Quercus

CONTENTS

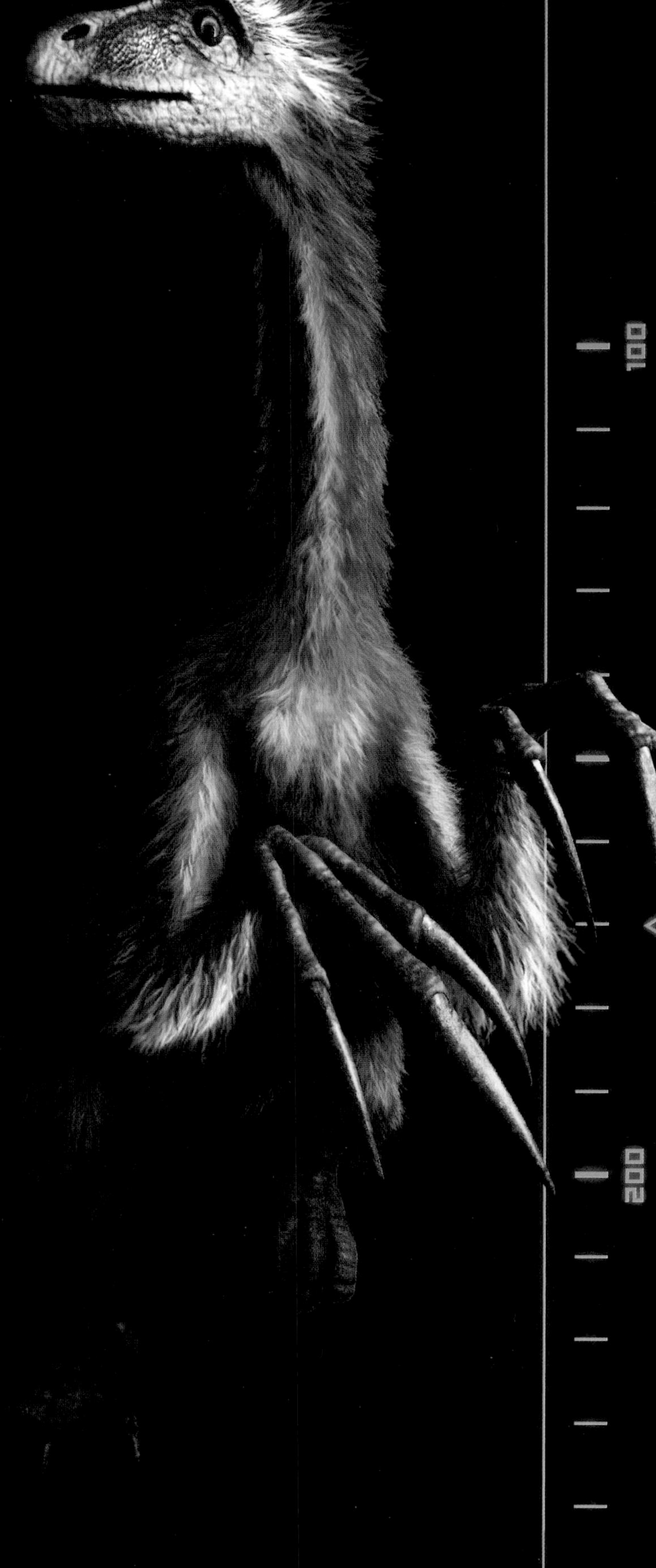

INTRODUCTION

Prepare yourself for the most incredible safari imaginable: a journey back in time through the Triassic, Jurassic and Cretaceous worlds to meet the most astonishing creatures ever to have walked the Earth. Emerging as small carnivores over 230 million years ago, the dinosaurs expanded into a dizzying array of species that dominated the Earth for 160 million years until a sudden catastrophe ended their reign.

On this journey you will observe nearly 90 dinosaurs in close-up using ultra high-tech imaging equipment from the safety of a time-travelling armoured personnel carrier. Data streams and digital displays provide the very latest information on these creatures: from their height, weight, habitats and habits to their formidable attack and defence systems, making this the ultimate field guide to dinosaurs.

SPOTTER GUIDE

Designed for quick and easy identification of several species at a glance, these pages provide key information that allows you to pinpoint distinguishing features of similar animals.

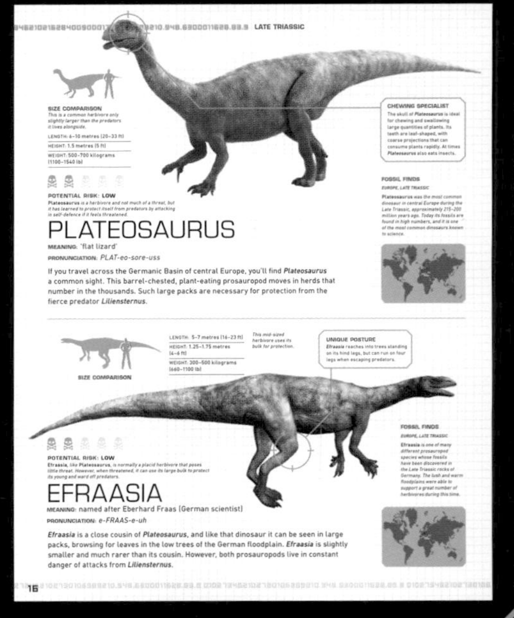

SITTING UP FRONT

Our time machine allows you to view dinosaurs in several different ways. The first of these is through the toughened glass of the windows, allowing you to get thrillingly close to ferocious teeth and powerful claws while remaining safe inside the vehicle's armoured plating.

DIGITAL DISPLAY

When a dinosaur comes into view, you can consult a fold-out digital screen to get the basic facts about the species right in front of you.

FOSSIL FINDS

Want to know where a particular dinosaur has been discovered? This box tells you where palaeontologists have unearthed the bones and pinpoints the place on a present-day map.

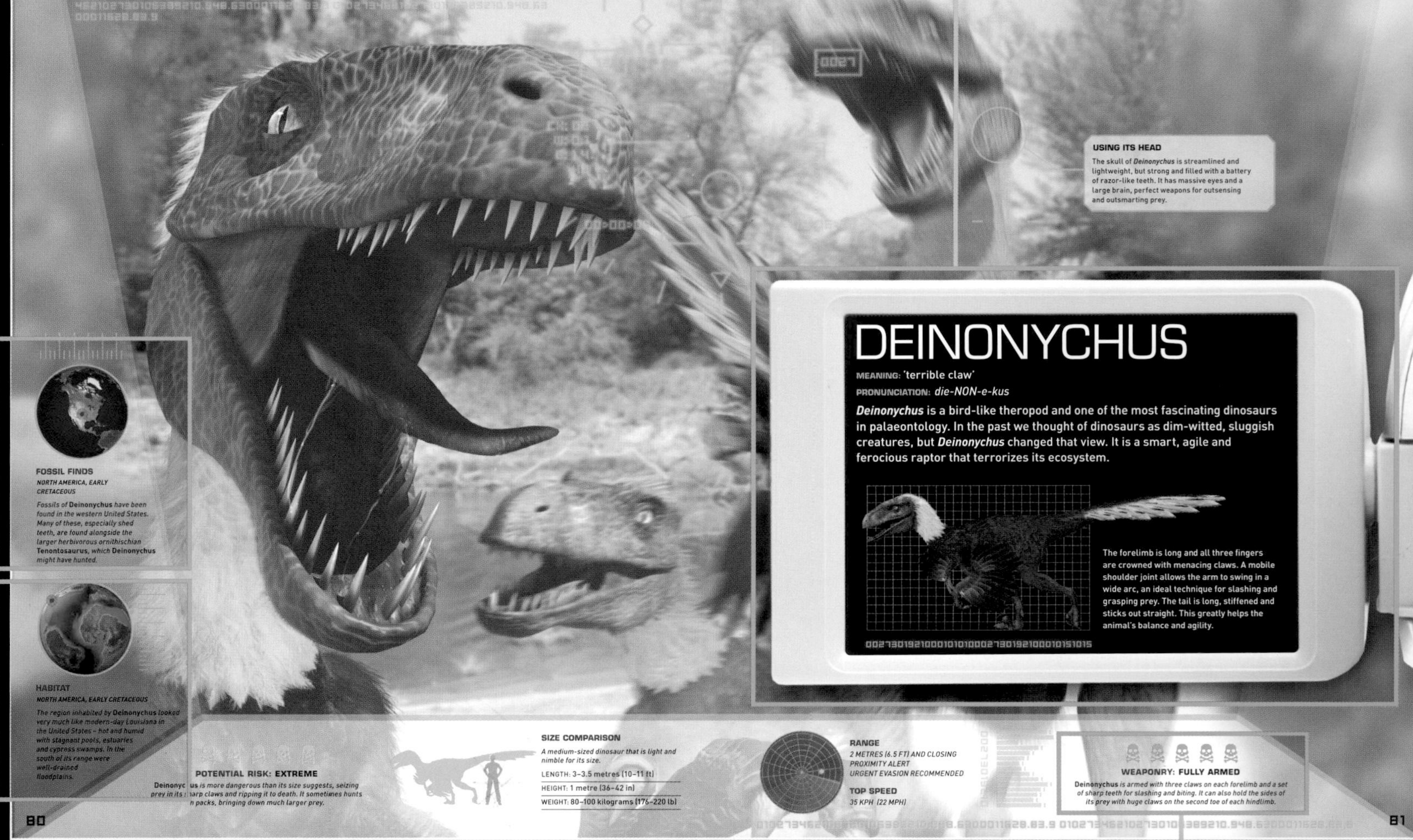

USING ITS HEAD
The skull of Deinonychus is streamlined and lightweight, but strong and filled with a battery of razor-like teeth. It has massive eyes and a large brain, perfect weapons for outsensing and outsmarting prey.
DEINONYCHUS
MEANING: 'terrible claw'
PRONUNCIATION: die-NON-e-kus
Deinonychus is a bird-like theropod and one of the most fascinating dinosaurs in palaeontology. In the past we thought of dinosaurs as dim-witted, sluggish creatures, but Deinonychus changed that view. It is a smart, agile and ferocious raptor that terrorizes its ecosystem.
The forelimb is long and all three fingers are crowned with menacing claws. A mobile shoulder joint allows the arm to swing in a wide arc, an ideal technique for slashing and grasping prey. The tail is long, stiffened and sticks out straight. This greatly helps the animal's balance and agility.
FOSSIL FINDS
HABITAT
POTENTIAL RISK: EXTREME
SIZE COMPARISON
LENGTH: 3–3.5 metres (10–11 ft)
HEIGHT: 1 metre (36–42 in)
WEIGHT: 80–100 kilograms (176–220 lb)
RANGE
TOP SPEED
WEAPONRY: FULLY ARMED
80
81

WHERE IN THE WORLD?

Maps of the ancient landmasses show the shape of the world at the time of the dinosaurs and how the places they lived in have shifted around.

ARMED AND DANGEROUS?

Consult the weaponry box to check how well an animal is armed. Skulls rank this on a scale from 1 (no weapons) to 5 (extremely dangerous weapons).

THROUGH THE PERISCOPE

An alternative way of viewing dinosaurs from our time machine is through a high-tech periscope with a lens so powerful that you can see the pores in a creature's skin, the evil glint in its eyes and the salivating jaws ever ready to snap up prey. Big bad wolves seem tame by comparison.

KEY FEATURES

Use the magnification of the periscope to examine distinguishing details, such as head crests, and read about them in pop-up captions.

DILOPHOSAURUS

MEANING: 'double-crested reptile'
PRONUNCIATION: *di-loh-fo-SORE-uss*

One of the strangest carnivores in the dinosaur kingdom is *Dilophosaurus*. This hunter is the largest predator in its ecosystem. It terrorizes prey with its sharp weapons and rapid speed. Its head is adorned with a crest, which it uses to attract mates.

The head crests of *Dilophosaurus* give this predator a comical appearance, but its sharp teeth, pointed claws, cunning senses and agility combine to create a killing machine unmatched in its environment. There is no evidence that this species had a fleshy neck frill or could spit venom as is sometimes portrayed.

POTENTIAL RISK: EXTREME

HEAD ORNAMENTS

FAST-MOVING PREDATOR

RANGE

TOP SPEED

SIZE COMPARISON

HABITAT

FOSSIL FINDS

DEGREE OF RISK

It's important to know when it might be safe to step outside the time machine. Just look at the number of skulls in the Potential Risk box and stay put if it shows three or above.

HOW CLOSE?

The Range Finder is similar to a radar gun and can be pointed at an animal to gauge its speed and trajectory. Keep yours handy when dinosaurs are on the loose.

CAPTURED ON CAMERA

Explorers always need a record of where they've been and what they've seen. The turret camera, with its computerized information, provides this.

UP CLOSE

Scales or skin? Spots or stripes? You're in no doubt about the details when you can focus as closely as this.

TURRET VIEW

Tired of being eyeball to eyeball with dinosaurs? Want to know exactly what their habitat is like and how they live within it? Then step into the turret of our time machine and get an elevated view that shows you the animals interacting with each other in their particular ecosystem. Their diet and habits will be crystal clear.

HOW BIG?

Consult the Size Comparison box for basic measurements of the dinosaur you're looking at and see how it compares to an average human adult shown for scale.

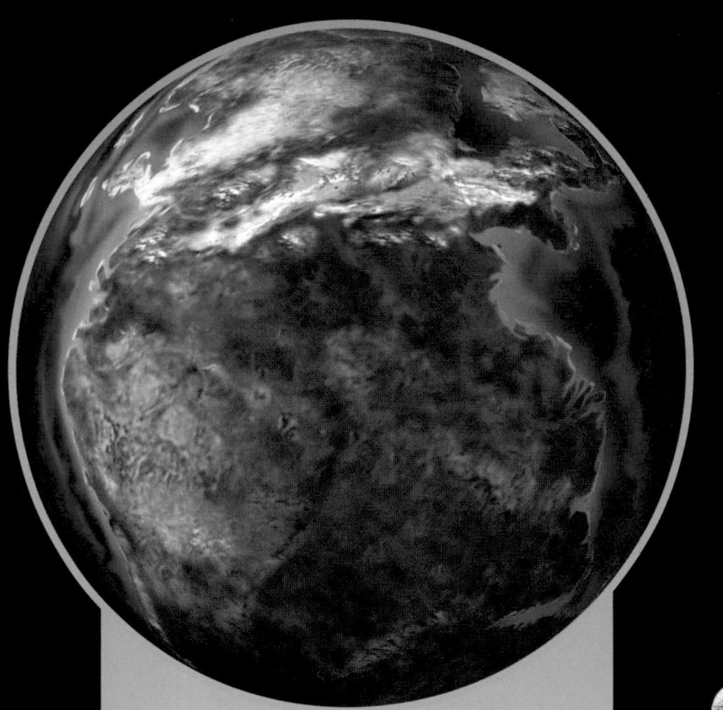

TRAVELLING BACK IN TIME

Our Mesozoic safari allows you to travel back in time throughout the 160-million-year reign of dinosaurs during the Triassic, Jurassic and Cretaceous Periods. The world was very different then, as climates were warmer, many regions were more arid, and the continents were gradually drifting apart. Dinosaurs lived all across the world for most of this time, and time travellers are able to transport themselves anywhere to see the wonderful creatures that used to call Earth home.

TRIASSIC

The Triassic Period (251–199.6 million years ago) was an alien world. All the Earth's land was gathered together into a single supercontinent called Pangaea, which was centred on the equator. Climates were hot and dusty; arid deserts engulfed much of the Pangaean interior. It was in this difficult environment that the first dinosaurs evolved, as well as mammals, crocodiles and turtles. Many of the first dinosaurs, such as Eoraptor, were small predators that ran quickly on two legs. Later, they evolved into a fantastic array of shapes and sizes.

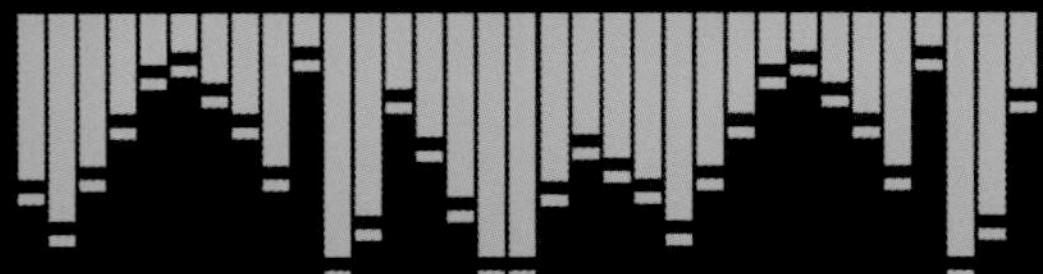

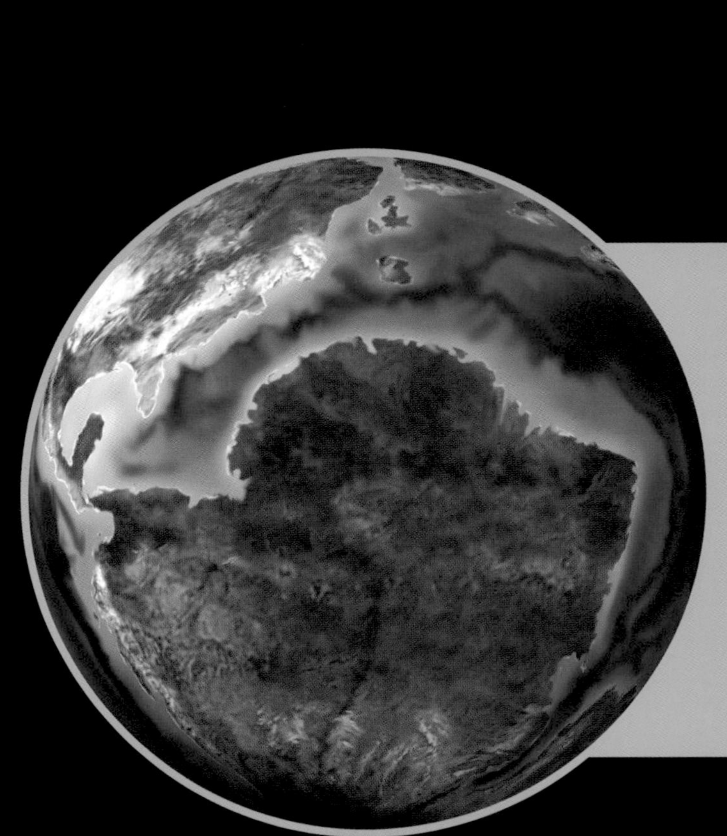

JURASSIC

The once great Pangaean supercontinent began to fragment during the Jurassic (199.6–145.5 million years ago). Throughout that time, dinosaurs lived on drifting lands, and evolved alongside the changing Earth. Climates were still warm, but much wetter, and many of the Triassic deserts were mere memories. The Jurassic was the age of dinosaur giants, as many colossal plant-eating sauropods thundered across the landscape.

WHEN DINOSAURS RULED THE WORLD

The Mesozoic (251–65.6 million years ago – MYA) is divided into the Triassic, Jurassic and Cretaceous Periods. Dinosaurs lived all around the world during these times, but our safari focuses on interesting groupings of them. For instance, during the Triassic, an array of early dinosaurs inhabited the lush river bottoms of Argentina and the arid badlands of the southwestern United States. These dinosaurs included ***Coelophysis***, a graceful predator that travelled in packs. Later, during the Jurassic Period, China, Africa and especially the western United States were home to a fantastic community of colossal dinosaurs. Chief among these were the thundering sauropods, such as ***Brachiosaurus*** and ***Diplodocus***, and the menacing theropod ***Allosaurus***. These three giants, along with over 50 other dinosaurs, lived in the warm and wet Morrison

Period	Epoch	Stage
TRIASSIC 251.0 – 199.6 MYA	Early Triassic 251.0 – 245.9 MYA	Induan 251.0 – 249.5 MYA
		Olenekian 249.5 – 245.9 MYA
	Middle Triassic 245.9 – 228.7 MYA	Anisian 245.9 – 237.0 MYA
		Ladinian 237.0 – 228.7 MYA
	Late Triassic 228.7 – 199.6 MYA	Carnian 228.7 – 216.5 MYA
		Norian 216.5 – 203.6 MYA
		Rhaetian 203.6 – 199.6 MYA
JURASSIC 199.6 – 145.5 MYA	Early Jurassic 199.6 – 175.6 MYA	Hettangian 199.6 – 196.5 MYA
		Sinemurian 196.5 – 189.6 MYA
		Pliensbachian 189.6 – 183.0 MYA
		Toarcian 183.0 – 175.6 MYA
	Middle Jurassic 175.6 – 161.2 MYA	Aalenian 175.6 – 171.6 MYA
		Bajocian 171.6 – 167.7 MYA
		Bathonian 167.7 – 164.7 MYA
		Callovian 164.7 – 161.2 MYA
	Late Jurassic 161.2 – 145.5 MYA	Oxfordian 161.2 – 155.6 MYA
		Kimmeridgian 155.6 – 150.8 MYA
		Tithonian 150.8 – 145.5 MYA

During the Mesozoic, dinosaurs ranged from the size of a chicken to nearly the length of a football pitch. Some ate meat while others ate plants. Some formed herds while others were loners. And some, like the Microraptor *(right), evolved into birds.*

CRETACEOUS

Continents continued to fragment during the Cretaceous (145.5–65.5 million years ago), and by the end of this period the world looked similar to how it does today. Many familiar dinosaurs, including Tyrannosaurus *and* Triceratops, *flourished in the warm, wet climate.*

ecosystem of the western United States about 150 million years ago. (This area, named after the town of Morrison in Colorado, is now a rich source of fossils. The rocks in which they are found are called the Morrison Formation.) The Cretaceous Period was the height of dinosaur diversity. During the early Cretaceous, South America and Africa supported some of the largest predators ever to walk the Earth: ***Spinosaurus*** and ***Giganotosaurus***. During the closing stages of the Cretaceous, North America was home to familiar faces, such as ***Tyrannosaurus*** and ***Triceratops***, which lived right up to the devastating asteroid impact that snuffed out the Age of Dinosaurs. Their fossils are found in the famous Hell Creek Formation, named after Hell Creek, Montana, which covers much of the western United States.

Berriasian 145.5 – 140.2 MYA
Valanginian 140.2 – 133.9 MYA
Hauterivian 133.9 – 130.0 MYA
Barremian 130.0 – 125.0 MYA
Aptian 125.0 – 112.0 MYA
Albian 112.0 – 99.6 MYA
Cenomanian 99.6 – 93.6 MYA
Turonian 93.6 – 88.6 MYA
Coniacian 88.6 – 85.8 MYA
Santonian 85.8 – 83.5 MYA
Campanian 83.5 – 70.6 MYA
Maastrichtian 70.6 – 65.5 MYA

Early–Middle Cretaceous 145.5 – 99.6 MYA

Late Cretaceous 99.6 – 65.5 MYA

CRETACEOUS 145.5 – 65.5 MYA

DINOSAURS OF THE TRIASSIC

251–199.6 MILLION YEARS AGO

Arid deserts, fierce sandstorms, gruelling droughts – the Late Triassic world is not a hospitable place. The primitive dinosaurs of this period rely on a combination of speed, intelligence and a warm-blooded metabolism to survive. Sleek predators, such as ***Coelophysis***, wander freely across the globe since all the world's continents are joined together in a single supercontinent known as Pangaea, meaning 'all earth'. Blistering heat blights the interior of this sprawling landmass, and flash floods pummel the coasts. In these savage climates it is important to beware ambushes from large predators known as rauisuchians, early relatives of crocodiles. Few dinosaurs can outmuscle these fierce hunters, but they can outwit and outrun them. Other early dinosaurs, such as the bulky and long-necked sauropodomorphs (e.g. ***Mussaurus***) and the bipedal and herbivorous ornithischians (e.g. ***Heterodontosaurus***), use their keen senses to avoid a gruesome fate at the hands of their enemies.

COELOPHYSIS

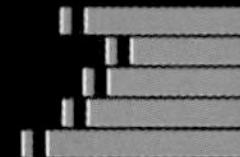

MEANING: 'hollow form' in reference to its hollow bones
PRONUNCIATION: *see-low-FYSS-iss*

Coelophysis is a small predator that appears meek at first sight. However, looks are deceiving. Although ***Coelophysis*** weighs much less than an average man, this theropod dinosaur is a sleek carnivore that hunts in packs to overwhelm prey.

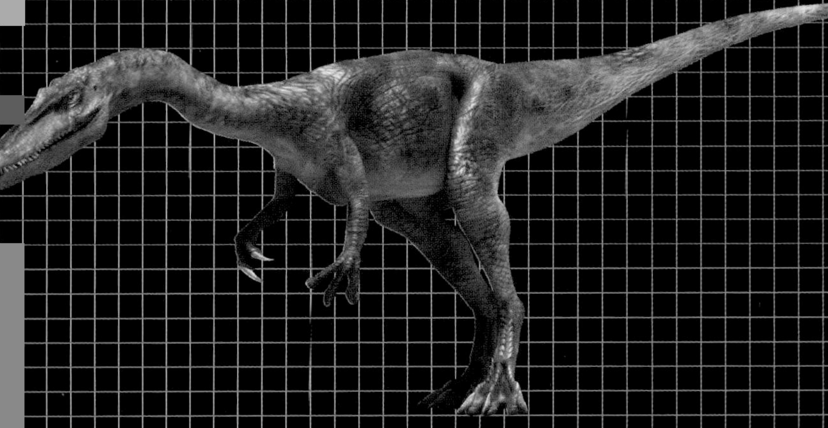

Coelophysis is the most primitive of the theropod dinosaurs. Unlike its more advanced cousins, it does not have any bizarre adaptations, such as the steak-knife teeth of ***Tyrannosaurus*** or the killer claws of ***Deinonychus***. However, it uses its blazing speed to outrun large, herbivorous prey.

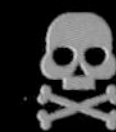

POTENTIAL RISK: MEDIUM

Coelophysis *is more dangerous than its graceful form suggests. It has all the important weapons necessary for any predator: numerous sharp teeth, piercing claws on its hands and feet, and keen eyesight, along with the advantage of speed and agility.*

SIZE COMPARISON

Coelophysis *is a small dinosaur that is light and nimble, but strong and fierce.*

LENGTH: 2–3 metres (6–9 ft)

HEIGHT: 0.5–1 metre (20–36 in)

WEIGHT: 25–75 kilograms (55–165 lb)

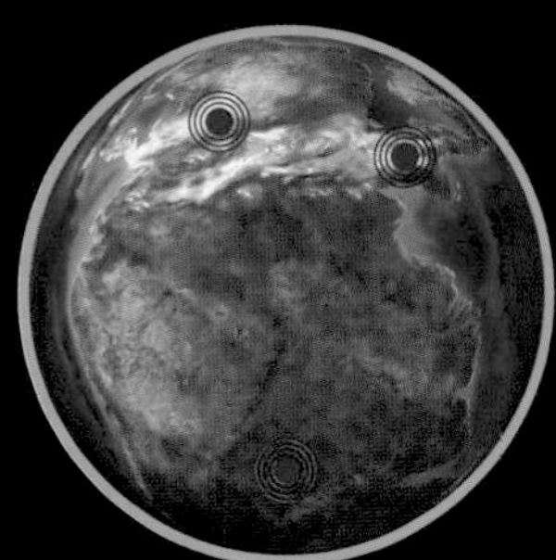

HABITAT

GLOBAL, LATE TRIASSIC

Coelophysis *lived about 215–200 million years ago, at a time when all the world's continents were joined in the supercontinent of Pangaea.* **Coelophysis** *was able to range across the entire planet, but was especially common in arid desert regions.*

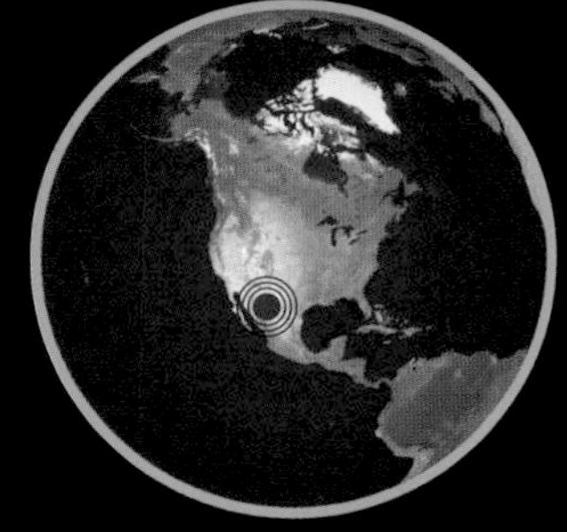

FOSSIL FINDS

NORTH AMERICA, AFRICA, CHINA

Fossils of **Coelophysis** *are very common in the Late Triassic rocks of the southwestern United States. One fossil deposit in New Mexico contains the skeletons of hundreds of* **Coelophysis** *that drowned when their pack was overtaken by a swollen river.*

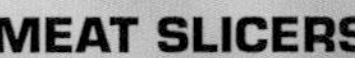

MEAT SLICERS

Coelophysis has more than 50 small, sharp teeth in its jaws, which are perfect for piercing the flesh of prey. The teeth at the front of the snout curve downwards, allowing ***Coelophysis*** to rip through skin and muscle with alarming efficiency.

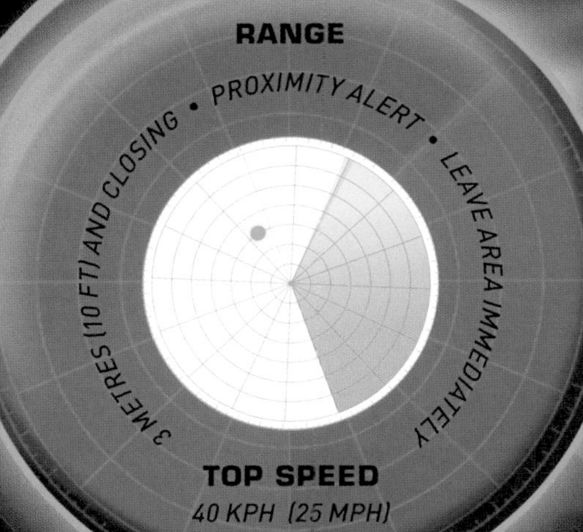

TERROR CLAWS

Like all carnivorous dinosaurs, ***Coelophysis*** has fingers on its hand. Only the first three fingers are functional, but together they form a large, muscular hand that ends in scythe-like claws.

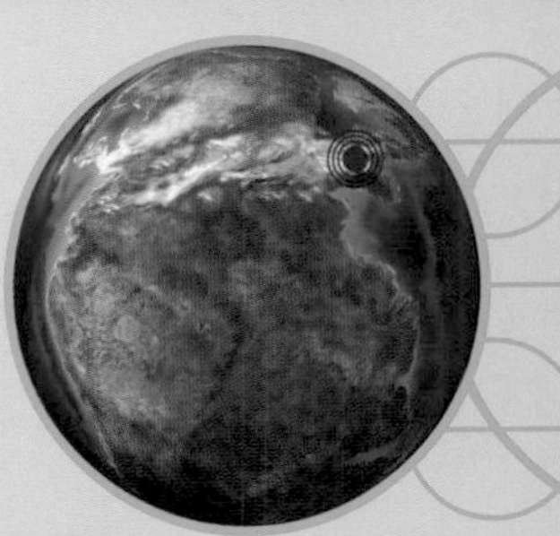

HABITAT

EUROPE, LATE TRIASSIC

Liliensternus *lived in central Europe during the Late Triassic, about 210 million years ago. At this time, Germany lay deep in the interior of the supercontinent Pangaea – a low-lying region choked with rivers and floodplains.*

POTENTIAL RISK: HIGH

Liliensternus *is the megapredator of its time and habitat. The meagre defences of* **Plateosaurus** *and other herbivores are no match for the teeth, claws and speed of* **Liliensternus**.

LILIENSTERNUS

MEANING: named after Hugo Rühle von Lilienstern (German scientist)

PRONUNCIATION: *lily-IN-stern-us*

Liliensternus is a close cousin of ***Coelophysis***, and shares many of the same adaptations for attacking and killing prey. However, there is one major difference between these two predators: ***Liliensternus*** is much larger and stronger, and can handle bigger prey.

250

0

ENEMY OF THE PLATEOSAURS

Liliensternus is the mortal enemy of ***Plateosaurus***, a plodding herbivore that must gather in herds for protection. ***Plateosaurus*** does have thick claws on its hands, but they are not much of a match for the larger and sharper claws of ***Liliensternus***. These, combined with piercing teeth and nimble speed, enable ***Liliensternus*** to rule its ecosystem.

The features of the vertebrae and pelvis identify **Liliensternus** *as a member of the same family as* **Coelophysis**.

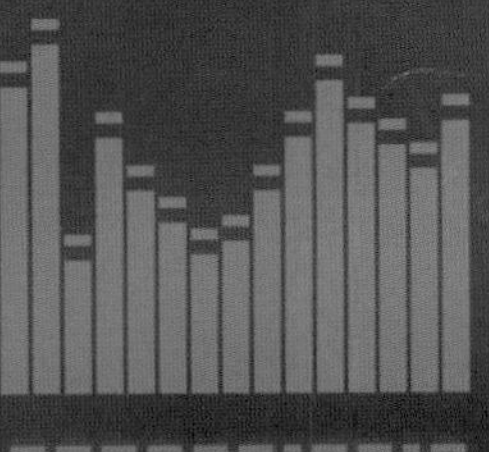

RANGE

10 METRES (33 FT) AND CLOSING
PROXIMITY ALERT
RETREAT SLOWLY

TOP SPEED

35 KPH (22 MPH)

FOSSIL FINDS

GERMANY

Only two skeletons of **Liliensternus** *have been found. Both were discovered in central Germany, within a thick sandwich of Late Triassic rocks that also included many prosauropod dinosaurs, such as* **Plateosaurus**.

DINO-RIPPER

Like all theropod dinosaurs, ***Liliensternus*** walks only on its hind legs. The arms are free to perform two functions important for any predator: balance during high-speed chases and dismembering prey once the chase comes to a bloody end.

DEADLY TEETH

This primitive dinosaur is a seriously dangerous predator with a battery of long, sharp teeth. Its bite is fatal to the lumbering herds of herbivores roaming the Late Triassic German floodplains.

SIZE COMPARISON

The largest predator of its time, outmatching prey with its strength.

LENGTH: 5–6 metres (16–20 ft)

HEIGHT: 1.5–2 metres (5–6 ft)

WEIGHT: 200–400 kilograms (440–880 lb)

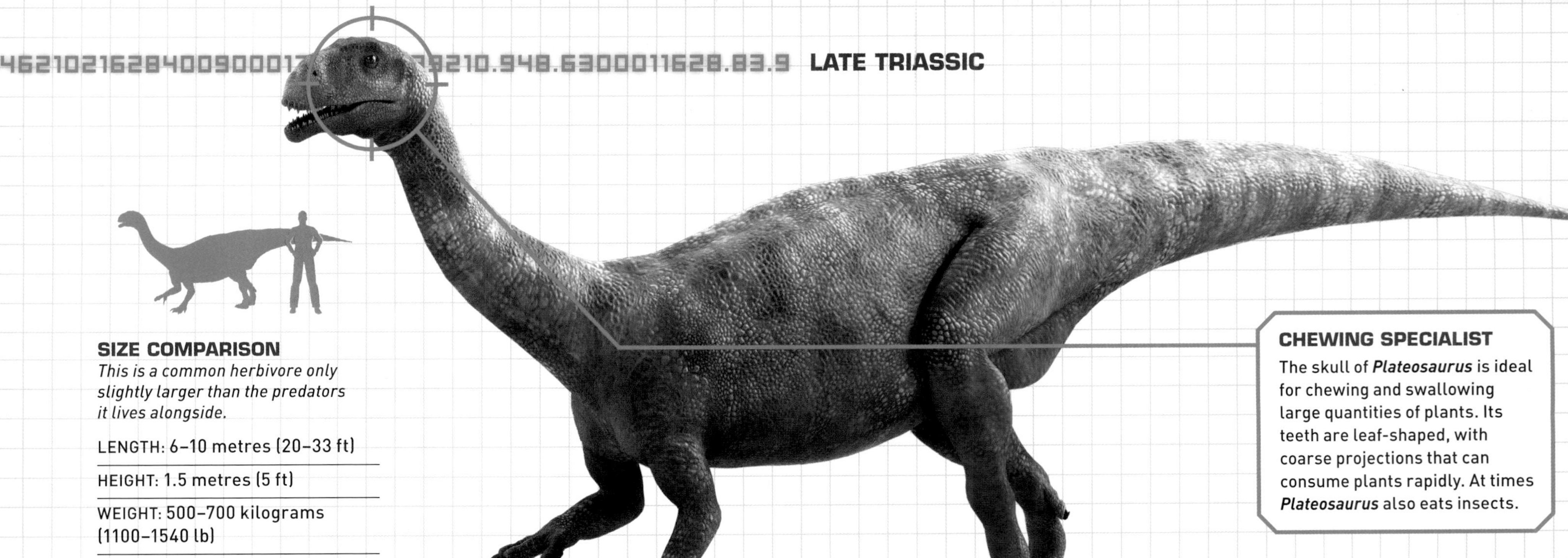

SIZE COMPARISON
This is a common herbivore only slightly larger than the predators it lives alongside.

LENGTH: 6–10 metres (20–33 ft)

HEIGHT: 1.5 metres (5 ft)

WEIGHT: 500–700 kilograms (1100–1540 lb)

CHEWING SPECIALIST
The skull of ***Plateosaurus*** is ideal for chewing and swallowing large quantities of plants. Its teeth are leaf-shaped, with coarse projections that can consume plants rapidly. At times ***Plateosaurus*** also eats insects.

POTENTIAL RISK: LOW
Plateosaurus *is a herbivore and not much of a threat, but it has learned to protect itself from predators by attacking in self-defence if it feels threatened.*

PLATEOSAURUS

MEANING: 'flat lizard'

PRONUNCIATION: *PLAT-eo-sore-uss*

If you travel across the Germanic Basin of central Europe, you'll find ***Plateosaurus*** a common sight. This barrel-chested, plant-eating prosauropod moves in herds that number in the thousands. Such large packs are necessary for protection from the fierce predator ***Lilienesternus***.

FOSSIL FINDS
EUROPE, LATE TRIASSIC

Plateosaurus *was the most common dinosaur in central Europe during the Late Triassic, approximately 215–200 million years ago. Today its fossils are found in high numbers, and it is one of the most common dinosaurs known to science.*

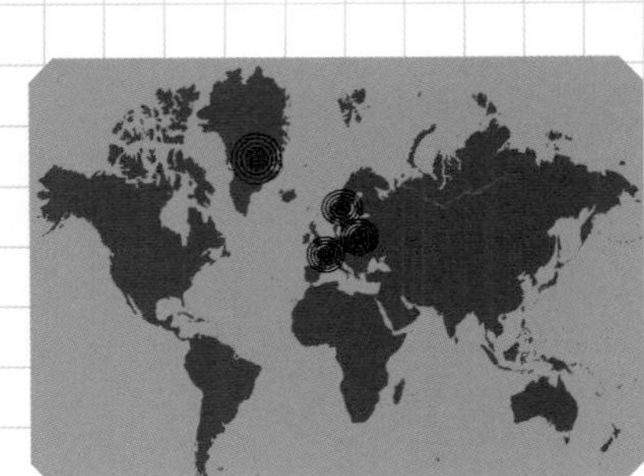

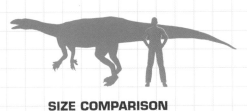

SIZE COMPARISON

LENGTH: 5–7 metres (16–23 ft)

HEIGHT: 1.25–1.75 metres (4–6 ft)

WEIGHT: 300–500 kilograms (660–1100 lb)

This mid-sized herbivore uses its bulk for protection.

UNIQUE POSTURE
Efraasia reaches into trees standing on its hind legs, but can run on four legs when escaping predators.

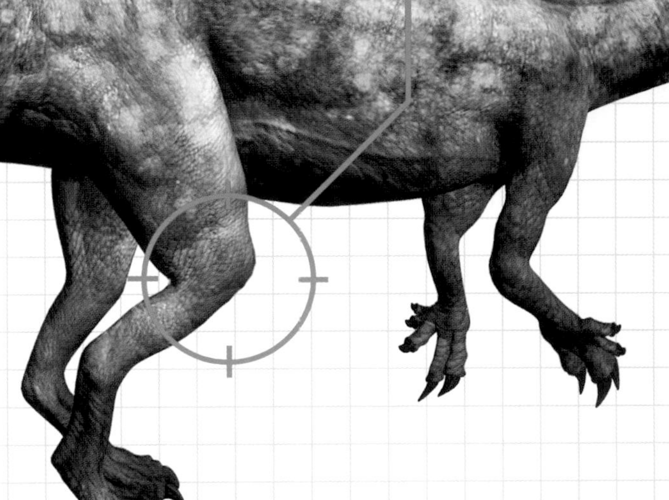

POTENTIAL RISK: LOW
Efraasia, *like* **Plateosaurus**, *is normally a placid herbivore that poses little threat. However, when threatened, it can use its large bulk to protect its young and ward off predators.*

EFRAASIA

MEANING: named after Eberhard Fraas (German scientist)

PRONUNCIATION: *e-FRAAS-e-uh*

Efraasia is a close cousin of ***Plateosaurus***, and like that dinosaur it can be seen in large packs, browsing for leaves in the low trees of the German floodplain. ***Efraasia*** is slightly smaller and much rarer than its cousin. However, both prosauropods live in constant danger of attacks from ***Lilienesternus***.

FOSSIL FINDS
EUROPE, LATE TRIASSIC

Efraasia *is one of many different prosauropod species whose fossils have been discovered in the Late Triassic rocks of Germany. The lush and warm floodplains were able to support a great number of herbivores during this time.*

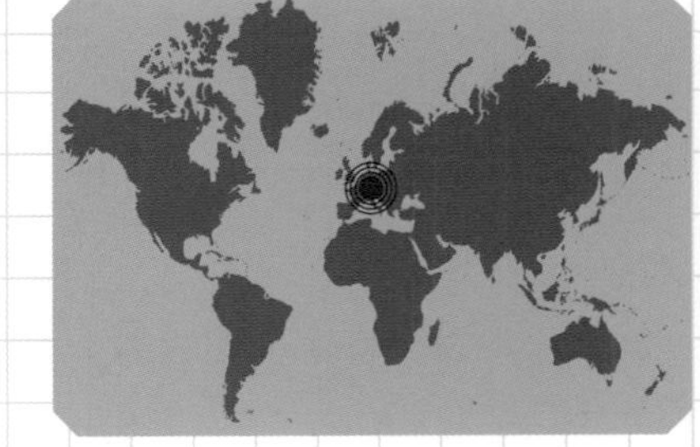

POTENTIAL RISK: VERY LOW

Thecodontosaurus is one of the smallest, meekest and gentlest of dinosaurs. It poses no risk.

THECODONTOSAURUS

MEANING: 'socket-toothed lizard'

PRONUNCIATION: *the-ko-DON-to-sore-uss*

This dinosaur is a minuscule herbivore, rarely larger than a mid-sized dog.

SIZE COMPARISON

LENGTH: 1–1.5 metres (3–5 ft)

HEIGHT: 20 centimetres (8 in)

WEIGHT: 18–44 kilograms (8–20 lb)

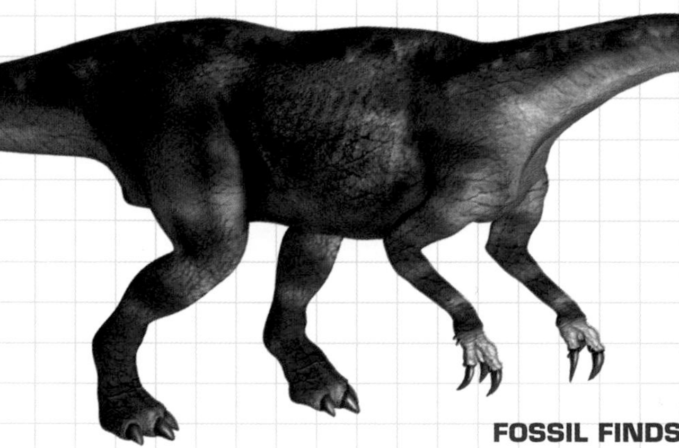

Thecodontosaurus is one of the smallest and most primitive of the sauropodomorphs, the group of dinosaurs that includes giant long-necked herbivores such as ***Brachiosaurus*** and ***Diplodocus***. Weighing no more than a five-year-old child, this diminutive herbivore makes its home in small caves, where it can hide from predators.

FOSSIL FINDS

EUROPE, LATE TRIASSIC

*While **Thecodontosaurus** believed it was safe in caves, these dark, damp hiding places sometimes collapsed, trapping the gentle plant-eaters inside. Their fossils were first found in the remains of such caves near Bristol, in southwest England.*

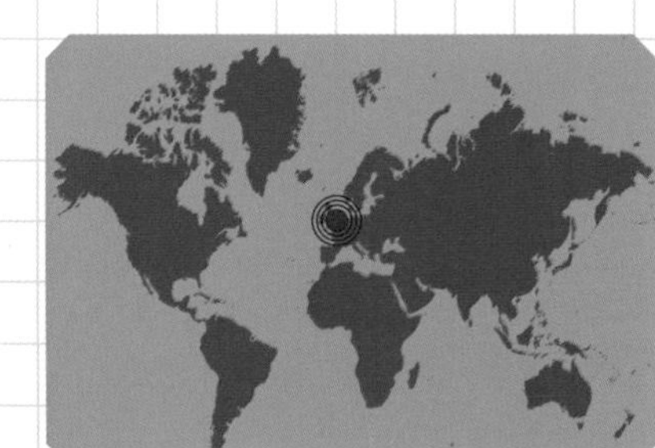

FOREIGN COUSINS

Riojasaurus is a very close cousin of ***Plateosaurus***, which might seem strange since they live so far apart. However, during the Triassic, all the world's continents were joined together, making it easy for animals to migrate across the planet.

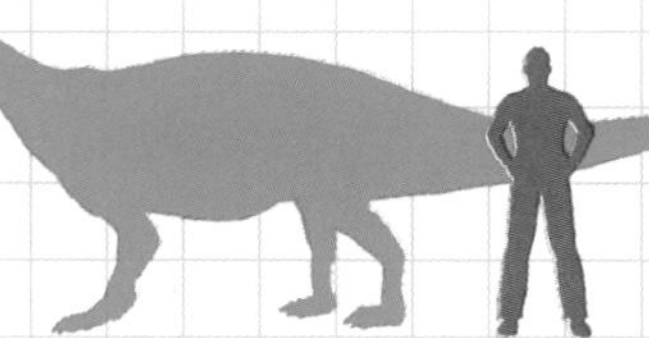

SIZE COMPARISON

LENGTH: 9–11 metres (30–36 ft)

HEIGHT: 2.25–2.75 metres (7–9 ft)

WEIGHT: 500–800 kilograms (1100–1760 lb)

Riojasaurus is the largest animal in its environment.

POTENTIAL RISK: LOW

Riojasaurus is a gentle beast unless it feels threatened, at which point others must be careful not to be crushed by its hulking frame.

RIOJASAURUS

MEANING: named after La Rioja Province, Argentina

PRONUNCIATION: *re-o-hah-SORE-uss*

One of the largest land animals of the Late Triassic, ***Riojasaurus*** is a heavy, plant-eating machine that inhabits the arid forests of Argentina. It is also a prosauropod, but unlike ***Thecodontosaurus***, it does not have to hide from predators. Instead, it can face its rivals head-on, hiding behind its bulk for protection.

FOSSIL FINDS

ARGENTINA, LATE TRIASSIC

*More than 20 skeletons of **Riojasaurus** have been found in Late Triassic rocks in Argentina, making it one of the best-known dinosaurs of this period. The longer bones in its neck distinguish it from other prosauropods of the region.*

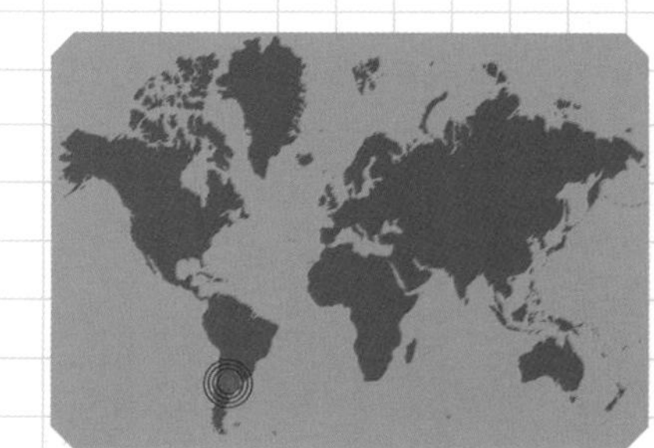

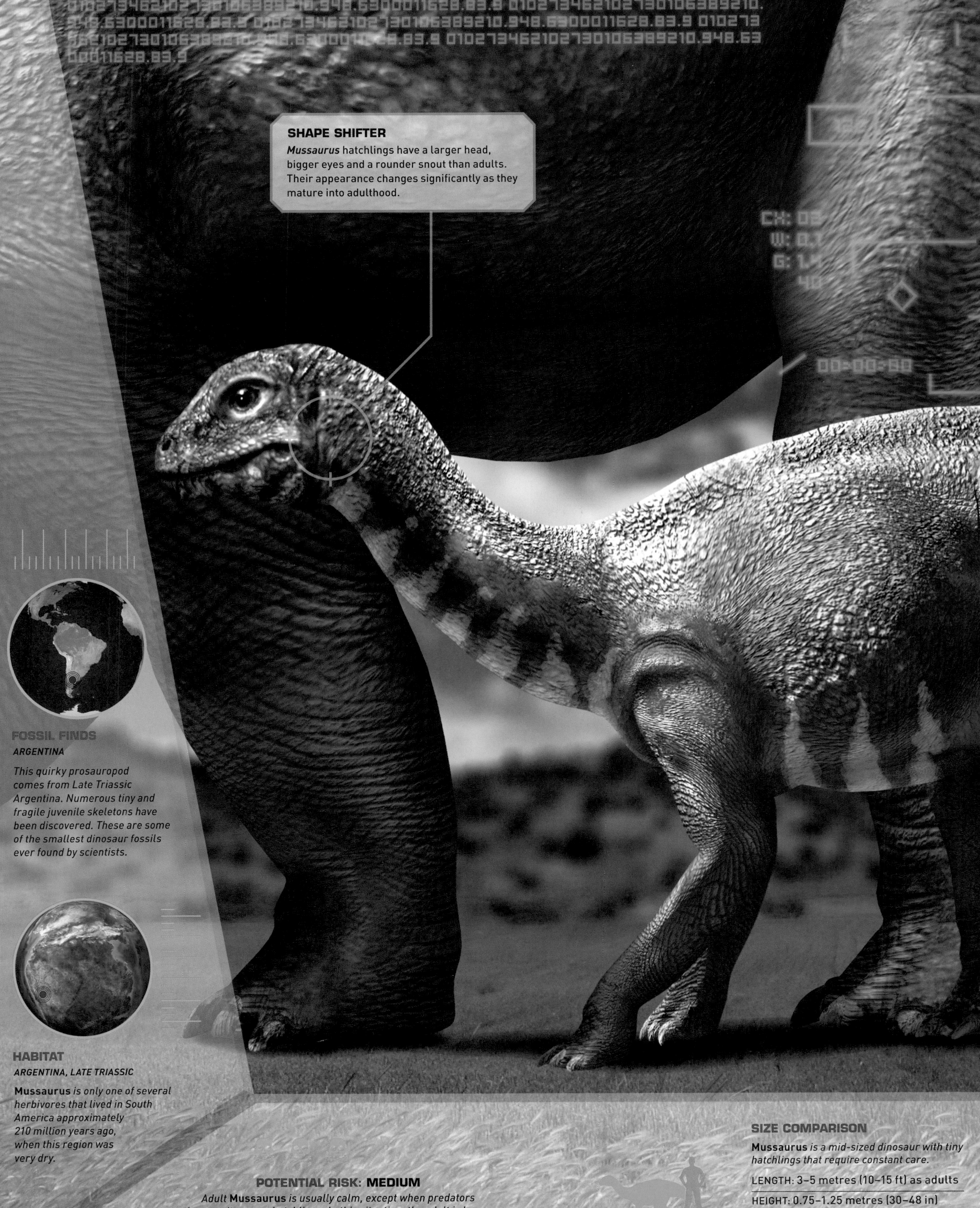

SHAPE SHIFTER
Mussaurus hatchlings have a larger head, bigger eyes and a rounder snout than adults. Their appearance changes significantly as they mature into adulthood.
00:00:00

FOSSIL FINDS

ARGENTINA

This quirky prosauropod comes from Late Triassic Argentina. Numerous tiny and fragile juvenile skeletons have been discovered. These are some of the smallest dinosaur fossils ever found by scientists.

HABITAT

ARGENTINA, LATE TRIASSIC

Mussaurus *is only one of several herbivores that lived in South America approximately 210 million years ago, when this region was very dry.*

POTENTIAL RISK: MEDIUM

Adult **Mussaurus** *is usually calm, except when predators threaten its young hatchlings. In this situation, the adult is known to strike back in order to save its children.*

SIZE COMPARISON

Mussaurus *is a mid-sized dinosaur with tiny hatchlings that require constant care.*

LENGTH: 3–5 metres (10–15 ft) as adults

HEIGHT: 0.75–1.25 metres (30–48 in)

WEIGHT: 80–120 kilograms (176–265 lb)

MUSSAURUS

MEANING: 'mouse lizard'

PRONUNCIATION: *muh-SORE-uss*

The name 'mouse lizard' might seem a bit strange for a dinosaur, but ***Mussaurus*** is simply another species of prosauropod herbivore. Its strange name refers to its hatchlings, which are very small, meek and helpless when first born.

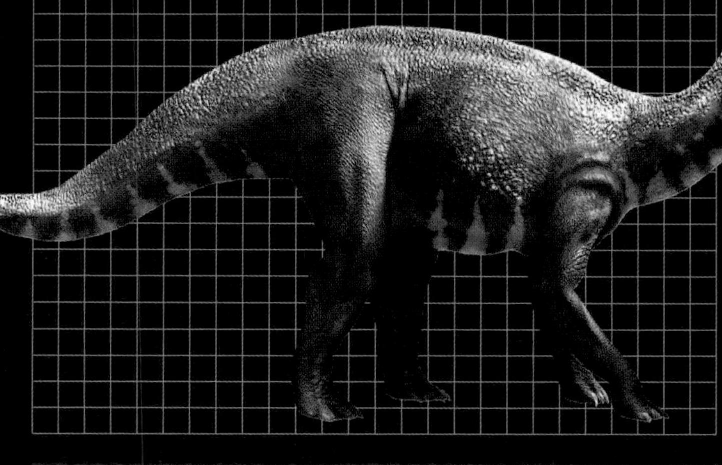

002730192100010101000273019210001015101 5

Mussaurus is a close cousin of the plant-eating prosauropods ***Plateosaurus***, ***Efraasia*** and ***Riojasaurus***. Adults grow to more than 5 metres (16 ft) in length, a large size necessary to stave off predators. On the other hand, hatchlings are only about 20 centimetres (8 in) long, no larger than a guinea pig. Adults must be careful to protect their offspring during the vulnerable period of childhood.

STRONG GROWN-UPS

Mussaurus adults are powerful animals that can stand on either two or four legs, depending on whether they need to run or reach high into trees for food. Hatchlings, on the other hand, have very weak limbs and rely on adults to bring food to the nests, much like many baby birds.

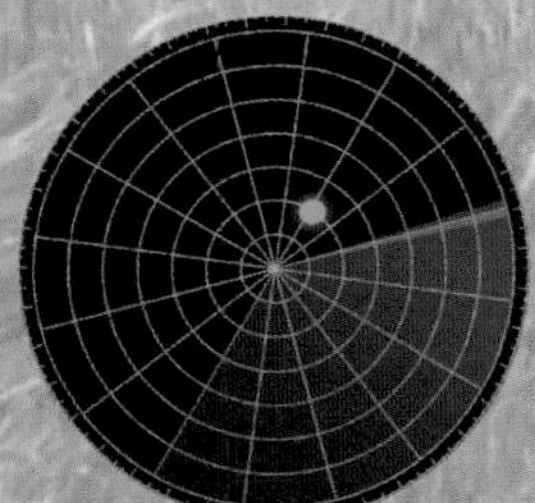

RANGE

2 METRES (6.5 FT) AND CLOSING
PROXIMITY ALERT
REMAIN STATIONARY

TOP SPEED

10 KPH (6 MPH)

WEAPONRY: UNARMED

Mussaurus *has no weapons except for its large bulk, which it can turn on any predator tempted to attack its helpless hatchlings.*

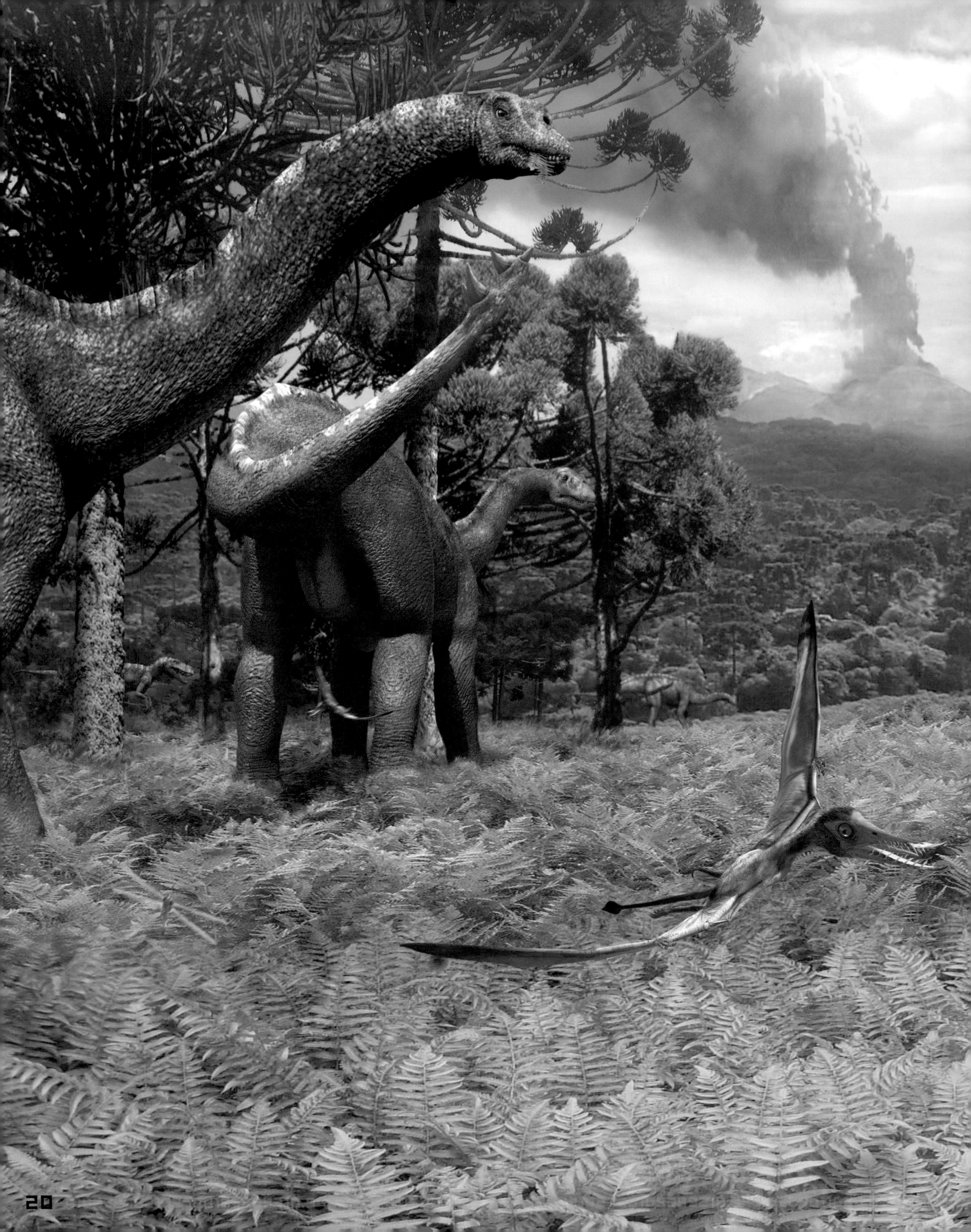

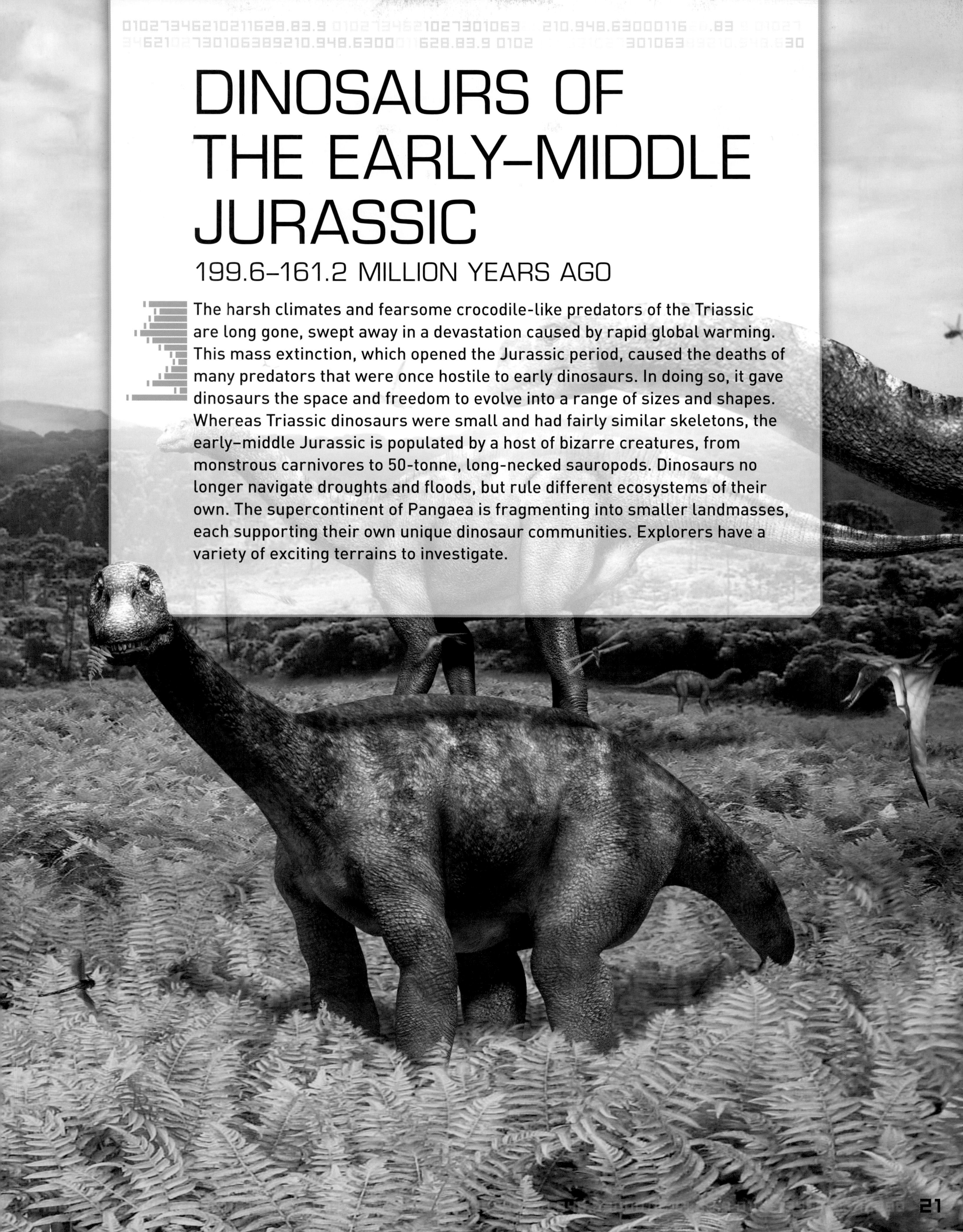

DINOSAURS OF THE EARLY–MIDDLE JURASSIC

199.6–161.2 MILLION YEARS AGO

The harsh climates and fearsome crocodile-like predators of the Triassic are long gone, swept away in a devastation caused by rapid global warming. This mass extinction, which opened the Jurassic period, caused the deaths of many predators that were once hostile to early dinosaurs. In doing so, it gave dinosaurs the space and freedom to evolve into a range of sizes and shapes. Whereas Triassic dinosaurs were small and had fairly similar skeletons, the early–middle Jurassic is populated by a host of bizarre creatures, from monstrous carnivores to 50-tonne, long-necked sauropods. Dinosaurs no longer navigate droughts and floods, but rule different ecosystems of their own. The supercontinent of Pangaea is fragmenting into smaller landmasses, each supporting their own unique dinosaur communities. Explorers have a variety of exciting terrains to investigate.

DILOPHOSAURUS

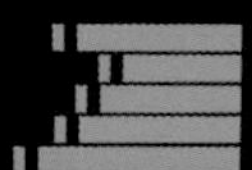

MEANING: 'double-crested reptile'

PRONUNCIATION: *di-loh-fo-SORE-uss*

One of the strangest carnivores in the dinosaur kingdom is ***Dilophosaurus***. This hunter is the largest predator in its ecosystem. It terrorizes prey with its sharp weapons and rapid speed. Its head is adorned with a crest, which it uses to attract mates.

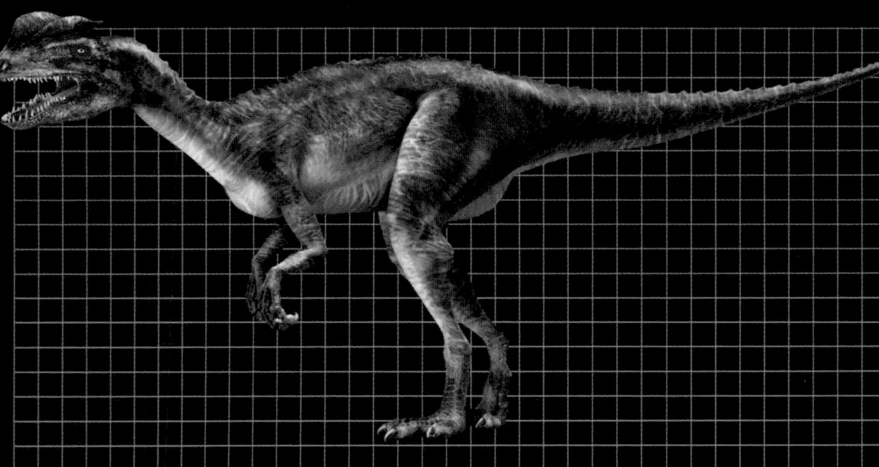

The head crests of ***Dilophosaurus*** give this predator a comical appearance, but its sharp teeth, pointed claws, cunning senses and agility combine to create a killing machine unmatched in its environment. There is no evidence that this species had a fleshy neck frill or could spit venom as is sometimes portrayed.

POTENTIAL RISK: EXTREME

There is no avoiding **Dilophosaurus** *in the arid and rugged hills of Arizona. The only defence against this predator is to run and hide.*

SIZE COMPARISON

Dilophosaurus *is a strong and fierce predator that can outmatch any prey.*

LENGTH: 5–6 metres (16–20 ft)

HEIGHT: 1.5–2 metres (5–6 ft)

WEIGHT: 400–500 kilograms (880–1100 lb)

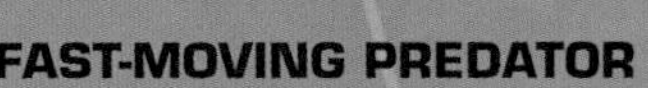

FAST-MOVING PREDATOR

Like all carnivorous dinosaurs, ***Dilophosaurus*** walks on two legs. Its hind legs are both sleek and strong at the same time. They have enough powerful muscle to allow for blazing speed, and are also streamlined for agility. Prey species have little chance of outrunning ***Dilophosaurus***.

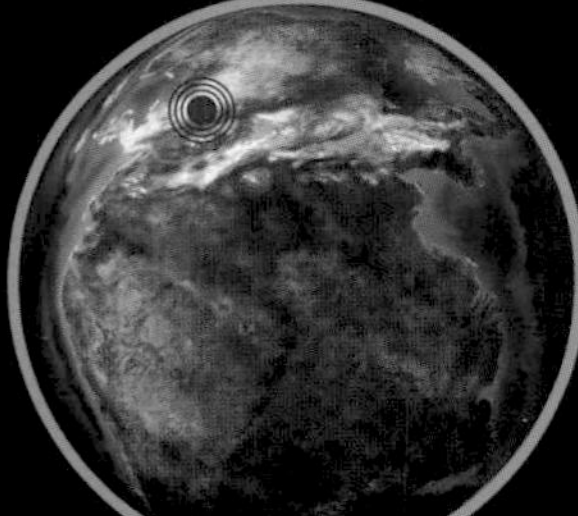

HABITAT

GLOBAL, EARLY JURASSIC

Dilophosaurus *lived about 195 million years ago, at a time when the continents were still gathered together into Pangaea but beginning to fragment. This predator probably ranged around the world, preferring environments teeming with prey.*

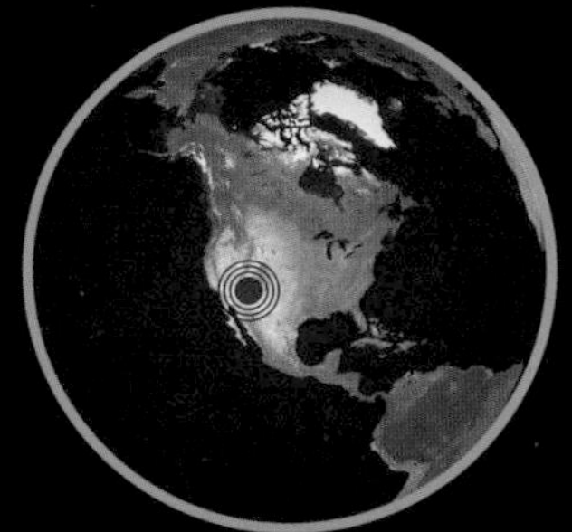

FOSSIL FINDS

NORTH AMERICA AND CHINA

Dilophosaurus *fossils are rare. A few fragmentary specimens are known from a Navajo Indian reservation in northern Arizona, and a single skeleton has been found in China, but footprints that might belong to* **Dilophosaurus** *are common.*

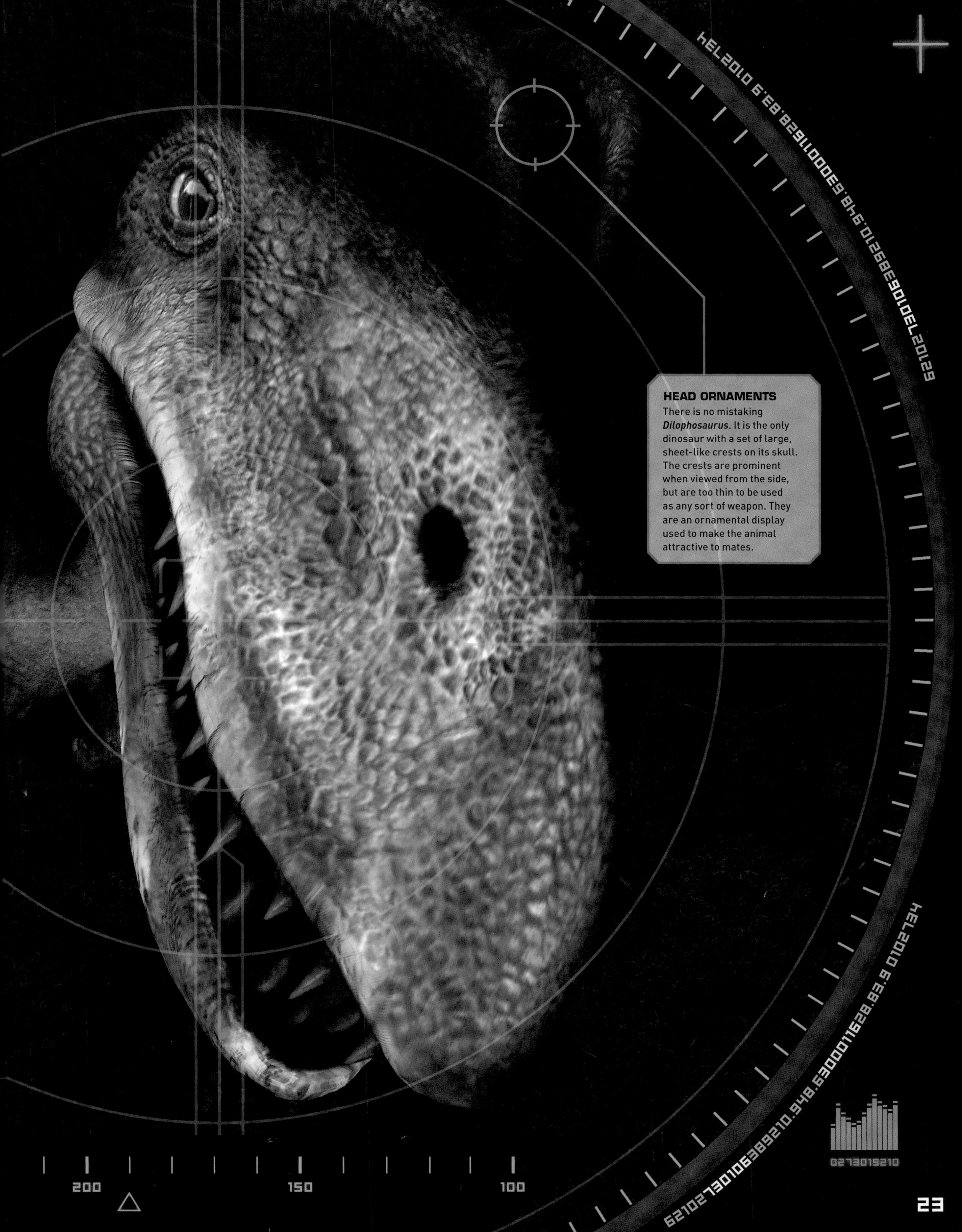

HEAD ORNAMENTS

There is no mistaking *Dilophosaurus*. It is the only dinosaur with a set of large, sheet-like crests on its skull. The crests are prominent when viewed from the side, but are too thin to be used as any sort of weapon. They are an ornamental display used to make the animal attractive to mates.

FOSSIL FINDS

ANTARCTICA

***Cryolophosaurus** was the first dinosaur from Antarctica ever given a scientific name. Only one fossil has been found, and half of the skull is missing because it was sheared off by a glacier before scientists could dig it out.*

HABITAT

GLOBAL, EARLY JURASSIC

***Cryolophosaurus** lived about 190 million years ago. At that time, Antarctica was not an icy, polar region as it is today, but was located several thousand kilometres closer to the equator. However, the environment was still quite cool.*

POTENTIAL RISK: EXTREME

*The prosauropods and lizards that live alongside **Cryolophosaurus** must remain alert throughout the day in order to avoid being hunted.*

SIZE COMPARISON

***Cryolophosaurus** is a strong and fierce predator that can outrun any prey.*

LENGTH: 6–8 metres (20–26 ft)

HEIGHT: 2–2.4 metres (6–8 ft)

WEIGHT: 400–600 kilograms (880–1320 lb)

COLOURFUL CREST

The head crest of *Cryolophosaurus* is a bizarre and unique feature. Many carnivorous dinosaurs, including *Dilophosaurus*, have crests, but only *Cryolophosaurus* has a crest that is clearly visible in a head-on view. The crest is fed by a supply of blood vessels, which nourish the colourful surrounding skin that is used to entice mates.

CRYOLOPHOSAURUS

MEANING: 'cold crested lizard'

PRONUNCIATION: *cry-oh-lo-fo-SORE-uss*

The colourful skull crest of *Cryolophosaurus* is a signal of doom to local plant-eating dinosaurs. For many prosauropods, this fan-like sheet above the nostrils is the last thing they will see before feeling the slicing jaws of death.

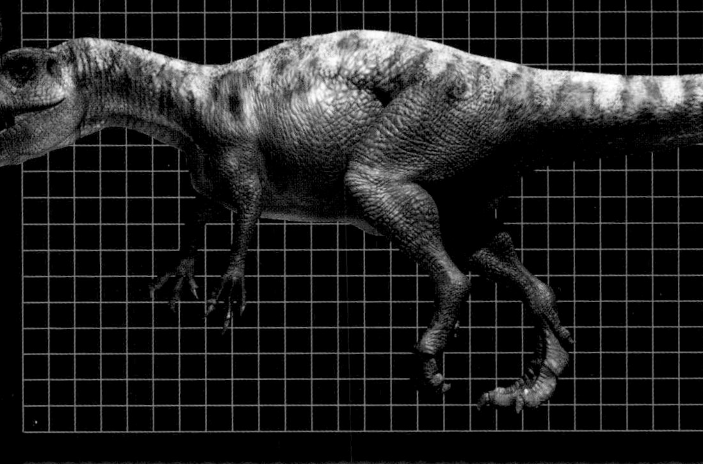

Cryolophosaurus is a close cousin of *Dilophosaurus*, even if they live in slightly different habitats. However, each is the master of its environment and the undisputed king of the food chain. Lizards, mammals and pterosaurs are common prey for *Cryolophosaurus*, but if given the choice, this mega-predator favours the fleshy corpses of prosauropods.

00273019210001010100027301921000101510 15

KNIFE TEETH

The teeth of *Cryolophosaurus* and other carnivorous dinosaurs are ideal for puncturing the flesh of prey. They resemble steak knives: they come to a sharp point, are covered with a fine array of serrations and are curved, which helps them cut smoothly through muscle and tendon.

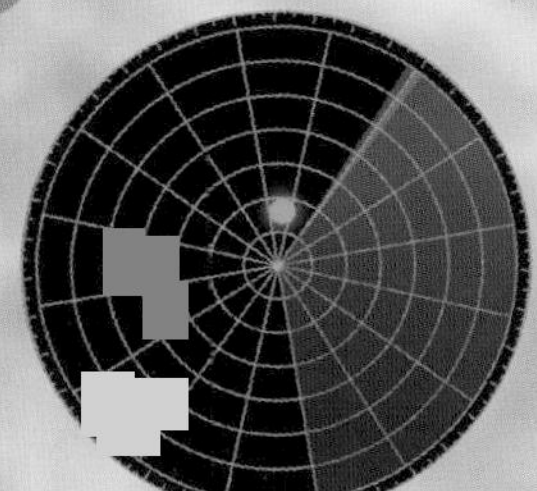

RANGE

2 METRES (6.5 FT) AND CLOSING
PROXIMITY ALERT
REMAIN COMPLETELY STILL

TOP SPEED

35 KPH (22 MPH)

WEAPONRY: FULLY ARMED

Cryolophosaurus *is armed with three claws on each forelimb and a set of sharp teeth for tearing off flesh. Its powerful legs can give it alarming speed.*

MONOLOPHOSAURUS

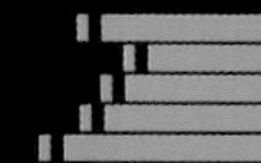

MEANING: 'single-crested reptile'

PRONUNCIATION: *mon-o-lo-fo-SORE-uss*

Another carnivorous dinosaur, another variety of peculiar skull crest. ***Monolophosaurus***, like ***Dilophosaurus*** and ***Cryolophosaurus***, uses its large cranial crest to attract mates, and its teeth and claws to attack prey.

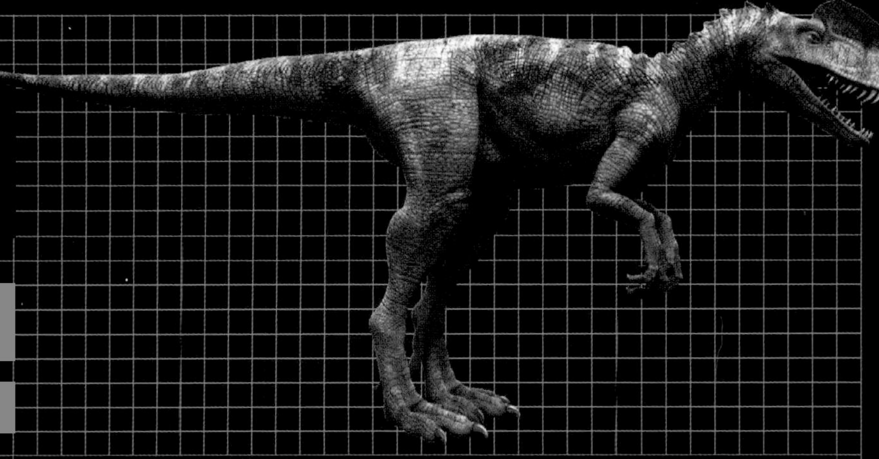

A more advanced theropod than the dinosaurs we have already met, ***Monolophosaurus*** is a large predator that uses its bulk, speed and arsenal of sharp weapons to ambush herds of long-necked sauropods. It will usually target small or weak animals, but may sometimes hunt in packs to take down adults.

BEST CREST

Dilophosaurus has two sheet-like crests, one on each side of its skull. ***Cryolophosaurus*** has a single fan-like crest that faces forward. ***Monolophosaurus*** is not unique in having a single crest, but its thickness is unusual, and it faces to the side. Potential mates are impressed.

POTENTIAL RISK: EXTREME

No other animal can match the predatory prowess of **Monolophosaurus.** *Sauropods, beware.*

SIZE COMPARISON

Monolophosaurus *is larger than all other contemporary predators.*

LENGTH: 5–6 metres (16–18 ft)

HEIGHT: 1.5–2 metres (5–6 ft)

WEIGHT: 400–600 kilograms (800–1320 lb)

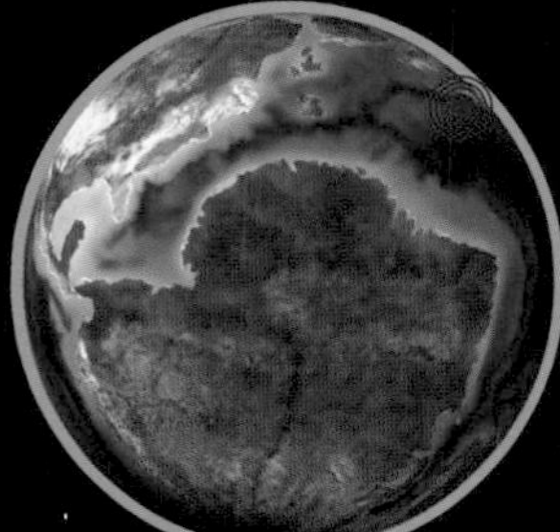

HABITAT

ASIA, MIDDLE JURASSIC

Monolophosaurus *lived approximately 165 million years ago. At this time, Asia had already broken free of the supercontinent Pangaea and was supporting its own unique species of dinosaurs.*

FOSSIL FINDS

CHINA

Only a single fossil of **Monolophosaurus** *is known, but this includes one of the best skulls ever found of a Middle Jurassic theropod. The skull and skeleton are from the Junggar Basin of far western China.*

CORRUGATED CRUNCHERS

The teeth of ***Monolophosaurus***, like those of other advanced theropods (tetanurans), have a series of 'wrinkles' that stretch across the tooth from one end to the other. Like the corrugations in a cardboard box, these wrinkles strengthen the teeth and make sure they do not break when ripping through flesh, muscle and bone.

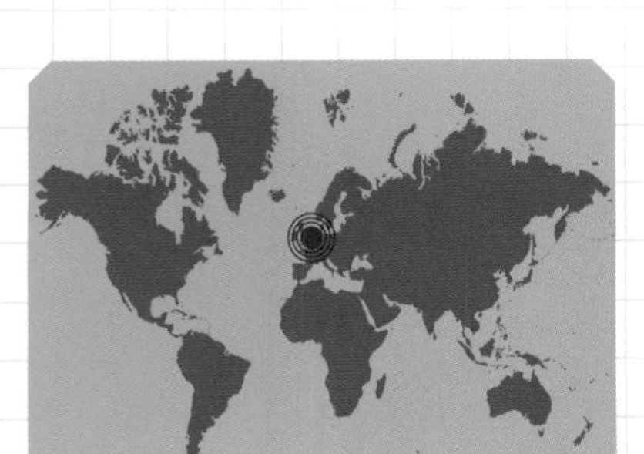

FOSSIL FINDS

EUROPE, MIDDLE JURASSIC

Eustreptospondylus *is a primitive member of the spinosaur group, which includes such beasts as* **Spinosaurus** *and* **Baryonyx**. *Its fossils were originally thought to be those of* **Megalosaurus**.

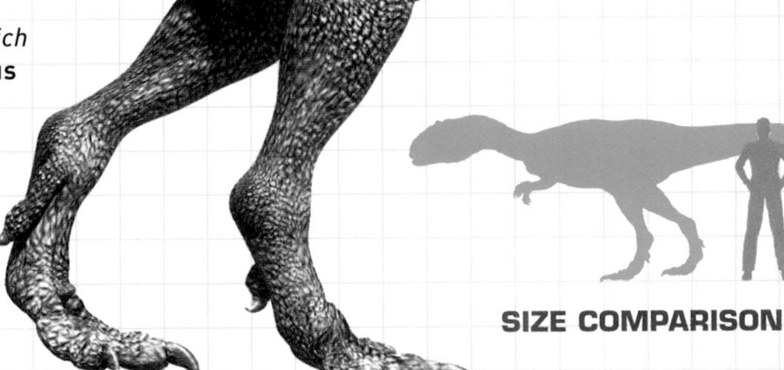

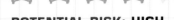

SIZE COMPARISON

LENGTH: 5–7 metres (16–23 ft)

HEIGHT: 1.5–2.1 metres (5–7 ft)

WEIGHT: 400–600 kilograms (880–1320 lb)

Eustreptospondylus *is smaller than its spinosaur cousins, but still a ferocious force.*

POTENTIAL RISK: HIGH

Eustreptospondylus *has the usual predatory array of razor teeth, killer claws and fast speed, along with sharpened senses.*

EUSTREPTOSPONDYLUS

MEANING: 'well-curved vertebra'

PRONUNCIATION: *you-strepto-SPOND-o-luss*

With large, bulging eyes and a keen sense of smell, ***Eustreptospondylus*** is a brainy predator that can dispatch large prey with relative ease. It has a particular fondness for long-necked sauropods and plate-backed stegosaurs.

SIZE COMPARISON

LENGTH: 5–6 metres (16–20 ft)

HEIGHT: 1.5–2 metres (5–6 ft)

WEIGHT: 400–600 kilograms (880–1320 lb)

A mid-sized predator, much smaller than its favourite prey.

POTENTIAL RISK: EXTREME

When **Megalosaurus** *gathers into a pack and goes on the prowl, sauropods and other plant-eaters should run for their lives.*

MEGALOSAURUS

MEANING: 'great lizard'

PRONUNCIATION: *meg-uh-low-SORE-uss*

Known as the 'great lizard', ***Megalosaurus*** is incredibly common in its environment. It is not a particularly large theropod, but what it lacks in size it makes up for in strength and agility. It often gathers in packs to take down large sauropods.

POTENTIAL RISK: HIGH

Risk lies in the size of the beholder. Large sauropods have little to fear, but baby dinosaurs and other small creatures should be on the lookout.

GASOSAURUS

MEANING: 'gas lizard'

PRONUNCIATION: *gas-o-SORE-uss*

SIZE COMPARISON

LENGTH: 3–4 metres (10–13 ft)

HEIGHT: 1–1.2 metres (3–4 ft)

WEIGHT: 100–400 kilograms (220–880 lb)

A small dinosaur, not much taller than an average five-year-old child.

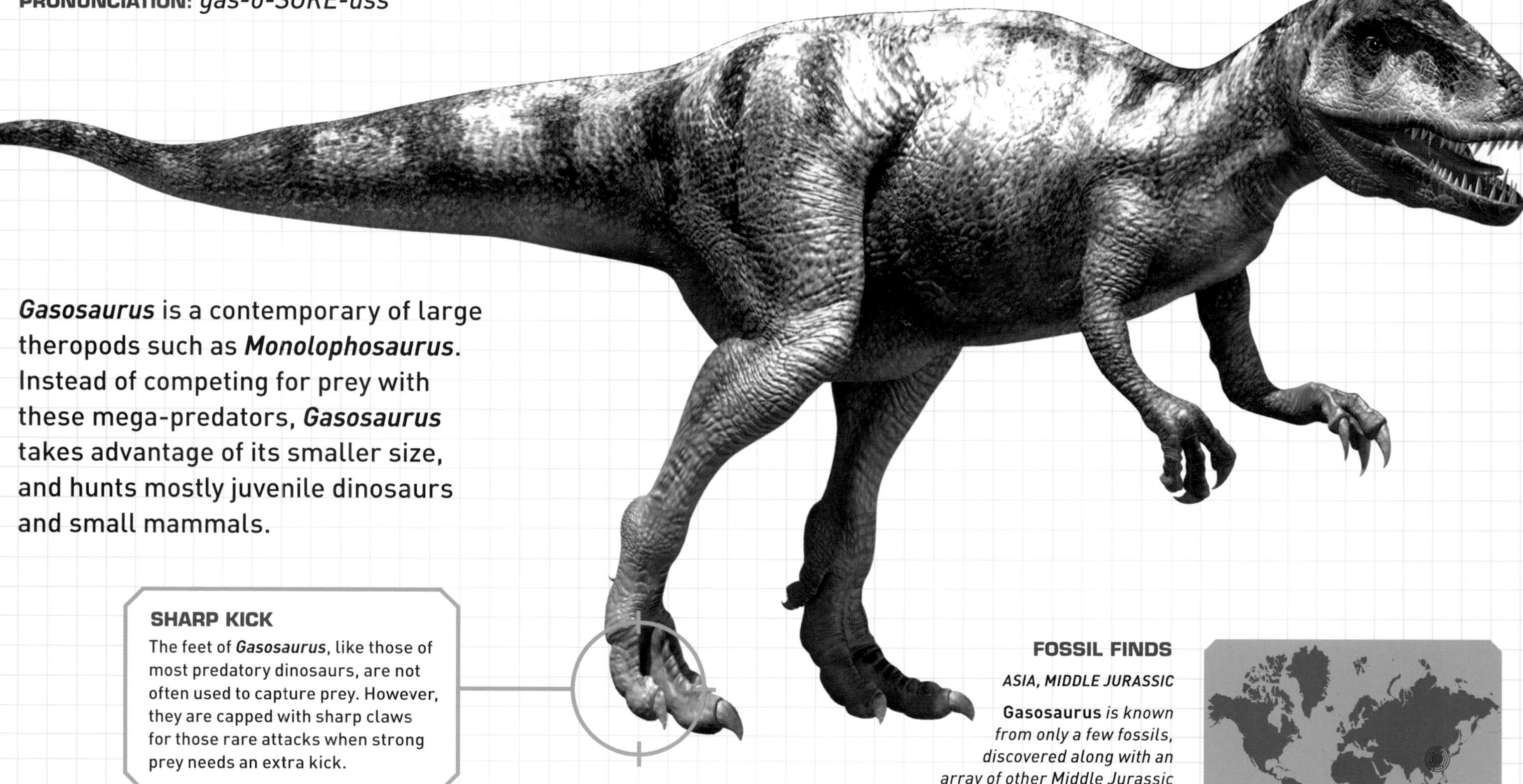

Gasosaurus is a contemporary of large theropods such as ***Monolophosaurus***. Instead of competing for prey with these mega-predators, ***Gasosaurus*** takes advantage of its smaller size, and hunts mostly juvenile dinosaurs and small mammals.

SHARP KICK

The feet of ***Gasosaurus***, like those of most predatory dinosaurs, are not often used to capture prey. However, they are capped with sharp claws for those rare attacks when strong prey needs an extra kick.

FOSSIL FINDS

ASIA, MIDDLE JURASSIC

Gasosaurus *is known from only a few fossils, discovered along with an array of other Middle Jurassic dinosaurs in the Sichuan Province of southern China. At this time, China was a lush, fertile terrain.*

BALANCING TAIL

The tails of theropods are stiffened and held high off the ground. This helps them provide balance, which is necessary for a fast-moving animal that runs on two legs.

CLAWS

The hands of carnivorous dinosaurs are primarily tools used to capture, kill, dismember and eat prey. Most theropods have three large fingers, each of which ends with an enlarged and sharpened claw.

FOSSIL FINDS

EUROPE, MIDDLE JURASSIC

Megalosaurus *was the first dinosaur ever named, and was described in 1824 by an English geologist, William Buckland. Its fossils are common in the Middle Jurassic rocks of England, which were laid down 160 million years ago by a series of raging rivers.*

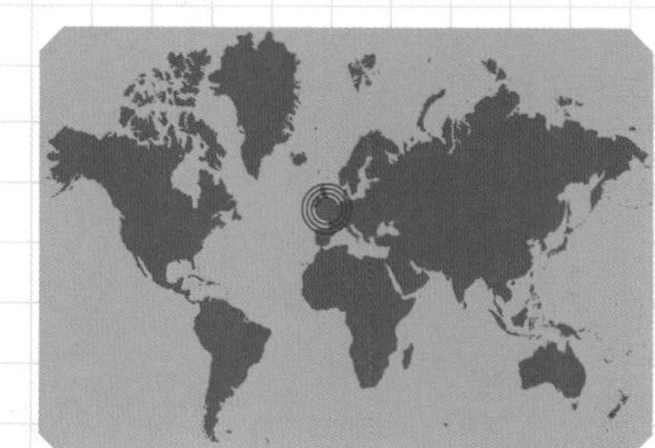

HABITAT

INDIA, EARLY JURASSIC

Barapasaurus *lived about 190 million years ago in the earliest part of the Jurassic Period, at about the time when the supercontinent Pangaea was beginning to split. It was one of many dinosaurs that enjoyed the lush floodplains of India.*

BENDY NECK

One of the trademark features of all sauropod dinosaurs is their greatly elongated neck. The individual vertebrae in the neck are stretched, giving the entire neck a snake-like appearance. Many sauropods use their necks to reach high into trees, but others use them as vacuum-cleaners to gobble up large swathes of low-lying bushes and ferns.

PRIMITIVE GIANT

Barapasaurus is one of the most primitive sauropods, the group of herbivorous dinosaurs that typically have long necks, small skulls, large guts and giant, column-like limbs. It uses its snake-like neck to reach high into tall trees, to reach leaves that are unavailable to smaller and shorter dinosaurs.

Barapasaurus *is one of the most common sauropods known to explorers of the Early Jurassic.*

RANGE

15 METRES (50 FT) AND CLOSING
PROXIMITY ALERT
WALK AWAY SLOWLY

TOP SPEED

8 KPH (5 MPH)

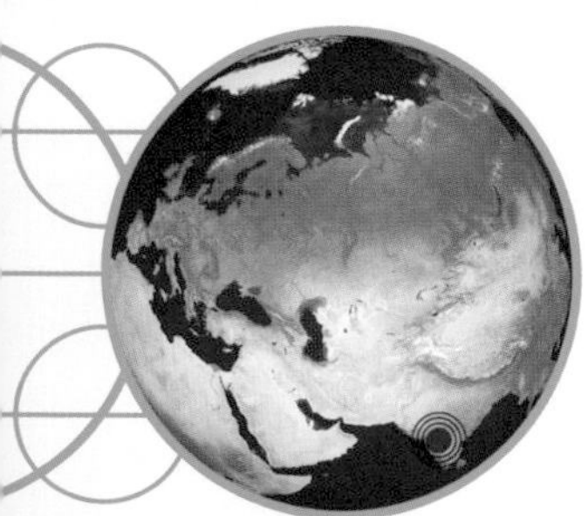

FOSSIL FINDS

INDIA

Dinosaur fossils are not very common in India, and **Barapasaurus** *is one of the better-known species from this subcontinent. It is the oldest large-bodied sauropod ever found.*

POTENTIAL RISK: LOW

Normally a gentle plant-eater, **Barapasaurus** *can crush predators when threatened.*

0102734621027301063892 10.948.6300011628.83.9

BARAPASAURUS

MEANING: 'big-legged reptile'

PRONUNCIATION: *bah-RAP-a-sore-uss*

Barapasaurus is the greatest giant of its time. It is the largest land animal in its ecosystem, and at 15–18 metres (50–60 ft) in length it can outmatch even the fiercest predator simply by standing its ground and staring down its foe.

BIG BACK

The individual neck and back vertebrae are huge, but lightened by many small cavities of air.

SIZE COMPARISON

The largest land animal of its time and place.

LENGTH: 15–18 metres (50–60 ft)

HEIGHT: 5–6 metres (17–20 ft)

WEIGHT: 50–55 tonnes

HETERODONTOSAURUS

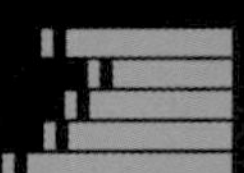

MEANING: 'different-toothed lizard'

PRONUNCIATION: *hett-er-o-don-to-SORE-uss*

Heterodontosaurus is a small and gentle dinosaur – one that is bound to appear cute to anyone who spots it. This animal eats mostly plants, but may also snack on small mammals and lizards during periods of stress.

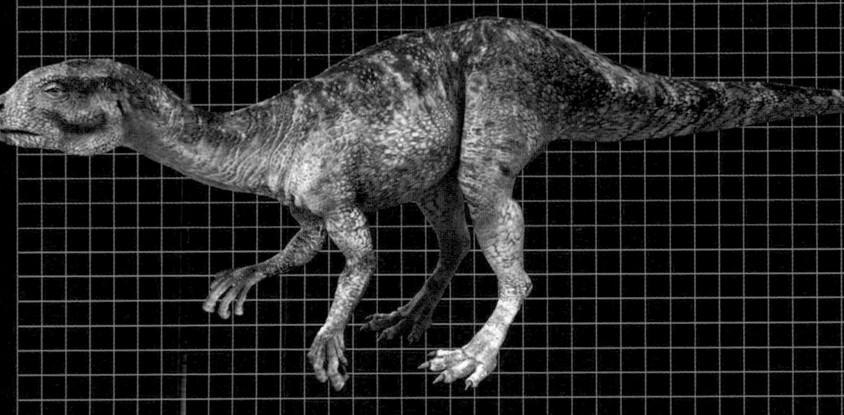

This small omnivore is one of the oldest and most primitive ornithischians. Ornithischia is the larger group of dinosaurs that includes species as varied as ***Stegosaurus***, ***Triceratops*** and ***Ankylosaurus***. Unlike many of its relatives, ***Heterodontosaurus*** is fast, sleek and also eats some meat.

HANDY OMNIVORE

The hands of ***Heterodontosaurus*** are in many respects similar to those of carnivorous theropods: they are large, have a wide range of motion and end in sharp claws. These are adaptations for catching and killing small mammals and lizards.

POTENTIAL RISK: VERY LOW

Under normal circumstances, ***Heterodontosaurus*** *poses no risk, but if hungry or tired, it may strike small prey.*

SIZE COMPARISON

A small, meek and quick little omnivore.

LENGTH: 1–1.25 metres (4–5 ft)

HEIGHT: 0.5–1 metres (2–3 ft)

WEIGHT: 20–30 kilograms (44–66 lb)

HABITAT

SOUTH AFRICA, EARLY JURASSIC

South Africa was teeming with a rich ecosystem during the Early Jurassic, about 195–190 million years ago. The presence of many close cousins around the world at this time is a testament to the free movement dinosaurs had across the Pangaean supercontinent.

FOSSIL FINDS

SOUTH AFRICA

A few specimens of this dinosaur, including a well-preserved adult and the skull of a small juvenile, are known from South Africa. Several close cousins are also known from South America, North America and Europe.

RANGE

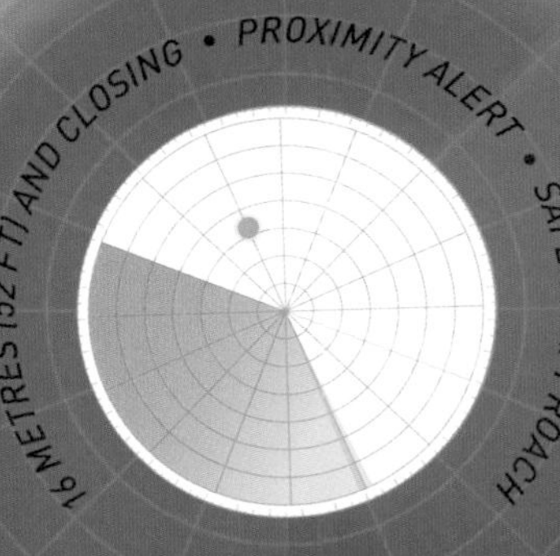

TOP SPEED

30 KPH (20 MPH)

ALL-ROUNDER

The snout of ***Heterodontosaurus*** is fine-tuned for its omnivorous diet. It has a beak at the front of its snout – perfect for nipping off leaves and stems. Also, most of its teeth are leaf-shaped, which is ideal for chewing plants. However, it also has two sharp 'canines' near the front of the jaws, which can puncture small prey.

SIZE COMPARISON

LENGTH: 6–7 metres (18–23 ft)

HEIGHT: 6 metres (20 ft)

WEIGHT: 5–7 tonnes

__Vulcanodon__ is a sauropod dinosaur, but less bulky than most.

FOSSIL FINDS

SOUTHERN AFRICA, EARLY JURASSIC

__Vulcanodon__ is one of the oldest and most primitive sauropods, and slightly less developed than its close cousin __Barapasaurus__. Only one decent fossil is known, from Zimbabwe.

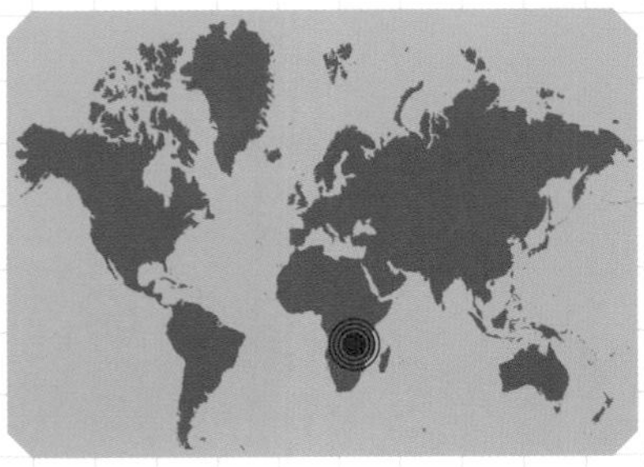

POTENTIAL RISK: VERY LOW

__Vulcanodon__ is neither fast nor fierce, and is not large enough to use its body mass as a weapon.

VULCANODON

MEANING: 'volcano tooth'

PRONUNCIATION: *vul-CAN-o-don*

One of the smallest of the long-necked sauropods, ***Vulcanodon*** is a little larger than a modern-day elephant. It feeds on the rich, green ferns and bushes that choke the riverbanks of southern Africa.

THICK ARMOUR

The most important feature linking ***Scelidosaurus*** to its later ankylosaur cousins is the extensive bony armour that covers most of the back. Parallel rows of thick scutes (plates) shield the back. One row guards each flank, and four rows enclose the tail.

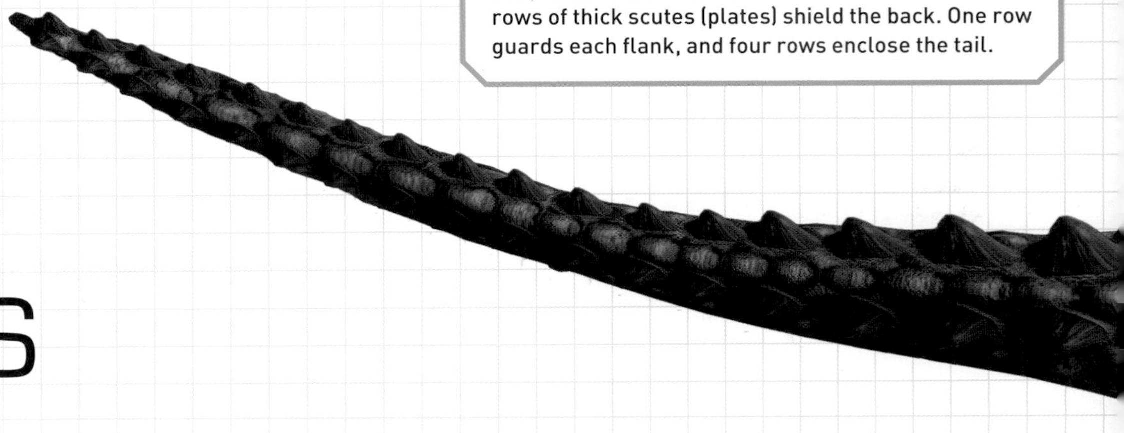

POTENTIAL RISK: LOW

Like a prickly cactus, __Scelidosaurus__ is harmless if left alone, but can be a spiky nightmare if provoked.

SCELIDOSAURUS

MEANING: 'limb lizard'

PRONUNCIATION: *skeh-lide-o-SORE-uss*

Some herbivorous dinosaurs are large enough to protect themselves from predators. Others have to be more creative. ***Scelidosaurus***, a primitive cousin to the ankylosaurs, shields itself from foes with a thick, bony coat of armour.

One of several sauropods that can terrify predators simply by flaunting its great size.

SIZE COMPARISON

LENGTH: 9–11 metres (30–35 ft)

HEIGHT: 4–5 metres (13–17 ft)

WEIGHT: 10 tonnes

POTENTIAL RISK: LOW

Although large in its ecosystem, **Shunosaurus** *is fairly small for a sauropod, and similar in many ways to* **Barapasaurus**.

SHUNOSAURUS

MEANING: 'Shu lizard' in reference to the Sichuan province of China

PRONUNCIATION: *shu-no-SORE-uss*

This hulking sauropod is the largest animal in the sweltering, wet ecosystems of central Asia. At nearly 10 tonnes, it is much larger than any contemporary predator, and can scare away even the fiercest theropods with its throaty roar.

FOSSIL FINDS

CHINA, MIDDLE JURASSIC

Shunosaurus *is remarkable among sauropods because it is known from numerous skeletons and even some skulls. It is only one of many dinosaurs that lived in Sichuan Province, China, during the Middle Jurassic.*

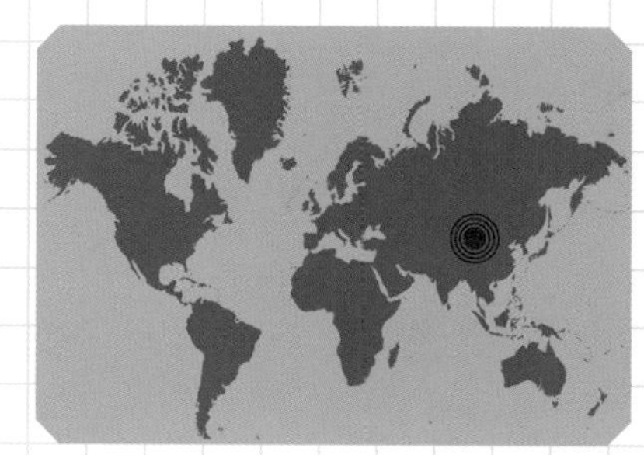

SIZE COMPARISON

LENGTH: 3.5–4.5 metres (10–15 ft)

HEIGHT: 0.5–1 metre (2–3 ft)

WEIGHT: 250–300 kilograms (550–660 lb)

Very long but quite squat, **Scelidosaurus** *weighs about three to four times as much as an average man.*

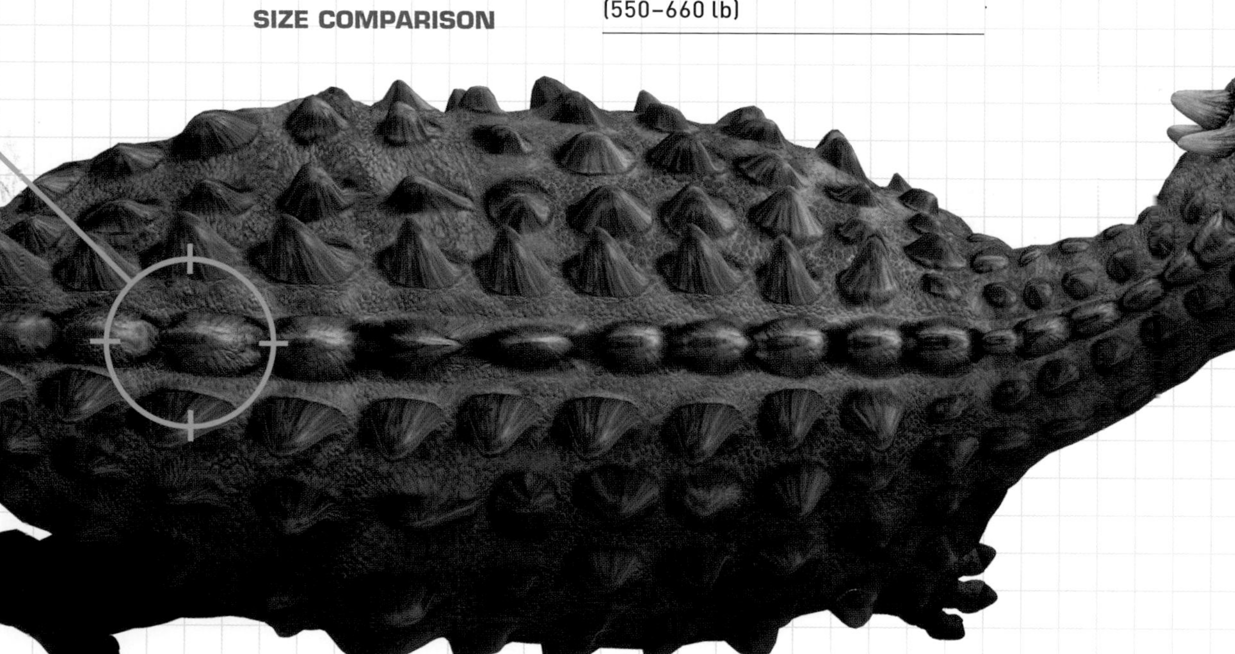

FOSSIL FINDS

EUROPE, EARLY JURASSIC

Scelidosaurus *is one of the oldest dinosaurs known to science. It was first found in England in the 1850s. It lived during the Early Jurassic, when Europe was a series of small, hot islands continually ravaged by waves and floods.*

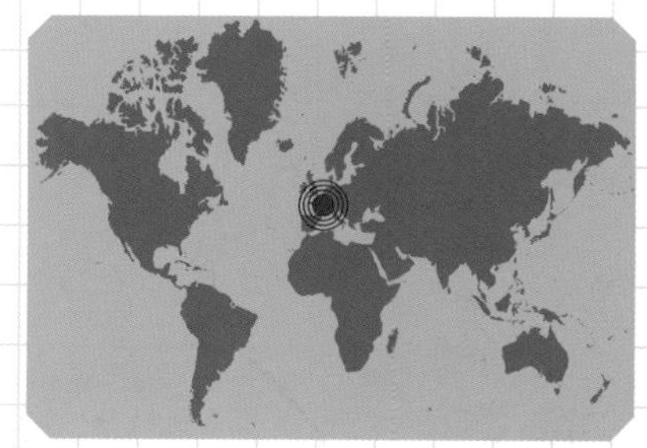

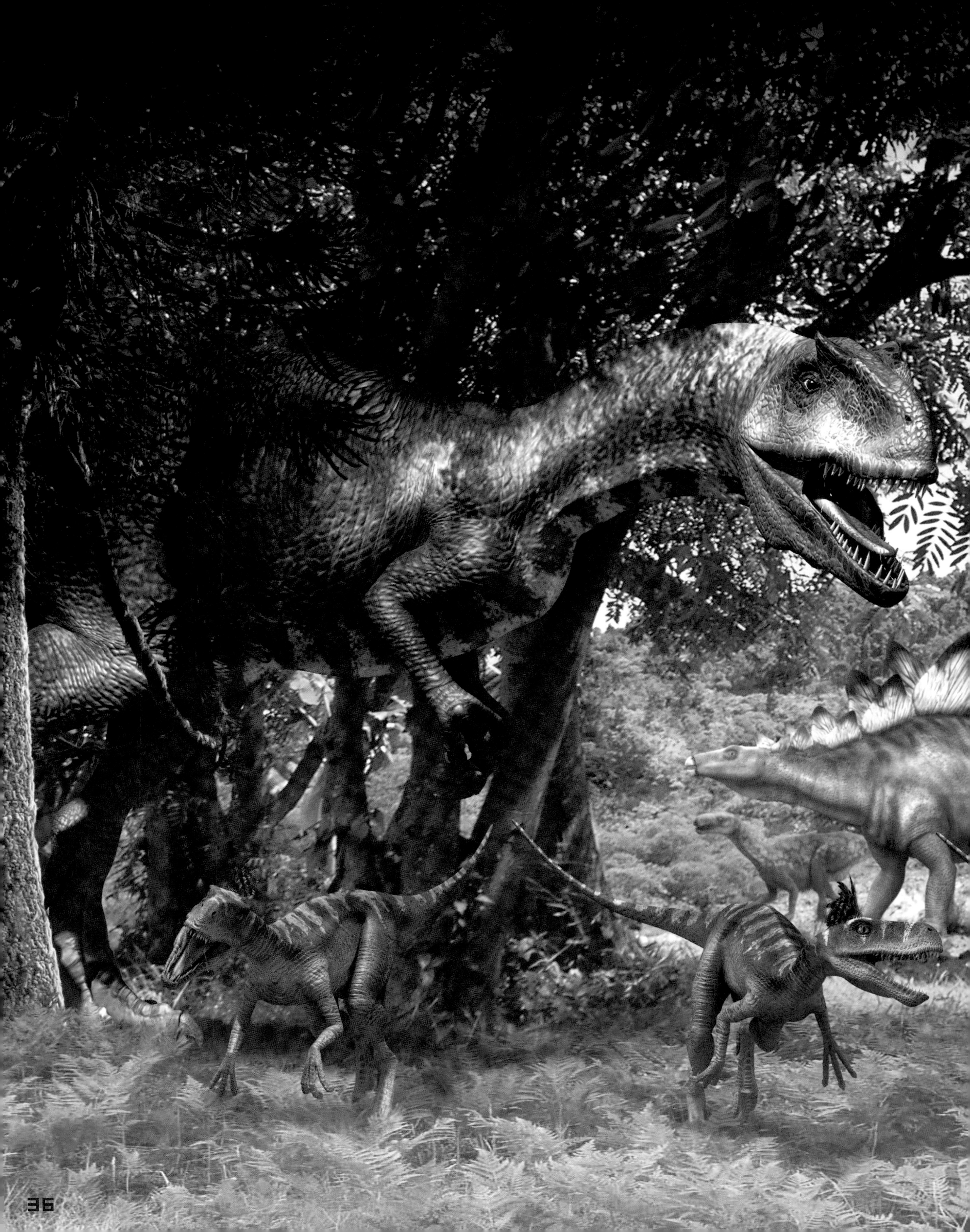

DINOSAURS OF THE LATE JURASSIC

161.2–145.5 MILLION YEARS AGO

In the world of the Late Jurassic, the climate is warm and dry. Pangaea is a distant memory, and as the continents continue to drift apart, the geography of the Earth is slowly beginning to resemble today's world. Advanced theropods, known as tetanurans, have spread worldwide, and among them is the ferocious ***Allosaurus*** – the heavy, meat-eating king of this period. But the Late Jurassic is truly the age of the giant-bodied sauropods on which ***Allosaurus*** preys. Never before or since have the long-necked, plant-eating animals been so enormous or so abundant. Some of these animals weigh more than 70 tonnes. The plains of North America and Africa shake as great herds of ***Brachiosaurus*** and ***Diplodocus*** roam thunderously in search of shrubs and conifers to eat, keeping together in large numbers to protect themselves from predators.

FOSSIL FINDS

AFRICA

Elaphrosaurus *is one of several dinosaurs known from the famous Tendaguru fossil beds of eastern Africa. During the early 1900s, large teams of collectors excavated more than 250 tonnes of dinosaur fossils from these sites.*

HABITAT

AFRICA, LATE JURASSIC

Elaphrosaurus *lived alongside the stegosaur* **Kentrosaurus** *and many other species on the fertile floodplains of eastern Africa about 150 million years ago.*

POTENTIAL RISK: EXTREME

Bulky sauropods can shield themselves with their size, but smaller herbivores are helpless when chased by **Elaphrosaurus**.

SIZE COMPARISON

A slender predator that is as tall as a man.

LENGTH: 4.5–6.5 metres (15–21 ft)

HEIGHT: 1.25–1.5 metres (4–5 ft)

WEIGHT: 200–250 kilograms (440–550 lb)

ELAPHROSAURUS

MEANING: 'lightweight lizard'

PRONUNCIATION: *e-LAF-ro-sore-uss*

One of the speediest predators of the dinosaur world, ***Elaphrosaurus*** can outrun even the quickest herbivorous dinosaurs. Like a cheetah, this fearsome predator relies on its agility and endurance to outrace its prey over long distances.

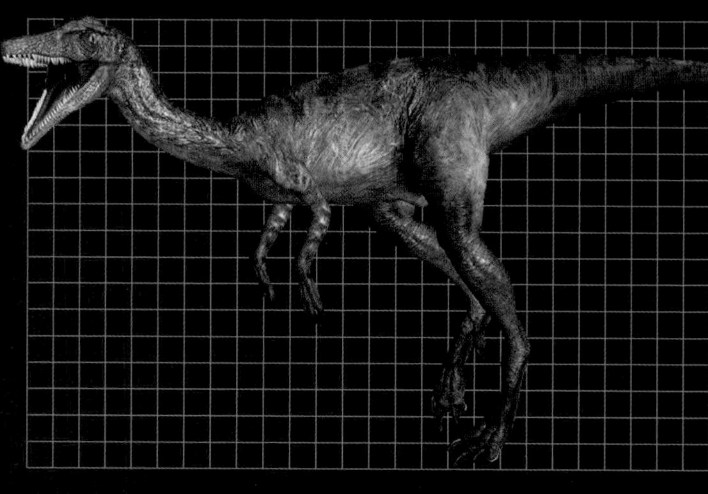

Elaphrosaurus lives in the shadow of the larger carnivorous dinosaurs, which rely on their large size and strong jaws to overpower their prey. The nimbler ***Elaphrosaurus*** has to be more creative. It is known to leap out of bushes to surprise young sauropods, which it then easily chases and outruns.

JAWS OF DEATH

An uncomfortably close view of the snout and teeth of ***Elaphrosaurus*** is often the last thing seen by many young sauropods in Africa. The glaring eyes, flaring nostrils and teeth dripping with saliva all mean that the chase is over and the end is near.

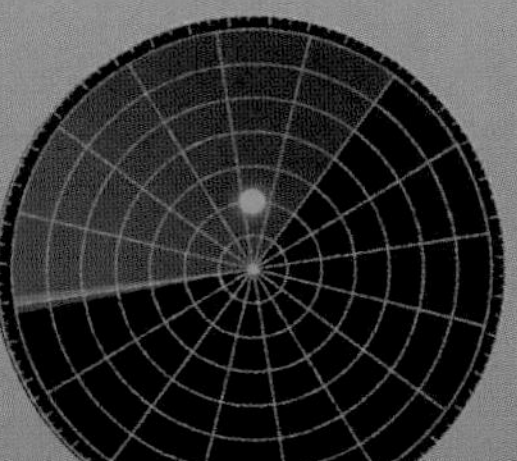

RANGE

1 METRE (3 FT) AND CLOSING
PROXIMITY ALERT
MAKE SPEEDY WITHDRAWAL

TOP SPEED

35 KPH (22 MPH)

WEAPONRY: FULLY ARMED

The rare combination of speed, sharp teeth, pointed claws and a keen brain makes **Elaphrosaurus** *a dangerous predator. All it lacks is size.*

POTENTIAL RISK: **EXTREME**

All other Late Jurassic dinosaurs live in fear of **Allosaurus***. Even the largest sauropods of the day avoid this most terrifying of predators.*

HABITAT

NORTHERN HEMISPHERE, LATE JURASSIC

Allosaurus *favoured the lowland floodplains near rivers and lakes, but was probably adapted to withstand almost any environment and roamed over many parts of the world.*

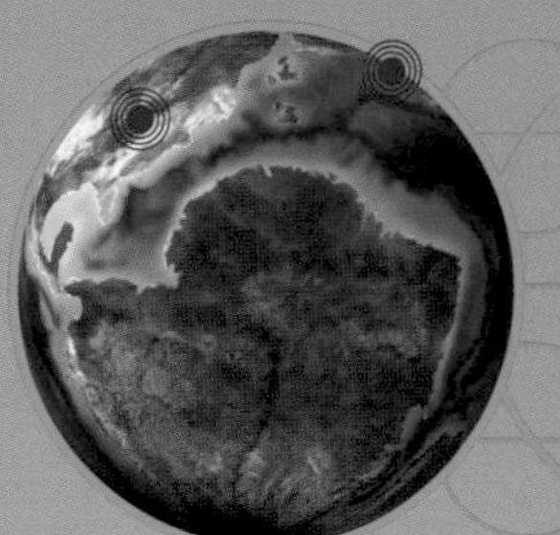

ALLOSAURUS

MEANING: 'different lizard'

PRONUNCIATION: *al-o-SAUR-uss*

Allosaurus is a major force of the Late Jurassic. This brawny carnivore is one of the most famous dinosaurs, earning its reputation as a terrifying predator by stalking large sauropods across the floodplains of North America.

BATTERED MEAT

Allosaurus is the largest carnivore in its ecosystem and is feared by everything that lives alongside it. Even other large theropods, such as ***Ceratosaurus*** and ***Torosaurus***, avoid ***Allosaurus*** at all costs. The reasons are simple: a skull 1 metre (3 ft) long that bristles with sharp teeth, powerful jaw muscles for ripping apart flesh and a neck so strong that the creature can grab prey in its mouth and batter it to death against the ground.

The leg and hip muscles of **Allosaurus** *are massive, allowing fast and sustained running.*

RANGE

10.5 METRES (35 FT) AND CLOSING
PROXIMITY ALERT
EVASIVE ACTION RECOMMENDED

TOP SPEED

30 KPH (20 MPH)

FOSSIL FINDS

NORTH AMERICA, EUROPE

Allosaurus *was an immensely successful dinosaur. Its fossils are common in the Late Jurassic rocks of North America, but it is also known from Europe and possibly Africa. Few other dinosaurs were as widespread.*

NECK CHOP

Allosaurus attacks in a particularly vicious way. Its head darts forwards, open-mouthed, towards the neck of its prey. It then strikes downwards with a deadly impact, just like a hatchet chopping a piece of wood.

SIZE COMPARISON

A muscular beast that could quickly dismember a man.

LENGTH: 7.5–12 metres (25–40 ft)

HEIGHT: 2 metres (6–7 ft)

WEIGHT: 1000–1800 kilograms (2200–3970 lb)

YANGCHUANOSAURUS

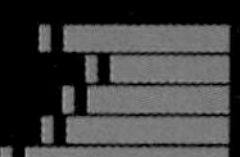

MEANING: named after its discovery site in China

PRONUNCIATION: *yang-CHOO-an-o-sore-uss*

Yangchuanosaurus, a close relative of ***Allosaurus,*** prowls the forests of Asia. Like ***Allosaurus,*** it is the largest and most feared predator in its ecosystem, and is especially fond of the many large sauropods that feed deep in the forests.

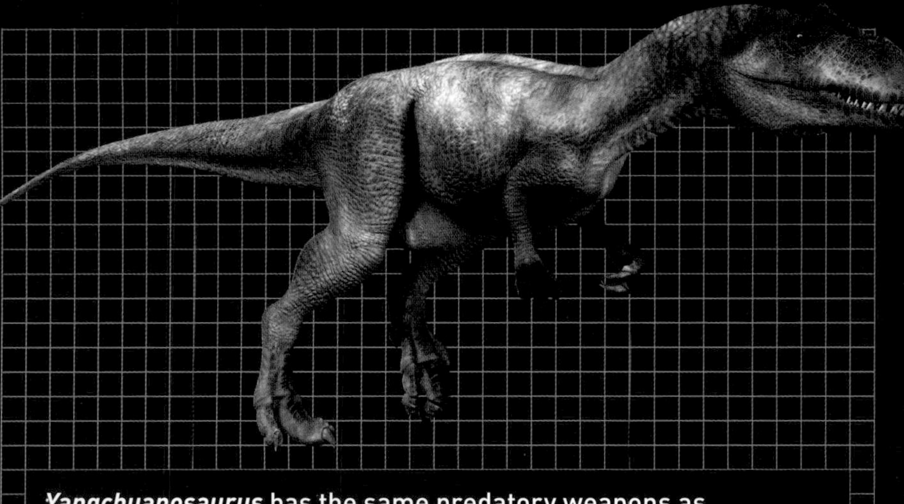

Yangchuanosaurus has the same predatory weapons as ***Allosaurus*** – claws, teeth and a strong neck. But the skull of ***Yangchuanosaurus*** is light and hollow. Many of the skull's bones have deep sinuses (hollow spaces). These help this predator to breathe more efficiently, giving it a stronger sense of smell.

POTENTIAL RISK: EXTREME

***Yangchuanosaurus** is even more dangerous than the terrifying **Allosaurus** because this predator's acute sense of smell can detect prey over great distances.*

SIZE COMPARISON

A muscular beast that can tackle any prey.

LENGTH: 7.5–9.75 metres (25–32 ft)

HEIGHT: 2 metres (6–7 ft)

WEIGHT: 900–1000 kilograms (1985–2200 lb)

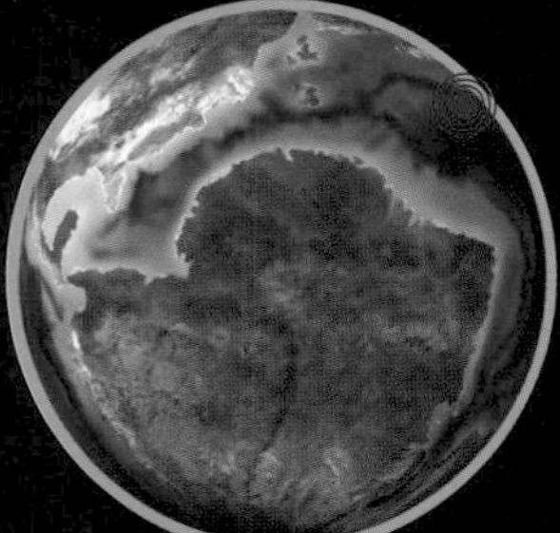

HABITAT

ASIA, LATE JURASSIC

*In the Late Jurassic, about 150–160 million years ago, Asia was home to a rich array of dinosaurs. **Yangchuanosaurus** preyed on sauropods and plate-backed stegosaurs.*

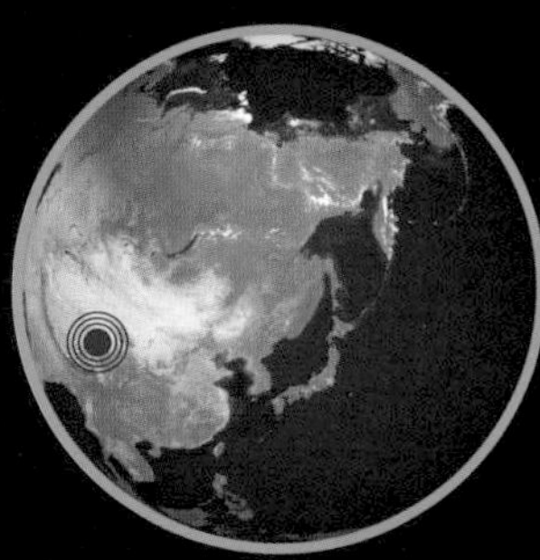

FOSSIL FINDS

ASIA

*Only two fossils of **Yangchuanosaurus** have been found, both from the southern Sichuan Province of China. One was discovered while workers were blasting rock to build a dam.*

HEAVY BREATHER

The deep and complex skull sinuses of ***Yangchuanosaurus*** not only give this predator a sharp sense of smell. They also allow it to breathe more efficiently, which means that it can run faster and for longer.

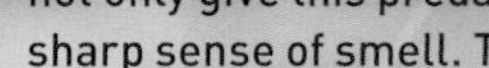

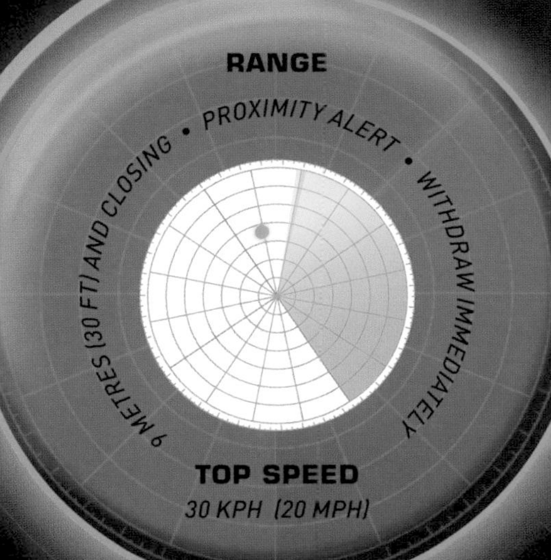

200
150
100
0273019210

IRREGULAR FEATHERS
Many dinosaurs have feathers, but only birds like Archaeopteryx have feathers that are asymmetrical (no regular shape). These give lift to its wings when flying.
FOSSIL FINDS
EUROPE
Archaeopteryx is probably the single most famous fossil animal in the world. A handful of beautiful specimens have been found in the 150-million-year-old limestones of Germany, many of which preserve exquisite details of the feathers.
WEAK CHEST
The flight muscles of birds are located on the chest and are anchored by a large breast-bone. Archaeopteryx lacks both the bone and the enlarged muscles, so is a poor flier.
HABITAT
EUROPE, LATE JURASSIC
Archaeopteryx lived along the rocky shores of a series of small lakes that dotted central Europe during the Late Jurassic. It ran across the ground, chasing small lizards and mammals.
POTENTIAL RISK: VERY LOW
Only insects and small mammals live in fear of this lightweight and shy bird.
SIZE COMPARISON
A crow-sized bird that is easy to miss.
LENGTH: 30–46 centimetres (12–18 in)
HEIGHT: 15 centimetres (6 in)
WEIGHT: 1–3 kilograms (2–7 lb)

ARCHAEOPTERYX

MEANING: 'ancient wing'

PRONUNCIATION: *ark-e-OP-ter-ix*

With its brightly coloured wing feathers, the meek little ***Archaeopteryx*** might easily be mistaken for a parrot. However, this insect-eater is one of the oldest and most primitive of all birds. Because of its importance in the evolution of dinosaurs into birds, an ***Archaeopteryx*** sighting is a must.

00273019210001010100027301921000101 51015

Archaeopteryx is a true bird – it is covered with feathers and has wings that enable powered, flapping flight. However, compared with most modern birds, ***Archaeopteryx*** is a weak flier. Its flight muscles are poorly developed, so it can flap for only short periods of time. Also, unlike other birds, the feet of ***Archaeopteryx*** do not allow it to perch in trees, so this creature spends most of its time on the ground.

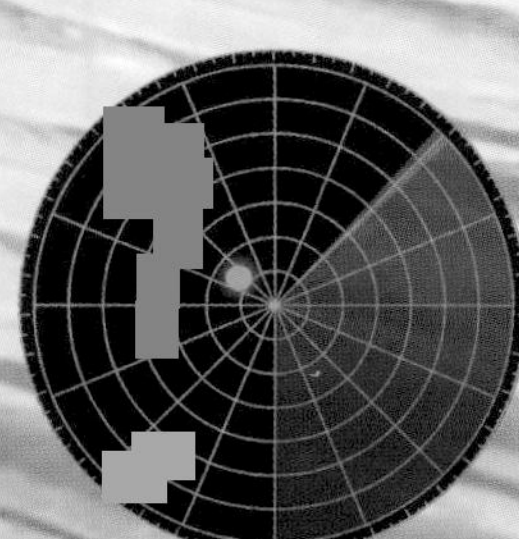

RANGE

1 METRE (3 FT) AND CLOSING
PROXIMITY ALERT
SAFE TO APPROACH

TOP SPEED

40 KPH (25 MPH)

WEAPONRY: VERY LOW

Archaeopteryx *is rare among birds in possessing sharp teeth and curved claws, which it uses to dispatch small prey.*

POTENTIAL RISK: **LOW**

Although only a gentle plant-eater, **Mamenchisaurus** *can crush unsuspecting animals with one misstep.*

HABITAT

ASIA, LATE JURASSIC

Along with **Yangchuanosaurus, Mamenchisaurus** *favoured the dense forests of Late Jurassic Asia, where it could munch plants throughout the day.*

0102734621027301063892 10.948.6300011628.83.9

MAMENCHISAURUS

MEANING: named after its discovery site in China

PRONUNCIATION: *ma-mench-is-SORE-uss*

Mamenchisaurus is one of the circus freaks of the dinosaur world. It holds the record for the longest neck of any dinosaur. This skinny, snake-like structure stretches nearly 12 metres (40 ft) and is longer than the rest of the body combined!

250

0

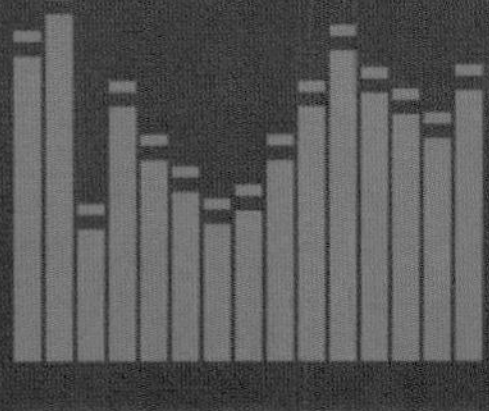

00273019210

RANGE

50.6 METRES (166 FT) AND CLOSING

APPROACH WITH CAUTION

TOP SPEED

8 KPH (5 MPH)

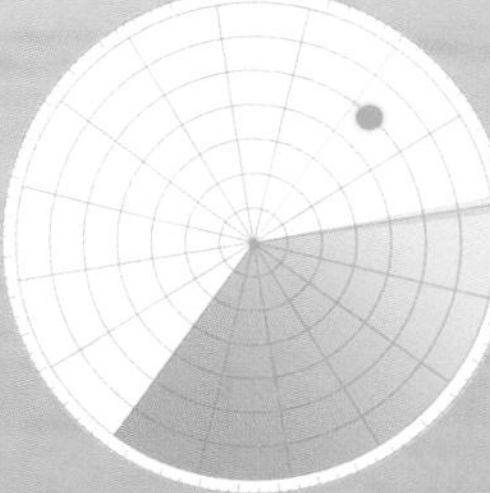

010273462102730106389

0102734621027301063892 10.948.6300011628.83.9 0102734621027301063892 10.948.6300011628.83.9

FOSSIL FINDS

ASIA

Countless fossils of **Mamenchisaurus** *have been found in China, clearly showing that this herbivore was one of the most common and successful animals of its time.*

CANOPY BROWSER

Mamenchisaurus's neck is so long because it needs to eat large amounts of vegetation. The length enables the animal to reach leaves and stems high in the canopy that are inaccessible to smaller sauropods.

MIGHTY BULK

This noodle-necked herbivore is one of the largest dinosaurs that ever lived. It is by far the biggest creature in its Asian ecosystem, and has to eat several tonnes of leaves and stems each day to provide the energy needs of its huge body. Even the mega-predator ***Yangchuanosaurus*** finds it difficult to take down ***Mamenchisaurus***.

The back and hip muscles are incredibly strong, helping to support the weight of the animal.

SIZE COMPARISON

Mamenchisaurus, *a true titan of a dinosaur, dominates the landscape.*

LENGTH: 20–25 metres (65–82 ft)

HEIGHT: 5–6 metres (16–20 ft)

WEIGHT: 20–25 tonnes

BRACHIOSAURUS

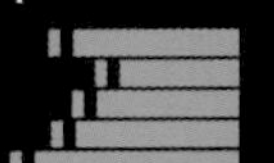

MEANING: 'arm lizard'

PRONUNCIATION: *BRACK-e-o-sore-uss*

The stocky, long-necked, strong-limbed ***Brachiosaurus*** is one of the better-known dinosaurs. It lives alongside the menacing ***Allosaurus*** but is able to avoid attack because of its bulky size and its habit of travelling in large herds.

Brachiosaurus is a giant among dinosaurs, and certainly the largest animal in its ecosystem. One of its most distinctive features is that the forelimbs are longer than the hindlimbs. These help ***Brachiosaurus*** to reach high into the trees in its search for leaves to eat.

POTENTIAL RISK: LOW

A peaceful herbivore, **Brachiosaurus** *can use its large size as a defensive weapon if provoked.*

SIZE COMPARISON

A hulking brute whose footsteps thunder across the plains.

LENGTH: 20–25 metres (65–82 ft)

HEIGHT: 5–6 metres (17–20 ft)

WEIGHT: 30–50 tonnes

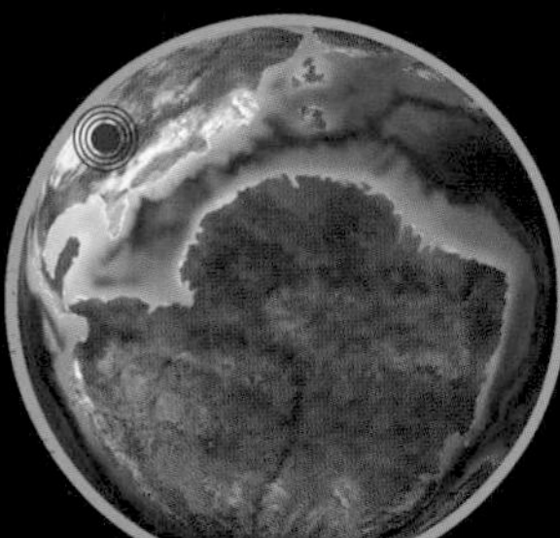

HABITAT

NORTH AMERICA AND AFRICA, LATE JURASSIC

Brachiosaurus *was a common sight along the riverbanks and in the wet forests of western North America during the Late Jurassic. It also lived in similar environments in Africa.*

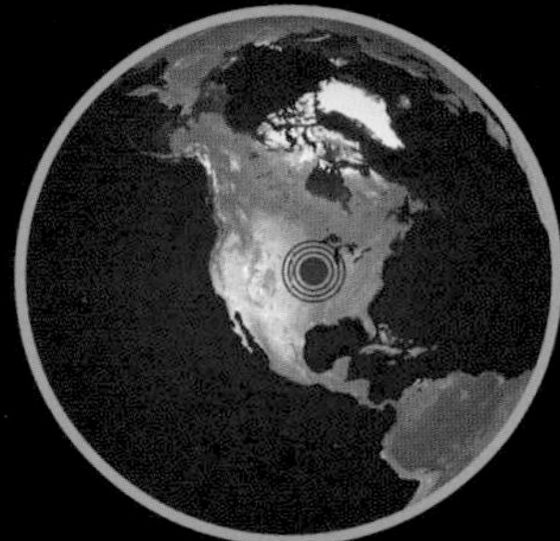

FOSSIL FINDS

NORTH AMERICA, AFRICA

Brachiosaurus *lived alongside a variety of giant sauropods, including* **Diplodocus, Apatosaurus** *and* **Barosaurus,** *during the Late Jurassic, about 150 million years ago.*

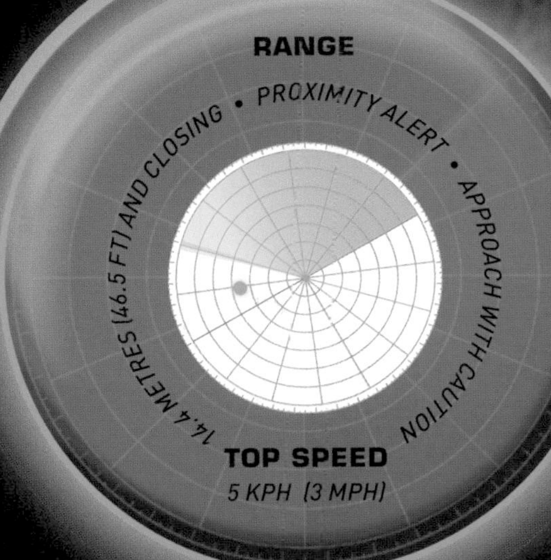

CALLING SYSTEM

The nostril of ***Brachiosaurus*** opens on top of the skull and is housed in a large dome. This hollow cavern is like a musical instrument, which ***Brachiosaurus*** uses to call out to mates and to scare off predators.

NECK OF THE WOODS

The neck of ***Brachiosaurus*** rises gracefully into the treetops. It can rise almost vertically because of the strong muscles and bones it contains.

POTENTIAL RISK: LOW

Like many other sauropods, **Diplodocus** *only uses its bulk as a weapon if threatened.*

HABITAT

NORTH AMERICA, LATE JURASSIC

Diplodocus *preferred the lowland areas near rivers, where there were vast quantities of bushes and ferns to graze on throughout the day.*

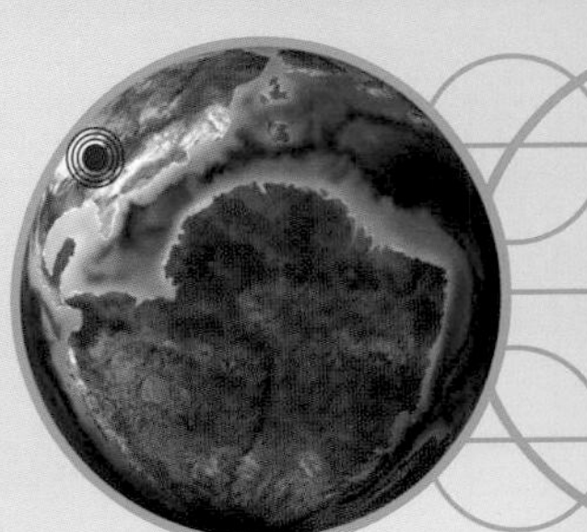

010273462102730106389210.948.6300011628.83.9

DIPLODOCUS

MEANING: 'double beam'

PRONUNCIATION: *dip-lo-do-KUSS*

Diplodocus is an unmistakable sight on the densely vegetated plains of North America. This sauropod herbivore is massive, with a long neck and an extremely long tail. The tail has tubular bones towards the end, which make it very flexible.

250

0

WHIP TAIL

The tail of ***Diplodocus*** has more than 80 separate bones, about double the number in other sauropods. It is used as a whip to fend off predators, and can deliver deadly blows if necessary.

RANGE

47.8 METRES (14.5 FT) AND CLOSING
PROXIMITY ALERT
APPROACH SLOWLY WITH CAUTION

TOP SPEED

5 KPH (3 MPH)

010273462102730106389

00273019210

FOSSIL FINDS

NORTH AMERICA

The first fossils of **Diplodocus** *were found in the late 1890s, when American business tycoon Andrew Carnegie dispatched a team of collectors to find a dinosaur for him.*

VARIETIES OF BIG

Diplodocus lives alongside ***Brachiosaurus***, another gargantuan sauropod. However, these herbivores are both large in different ways: ***Brachiosaurus*** is tall and heavy, whereas ***Diplodocus*** is lighter and extremely long. While ***Brachiosaurus*** reaches high into the treetops, ***Diplodocus*** uses its stretched neck to mow through low bushes and shrubs.

The forelimbs are strong and sturdy to support the weight of the animal.

SIZE COMPARISON

A long, low herbivore that lumbers across the plains.

LENGTH: 25–29 metres (82–95 ft)

HEIGHT: 3–4 metres (10–13 ft)

WEIGHT: 12–16 tonnes

FOSSIL FINDS

CHINA

One good fossil of **Huayangosaurus** *has been found in the Middle Jurassic rocks of western China.*

HABITAT

ASIA, MIDDLE JURASSIC

Huayangosaurus, *along with the theropod* **Gasosaurus** *and many other dinosaurs, thrived in the sweltering heat of western China about 160 million years ago.*

POTENTIAL RISK: MEDIUM

Huayangosaurus *is harmless if left alone, but will go on a deadly offensive if provoked.*

SIZE COMPARISON

A long, low, lumbering herbivore.

LENGTH: 4.5 metres (15 ft)

HEIGHT: 1.5 metres (5 ft)

WEIGHT: 900–1000 kilograms (1985–2200 lb)

SPIKED BLOW
The tail of *Huayangosaurus* is its most important weapon. It is very flexible, allowing the spikes on the end to be swung in a wide, lethal arc.

HUAYANGOSAURUS

MEANING: named after its discovery site in China

PRONUNCIATION: *hwa-yang-o-SORE-uss*

One of the oldest and most primitive of the plate-backed stegosaurs, ***Huayangosaurus*** is a gentle plant-eater with a taste for ferns. Its bristling armour is a clear warning that attacking predators should proceed at their own risk!

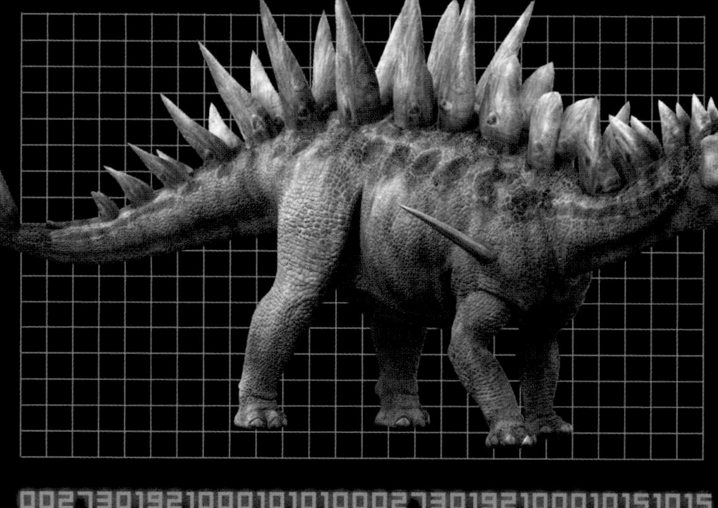

Huayangosaurus lives alongside a number of large and diverse theropods, but these predators rarely attack. The thick plates along the back of ***Huayangosaurus***, and the sharp spikes on the shoulder and tail, can injure or kill even the fiercest attackers.

0027301921000101010002730192100010151015

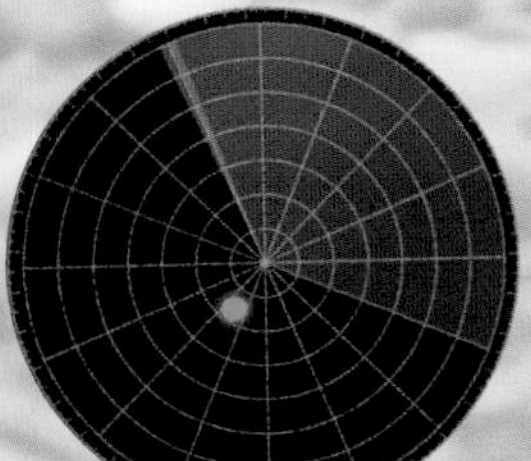

RANGE
4.4 METRES (14.4 FT) AND CLOSING KEEP YOUR DISTANCE

TOP SPEED
15 KPH (10 MPH)

WEAPONRY: FULLY ARMED
Thick, long and sharp spikes over the shoulders and on the tail can be instantly turned on this animal's rivals.

POTENTIAL RISK: MEDIUM

Allosaurus *and other predators live in fear of the tail spikes of* **Stegosaurus**.

HABITAT

NORTH AMERICA AND EUROPE, LATE JURASSIC

Herds of **Stegosaurus** *flocked to the riverbanks and other damp areas of western North America, where ferns and juicy shrubs grew in abundance.*

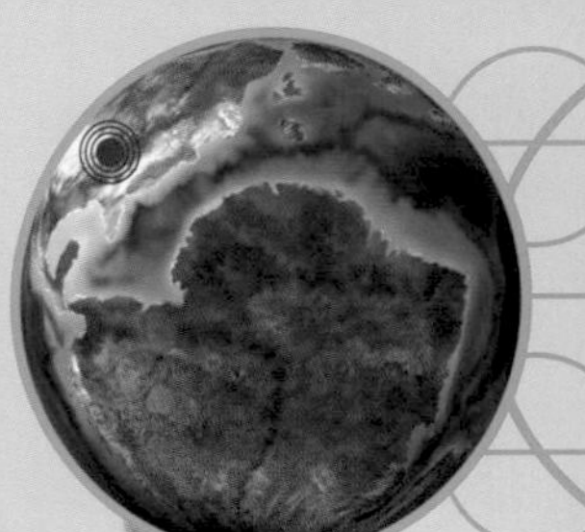

0102734621027301063892 10.948.6300011628.83.9

STEGOSAURUS

MEANING: 'roofed lizard'

PRONUNCIATION: *steg-o-SORE-uss*

Its huge plates and spikes make ***Stegosaurus*** one of the most recognizable dinosaurs. It peacefully grazes on ferns and other ground vegetation in the shadow of ***Allosaurus***, always keeping its tail spikes raised in anticipation of an attack.

250

0

UNIQUE DESIGN

Stegosaurus is a bulky animal with a striking appearance. However, compared with ***Brachiosaurus***, ***Diplodocus*** and other sauropods from the same time, it is a relatively small herbivore. ***Stegosaurus*** is able to avoid competing with these long-necked giants by eating soft shrubs that grow near the ground.

0027301921000101 51015

00273019210

RANGE

13.6 METRES (44.6 FT)

PROXIMITY ALERT

REMAIN STATIONARY

TOP SPEED

15 KPH (10 MPH)

FOSSIL FINDS

NORTH AMERICA, EUROPE

Stegosaurus *is known from numerous fossils discovered in the famous Morrison Formation of the United States, as well as from fragmentary specimens found in Portugal.*

TABLE-SIZED PLATES

The back plates of ***Stegosaurus*** are enormous – some are larger than a coffee table! They are not used for defence but rather as a display to impress mates.

SHRUB MUNCHER

With its beaky mouth that shears leaves and stems like scissors, ***Stegosaurus*** is perfectly adapted for chomping on soft plants.

SIZE COMPARISON

A low and bulky herbivore with enormous back plates.

LENGTH: 9 metres (30 ft)

HEIGHT: 2.5 metres (8 ft)

WEIGHT: 3–3.5 tonnes

SHAPE CHANGER

The body of ***Camarasaurus*** changes remarkably as it grows from hatchling into adult. Its neck gradually becomes longer and its bones slimmer as it matures.

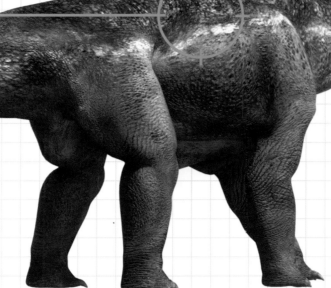

SIZE COMPARISON

LENGTH: 18–21 metres (59–69 ft)

HEIGHT: 3–5 metres (10–16 ft)

WEIGHT: 15–20 tonnes

Camarasaurus *is a short and stocky, long-necked sauropod.*

POTENTIAL RISK: VERY LOW

Camarasaurus *is a herbivorous dinosaur that poses no threat unless it feels cornered, when it may use its tail to swipe.*

CAMARASAURUS

MEANING: 'chambered lizard'

PRONUNCIATION: *kam-ah-ra-SORE-uss*

A short and stocky brute, ***Camarasaurus*** is the most common dinosaur on the leafy Morrison floodplains of North America. Thundering herds of ***Camarasaurus***, their footsteps echoing across the landscape, are a common sight.

FOSSIL FINDS

NORTH AMERICA, LATE JURASSIC

Over 20 specimens of **Camarasaurus** *fossils, including a complete skull, have been found in the Morrison Formation in Colorado. It was one of more than 10 species of sauropod that lived there about 150 million years ago.*

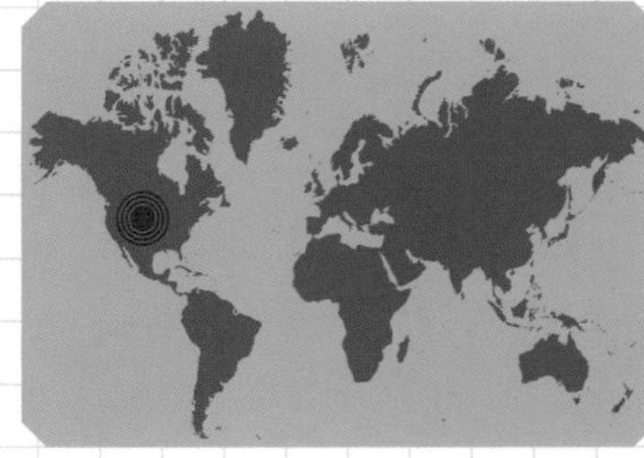

FAST GROWER

Apatosaurus reaches its huge size very quickly. It achieves full adulthood in only 13 years, meaning that a juvenile must gain about 15 kilograms (33 lb) every day of its young life!

SIZE COMPARISON

LENGTH: 19–25 metres (62–82 ft)

HEIGHT: 3–5 metres (10–16 ft)

WEIGHT: 25–28 tonnes

Apatosaurus *is a monstrous plant-eating machine.*

POTENTIAL RISK: LOW

Apatosaurus *can be dangerous because of its sheer size, so smaller animals should avoid its massive feet.*

APATOSAURUS

MEANING: 'deceptive lizard'

PRONUNCIATION: *a-pat-o-SORE-uss*

Apatosaurus is one of the largest animals ever to have walked the Earth. This enormous plant-guzzler, formerly known as ***Brontosaurus***, literally shakes the ground as it wanders the Morrison riverbanks of North America in search of new trees and bushes to eat.

FOSSIL FINDS

NORTH AMERICA, LATE JURASSIC

Apatosaurus *lived alongside* **Camarasaurus, Diplodocus** *and* **Brachiosaurus** *in western North America about 150 million years ago. Many of its fossils have been found in this region.*

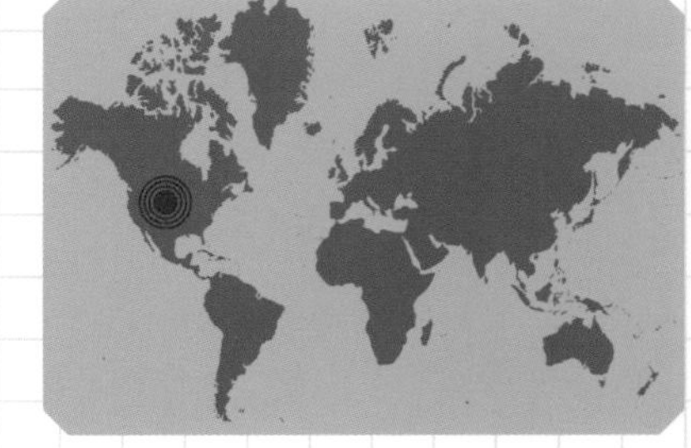

POTENTIAL RISK: LOW

Like many herbivores, **Dacentrurus** *is harmless if left alone, but could deliver a lethal strike with its spiky tail if threatened.*

DACENTRURUS

MEANING: 'very sharp tail'

PRONUNCIATION: *da-SEN-troo-russ*

SIZE COMPARISON

LENGTH: 4.5–10 metres (15–33 ft)
HEIGHT: 2 metres (6.5 ft)
WEIGHT: 1400–2000 kilograms (3090–4410 lb)

The body of **Dacentrurus** *is modest in size, but the back plates give a menacing profile.*

All across the European island, one small herbivore dominates the landscape: ***Dacentrurus***. This plate-backed stegosaur exists in huge numbers because it is remarkably successful at dodging predators. Large carnivores, such as ***Megalosaurus***, have learned to avoid the thick back plates and devastating tail spikes of ***Dacentrurus*** at all costs.

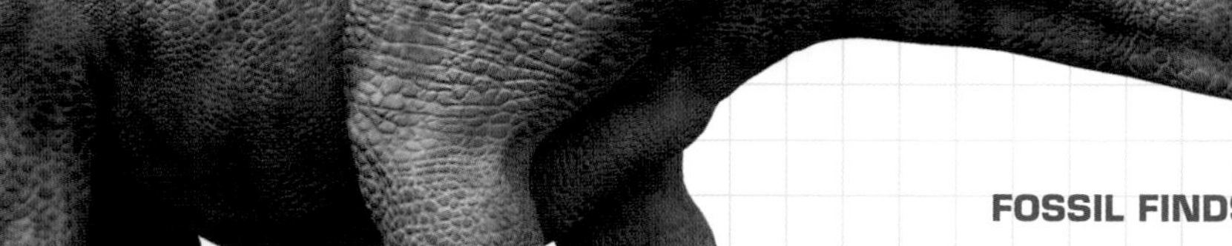

FOSSIL FINDS

EUROPE, LATE JURASSIC

The first fossils of **Dacentrurus** *were found in the 1870s. This stegosaur lived about 150 million years ago when Europe was fragmented into many small islands.*

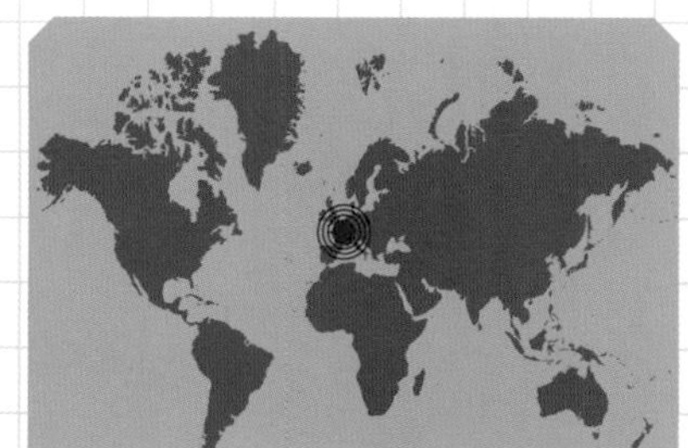

POTENTIAL RISK: LOW

Kentrosaurus *is normally gentle, but an attacking predator can expect a nasty jab from the shoulder spikes.*

SIZE COMPARISON

LENGTH: 4–5 metres (13–16 ft)
HEIGHT: 1.5 metres (5 ft)
WEIGHT: 1–1.5 tonnes

This small stegosaur needs sharp weapons to make up for its slender build.

KENTROSAURUS

MEANING: 'pointed lizard'

PRONUNCIATION: *ken-tro-SORE-uss*

FOSSIL FINDS

AFRICA, LATE JURASSIC

Kentrosaurus *lived in eastern Africa about 150 million years ago. Hundreds of its bones have been found in the famous fossil beds of Tanzania.*

Much smaller than most other stegosaurs, ***Kentrosaurus*** makes up for its lack of stature with a destructive arsenal of spikes and plates that can be used against any predators. The teeth of this herbivore are small and simple, used to ingest large quantities of soft plants along the banks of streams.

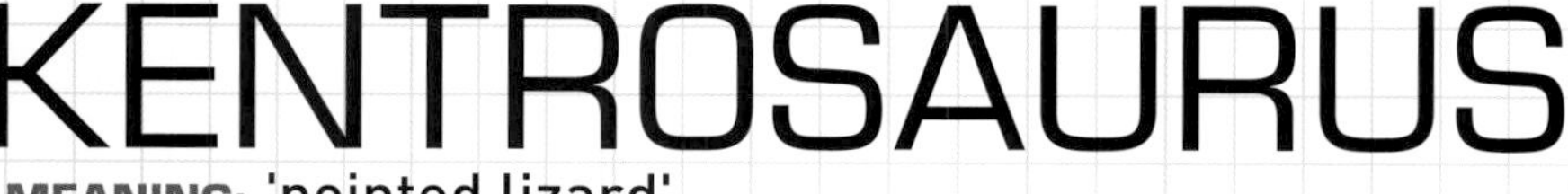

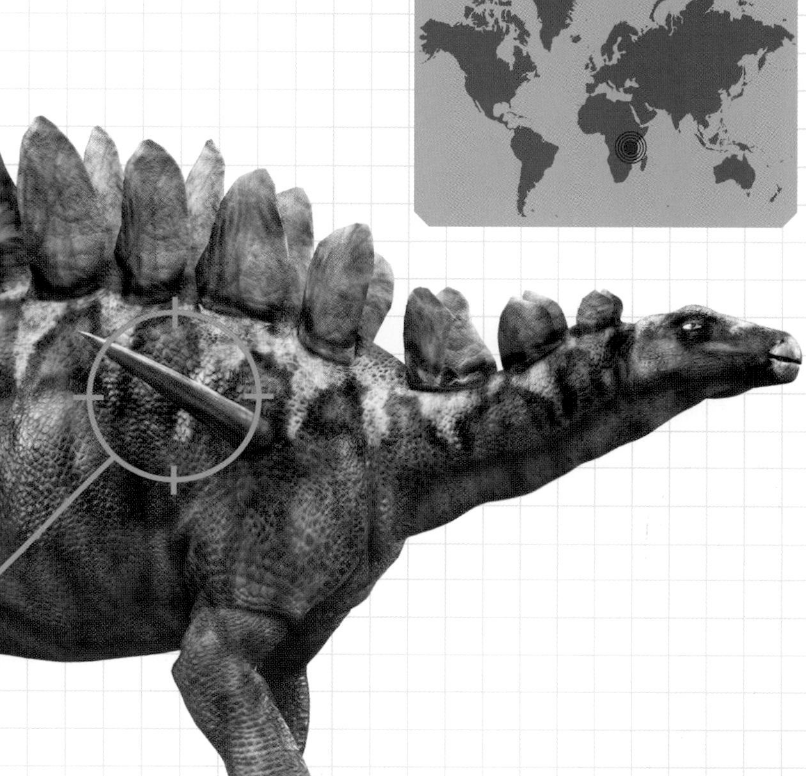

ARMOURED VEGETARIAN

The most important weapons of ***Kentrosaurus*** are the spikes that project backwards and sideways from each shoulder. Along with the tail spikes, these ward off dangerous predators, such as ***Elaphrosaurus***.

GARGOYLEOSAURUS

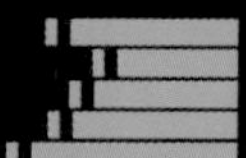

MEANING: 'gargoyle lizard'

PRONUNCIATION: *garh-GOYL-o-sore-uss*

Gargoyleosaurus is an ugly little creature. This lumbering herbivore is short and plump, and its face is covered with patches of swollen skin. In some ways it resembles a gargoyle from a Gothic cathedral, hence its name.

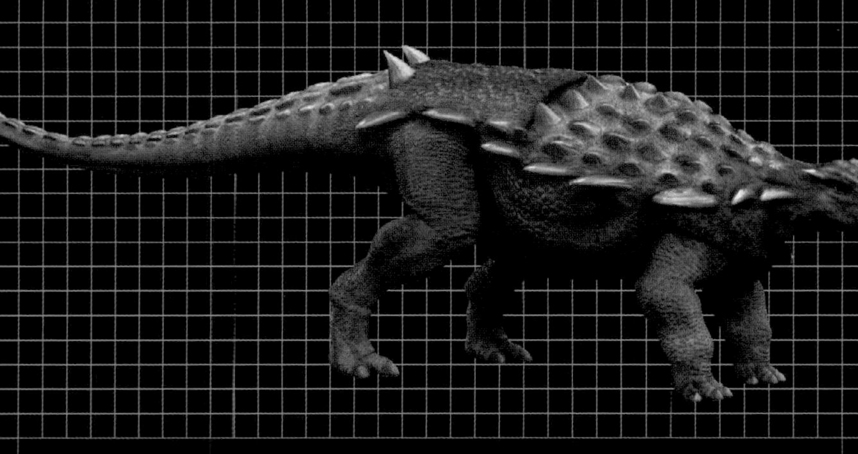

Gargoyleosaurus is one of the most dominant ankylosaurs, the large group of tank-like herbivores that plod about on four legs. Ankylosaurs are slow runners but avoid predators simply by crouching down. No attacker wants to break its teeth on the bony armour of ***Gargoyleosaurus***!

POTENTIAL RISK: VERY LOW

This primitive ankylosaur lacks the bony tail clubs and spikes of later relatives, but its thick armour is a defence against predators.

SIZE COMPARISON

One of the smallest ankylosaurs, with a tiny skull in comparison to its body.

LENGTH: 3 metres (10 ft)

HEIGHT: 1 metre (3.5 ft)

WEIGHT: 900–1100 kilograms (1985–2425 lb)

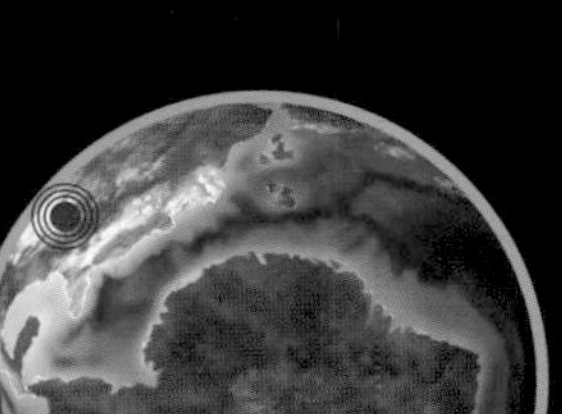

HABITAT

NORTH AMERICA, LATE JURASSIC

Gargoyleosaurus *probably lived in lowland areas alongside rivers and lakes, much like its cousin* **Stegosaurus**.

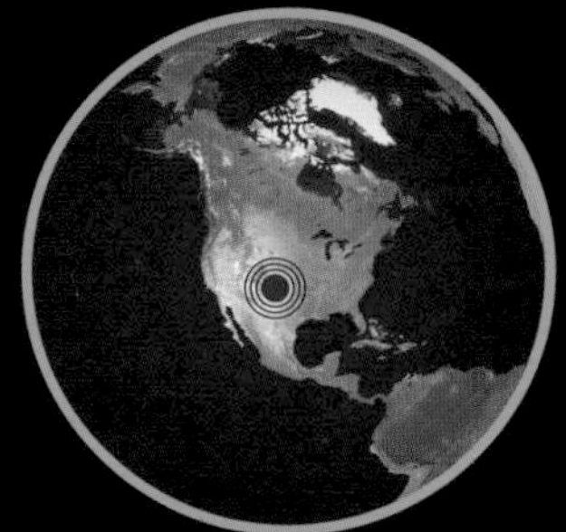

FOSSIL FINDS

NORTH AMERICA

The fossils of **Gargoyleosaurus**, *like those of* **Allosaurus** *and* **Stegosaurus**, *come from the Morrison Formation of western North America, which was deposited by rivers and lakes 150 million years ago.*

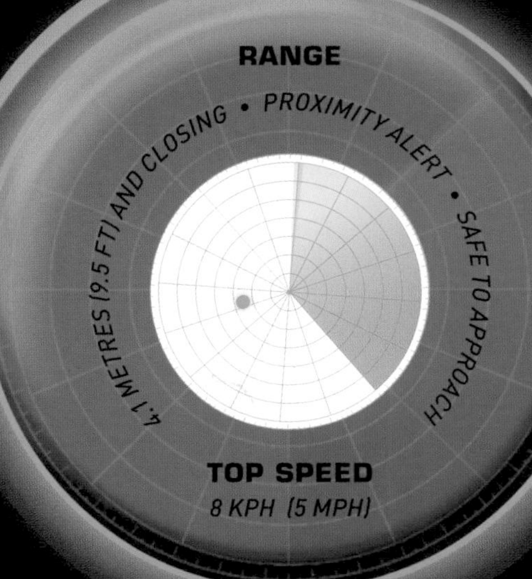

BOXY HEAD
The skull of *Gargoyleosaurus* is bizarre: it is small, box-like and covered with many small armour plates that are fused to the skull itself.
200
150
100

ADAPTABLE LEGS

Camptosaurus can walk on two or four legs. It usually stands on all four as it feeds, but can run faster if it rears up on its hindlegs.

FOSSIL FINDS

NORTH AMERICA, EUROPE

Fossils of **Camptosaurus** *are common in the Morrison Formation of the United States, and they have also been discovered thousands of kilometres away in England.*

HABITAT

NORTH AMERICA AND EUROPE, LATE JURASSIC

Camptosaurus *was able to reach the tops of mid-sized trees, so could browse at a height in between the low-grazing stegosaurs and the high-feeding sauropods.*

POTENTIAL RISK: VERY LOW

This herbivore is a gentle giant that never attacks other animals, unless threatened.

SIZE COMPARISON

An elephant-sized plant-muncher.

LENGTH: 5–7.5 metres (16–25 ft)

HEIGHT: 1.5–2.5 metres (5–8 ft)

WEIGHT: 880–1985 kilograms (1935–4370 lb)

CAMPTOSAURUS

MEANING: 'bent lizard'

PRONUNCIATION: *kamp-to-SORE-uss*

Of all the herbivores in the Morrison ecosystem of North America, ***Camptosaurus*** is the least spectacular. It lacks the long neck of a sauropod, the spikes of a stegosaur and the armour of an ankylosaur. It is, however, a mega-herbivore, well adapted to eating huge amounts of plants very quickly.

Camptosaurus is a slow-moving animal with a habit of fast eating. Its jaws contain several leaf-shaped teeth, which are perfect for grinding tough leaves, and its upper jaw can rotate outwards while feeding, which allows the animal to chew its food thoroughly.

0027301921000101010002730192100010151015

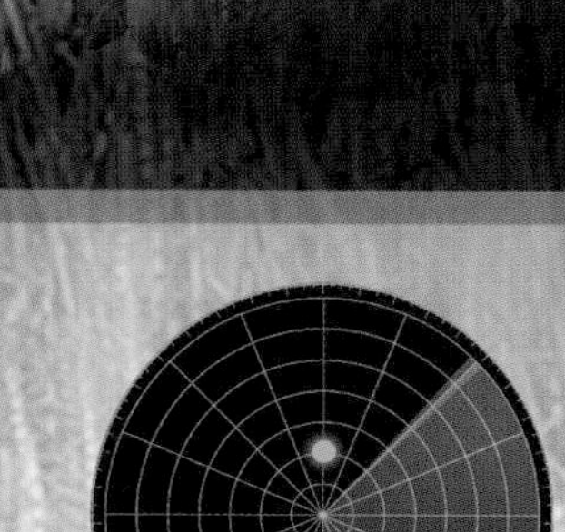

RANGE
3.7 METRES (12.1 FT) AND CLOSING
PROXIMITY ALERT
SAFE TO APPROACH

TOP SPEED
20 KPH (12 MPH)

WEAPONRY: NONE
Camptosaurus *has no sharp teeth, claws, spikes or armour. It is harmless.*

DRYOSAURUS

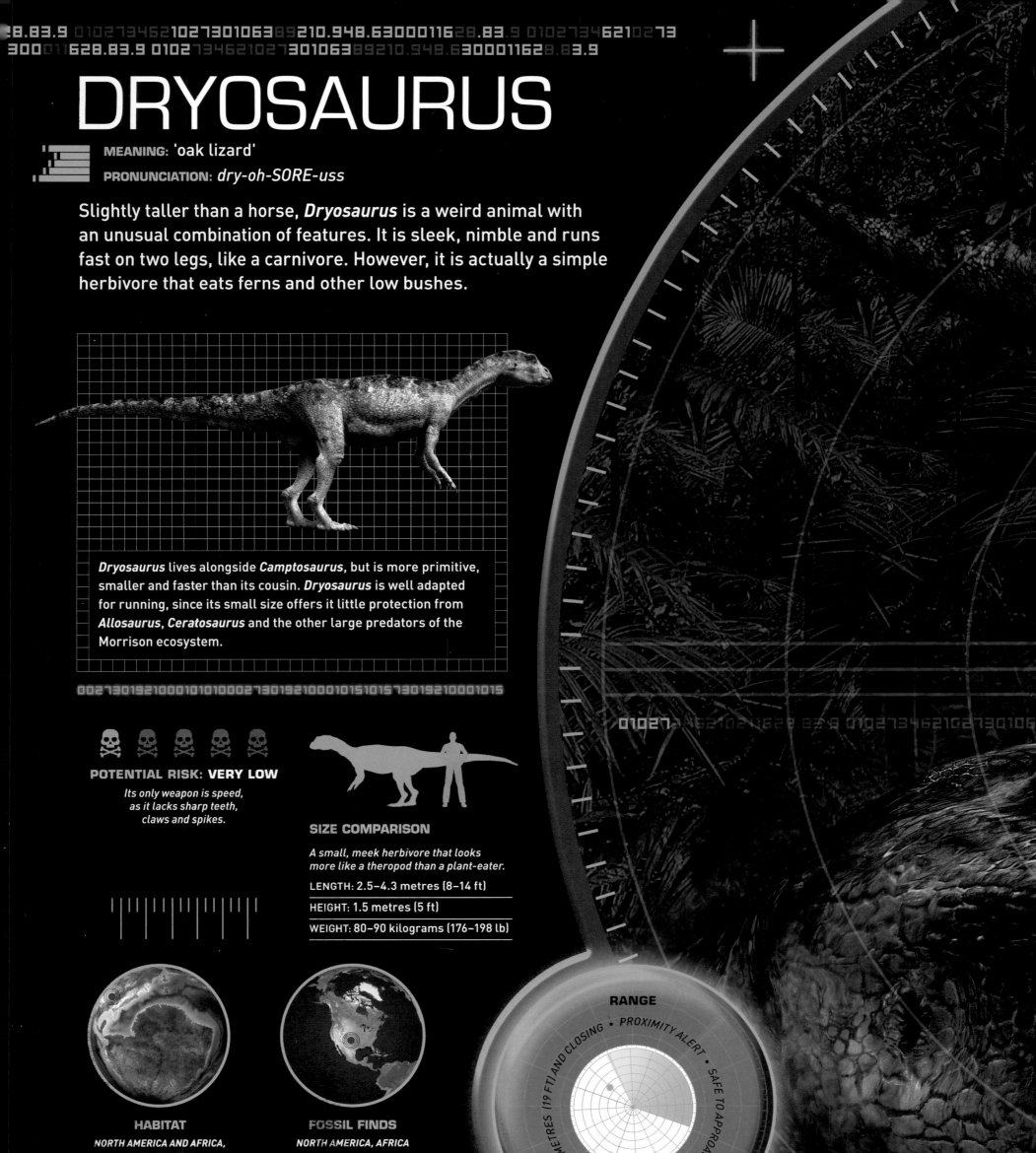

MEANING: 'oak lizard'

PRONUNCIATION: *dry-oh-SORE-uss*

Slightly taller than a horse, ***Dryosaurus*** is a weird animal with an unusual combination of features. It is sleek, nimble and runs fast on two legs, like a carnivore. However, it is actually a simple herbivore that eats ferns and other low bushes.

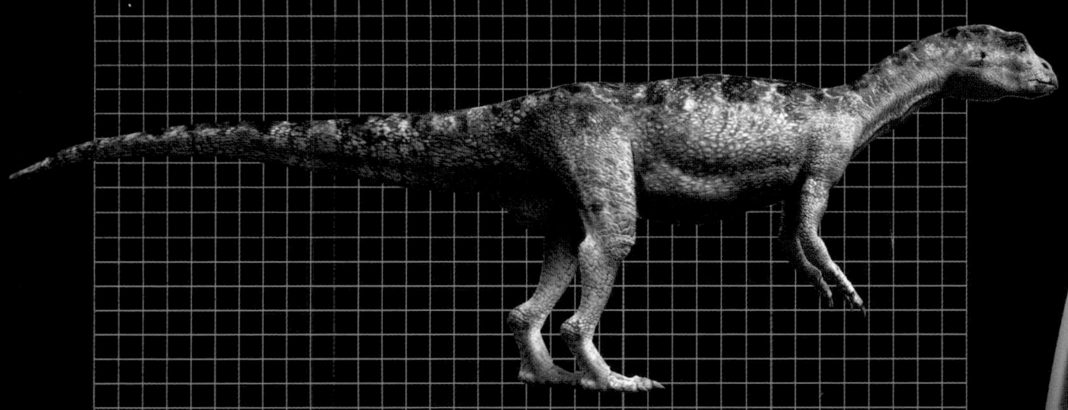

Dryosaurus lives alongside ***Camptosaurus***, but is more primitive, smaller and faster than its cousin. ***Dryosaurus*** is well adapted for running, since its small size offers it little protection from ***Allosaurus***, ***Ceratosaurus*** and the other large predators of the Morrison ecosystem.

POTENTIAL RISK: VERY LOW

Its only weapon is speed, as it lacks sharp teeth, claws and spikes.

SIZE COMPARISON

A small, meek herbivore that looks more like a theropod than a plant-eater.

LENGTH: 2.5–4.3 metres (8–14 ft)

HEIGHT: 1.5 metres (5 ft)

WEIGHT: 80–90 kilograms (176–198 lb)

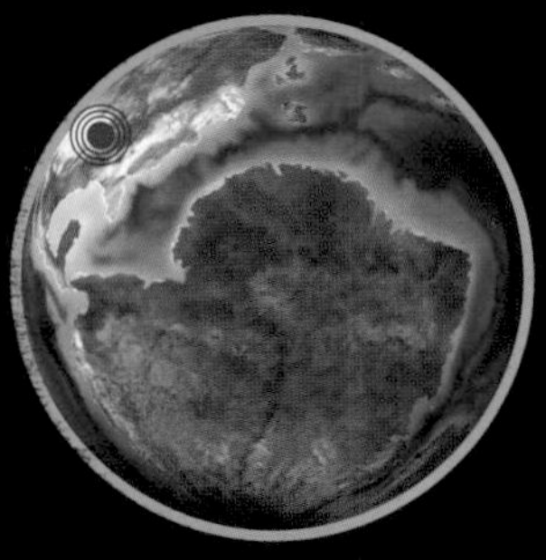

HABITAT

NORTH AMERICA AND AFRICA, LATE JURASSIC

***Dryosaurus** could not feed on the taller trees that its cousin **Camptosaurus** could reach, so it flocked to the fern-choked forest floors and river margins of the African and North American frontiers.*

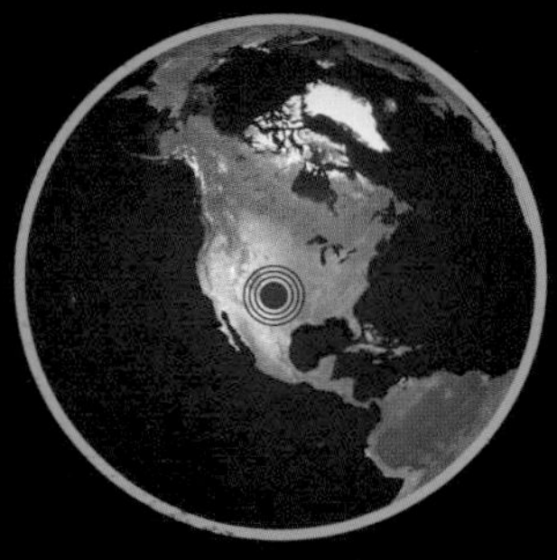

FOSSIL FINDS

NORTH AMERICA, AFRICA

***Dryosaurus** fossils have been found in the Morrison Formation of North America, as well as in the famous fossil beds of eastern Africa.*

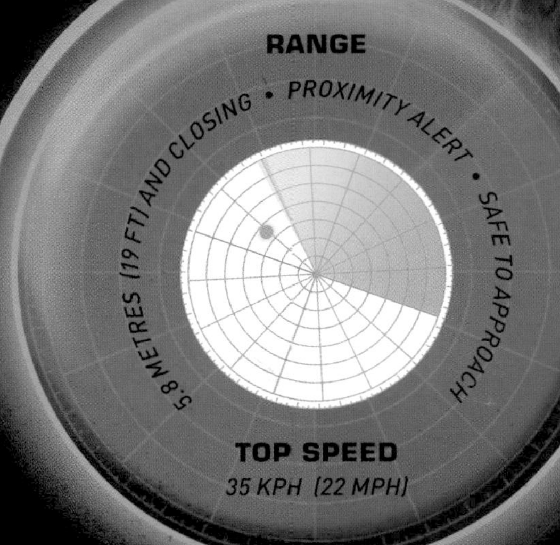

AGILE WALKER
Dryosaurus walks on two legs most of the time, just like theropod dinosaurs. It has an upright and agile posture – strange features for a gentle plant-eater.
BEAKY MOUTH
The front of the skull ends in a sharp beak, much like that of a bird. It is ideal for shearing and snipping plants.
200
150
100
0273019210

DINOSAURS OF THE EARLY–MIDDLE CRETACEOUS

145.5–99.6 MILLION YEARS AGO

The Cretaceous belonged to the dinosaurs. It was a time when they were so diverse and abundant that they dominated the world. No spot was left untouched by these giants. The planet was changing, too. By the middle of the Cretaceous, the supercontinent of Pangaea was just a distant memory. North America and Europe had drifted apart and were now separated by oceans. Animals no longer had complete freedom of movement around the world, so distinct communities of dinosaurs developed on different landmasses. Old groups, such as the coelurosaurs, diversified, and new groups, such as the ceratopsians, evolved. Global warming had turned the Earth into a giant greenhouse, and this led to the most significant change of the Cretaceous: the evolution of flowers and primitive grasses. Plant-eaters, such as hadrosaurs and pachycephalosaurs, thrived on this varied diet, and of course it also vastly changed the appearance of the planet.

POTENTIAL RISK: EXTREME

Spinosaurus *is a huge, powerful and aggressive predator. To be avoided on sight.*

HABITAT

NORTH AFRICA, CRETACEOUS

With its varied diet, **Spinosaurus** *could have lived in many different habitats. Those found in what is now Egypt might have lived alongside fellow giants* **Bahariasaurus** *and* **Paralititan** *in mangrove forests on tidal flats.*

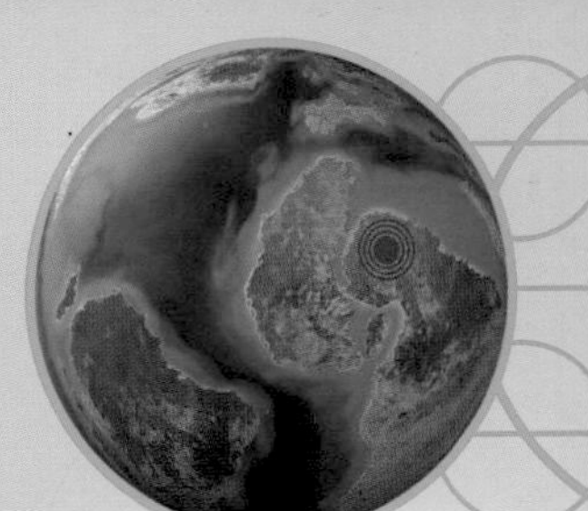

010273462102730106389210.948.6300011628.83.9

SPINOSAURUS

MEANING: 'spine lizard'

PRONUNCIATION: *spine-o-SORE-uss*

Possibly the largest carnivore ever to walk the Earth, ***Spinosaurus*** is a terrifying theropod. An opportunistic hunter, it is the Cretaceous equivalent of a grizzly bear, killing many different types of prey but with a particular liking for fish.

250

0

COOL CUSTOMER

The sail on ***Spinosaurus***'s back might serve several purposes. It makes the already enormous animal appear even larger and more fearsome. It might also help the creature to regulate its body temperature, either by absorbing heat from the sun to warm up, or by radiating excess heat if it becomes too hot in the warm climate of Cretaceous Africa.

The back vertebrae are extended into tall, thin sheets that support a sail.

002730192100010151015

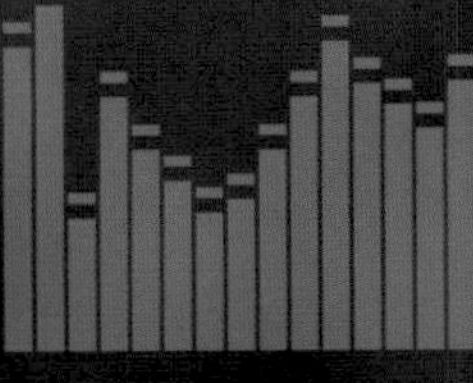

00273019210

RANGE

7.5 METRES (25 FT) AND CLOSING
PROXIMITY ALERT
EVASIVE ACTION RECOMMENDED

TOP SPEED

23 KPH (14 MPH)

010273462102730106389

010273462102730106389210.948.6300011628.83.9 010273462102730106389210.948.6300011628.83.9 01027

FOSSIL FINDS

AFRICA (EGYPT, MOROCCO, NIGER)

Remains were first discovered in North Africa in 1910 by the German aristocrat Ernst Stromer, but they were all destroyed during World War II. A handful of bones have recently been found, but no complete skeletons.

FLAT HEAD

Spinosaurus has a long, low cranium very similar to that of a modern-day crocodile, which probably means this dinosaur likes to gorge on fish, as well as large land-based prey.

SIZE COMPARISON

The largest **Spinosaurus** *is one and a half times as long as the largest* **T. rex**.

LENGTH: 10–18 metres (33–60 ft)

HEIGHT: 2.5–3 metres (8–10 ft)

WEIGHT: 6–9 tonnes

BARYONYX

MEANING: 'heavy claw'

PRONUNCIATION: *bah-ree-ON-icks*

The killer claws on each hand of ***Baryonyx*** are among the most feared weapons in the dinosaur kingdom. These multi-purpose tools are used to spear fish, fend off rivals and to rip through the flesh of large prey.

Baryonyx is a monstrous predator, but is only one of three large carnivores in its ecosystem. It lives alongside ***Neovenator***, a relative of the colossal carcharodontosaurids, and ***Eotyrannus***, a cousin of ***Tyrannosaurus***. These three predators stalk the river deltas and soggy lake basins of England, feeding on ***Iguanodon*** and other herbivorous dinosaurs.

KILLER CLAWS

All three fingers of ***Baryonyx*** are capped by powerful claws. The largest of these is 25 centimetres (10 inches) long! Only ***Baryonyx*** and its spinosaurid cousins have such large, thick and deadly claws.

POTENTIAL RISK: EXTREME

Aside from its teeth and claws, **Baryonyx** *is terrifying because it is in constant competition with its rivals for fresh meat.*

SIZE COMPARISON

A true monster that has to wrestle other large theropods for prey.

LENGTH: 9–13 metres (30–43 ft)

HEIGHT: 1.8–2.5 metres (6–8 ft)

WEIGHT: 2500–5400 kilograms (5500–11900 lb)

FOSSIL FINDS

ENGLAND, EARLY CRETACEOUS

***Baryonyx**, like its close cousin **Spinosaurus**, is a rare dinosaur. Only two good fossils have been found, in England.*

HABITAT

ENGLAND, EARLY CRETACEOUS

*As fish scales have been found in the gut of **Baryonyx** fossils, it is likely that they lived near water. Their streamlined head and strong, clawed arms would have been ideal for snapping up passing fish.*

RANGE

2 METRES (6.5 FT) AND CLOSING
PROXIMITY ALERT
IMMEDIATE EVASIVE ACTION

TOP SPEED

25 KPH (15 MPH)

WEAPONRY: FULLY ARMED

*While **Baryonyx** has deadly hand claws, it also possesses a long, narrow skull full of very sharp conical teeth.*

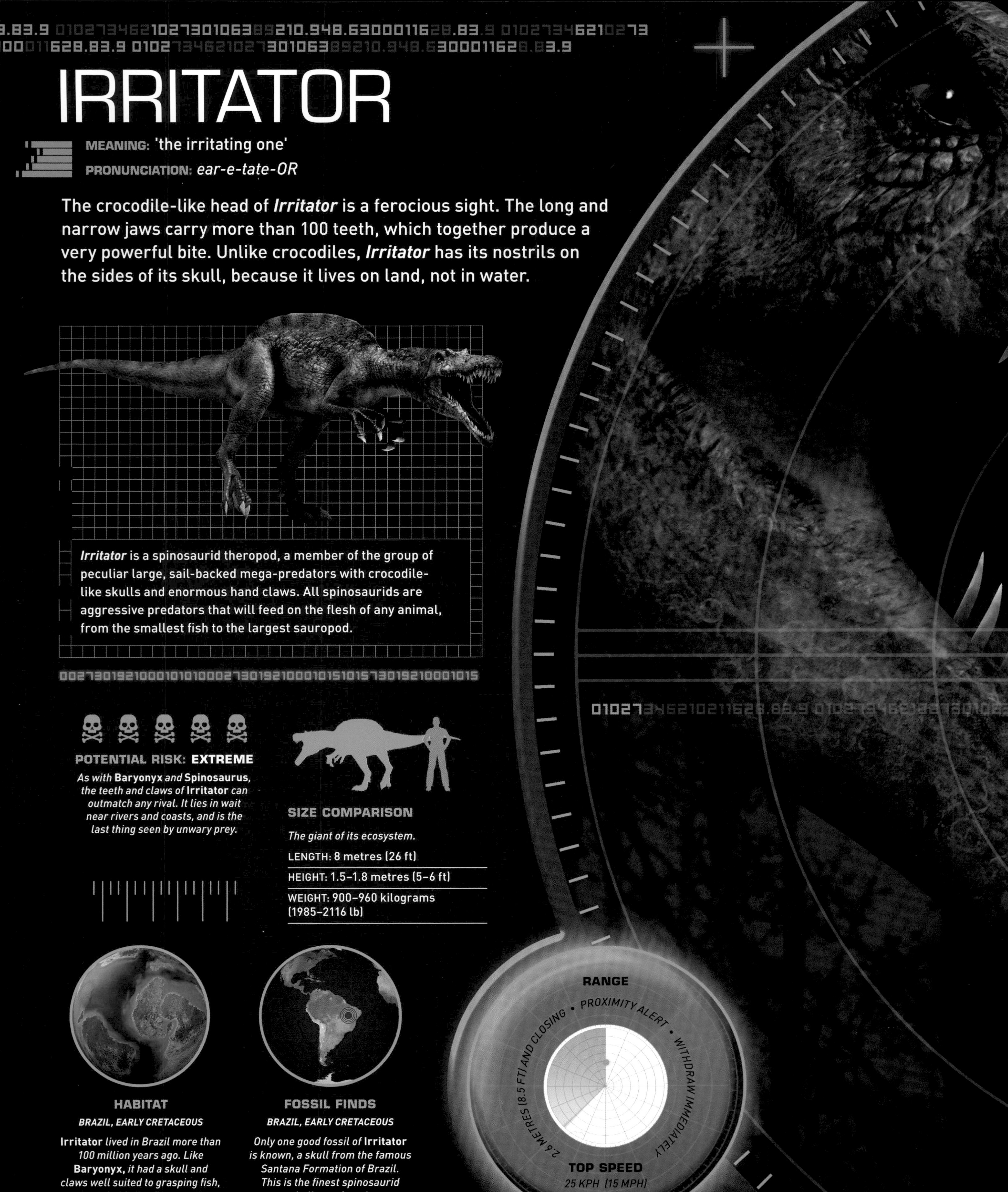

IRRITATOR

MEANING: 'the irritating one'

PRONUNCIATION: *ear-e-tate-OR*

The crocodile-like head of ***Irritator*** is a ferocious sight. The long and narrow jaws carry more than 100 teeth, which together produce a very powerful bite. Unlike crocodiles, ***Irritator*** has its nostrils on the sides of its skull, because it lives on land, not in water.

Irritator is a spinosaurid theropod, a member of the group of peculiar large, sail-backed mega-predators with crocodile-like skulls and enormous hand claws. All spinosaurids are aggressive predators that will feed on the flesh of any animal, from the smallest fish to the largest sauropod.

POTENTIAL RISK: EXTREME

As with **Baryonyx** *and* **Spinosaurus**, *the teeth and claws of* **Irritator** *can outmatch any rival. It lies in wait near rivers and coasts, and is the last thing seen by unwary prey.*

SIZE COMPARISON

The giant of its ecosystem.

LENGTH: 8 metres (26 ft)

HEIGHT: 1.5–1.8 metres (5–6 ft)

WEIGHT: 900–960 kilograms (1985–2116 lb)

HABITAT

BRAZIL, EARLY CRETACEOUS

Irritator *lived in Brazil more than 100 million years ago. Like* **Baryonyx,** *it had a skull and claws well suited to grasping fish, so it probably lived near water.*

FOSSIL FINDS

BRAZIL, EARLY CRETACEOUS

Only one good fossil of **Irritator** *is known, a skull from the famous Santana Formation of Brazil. This is the finest spinosaurid skull ever found.*

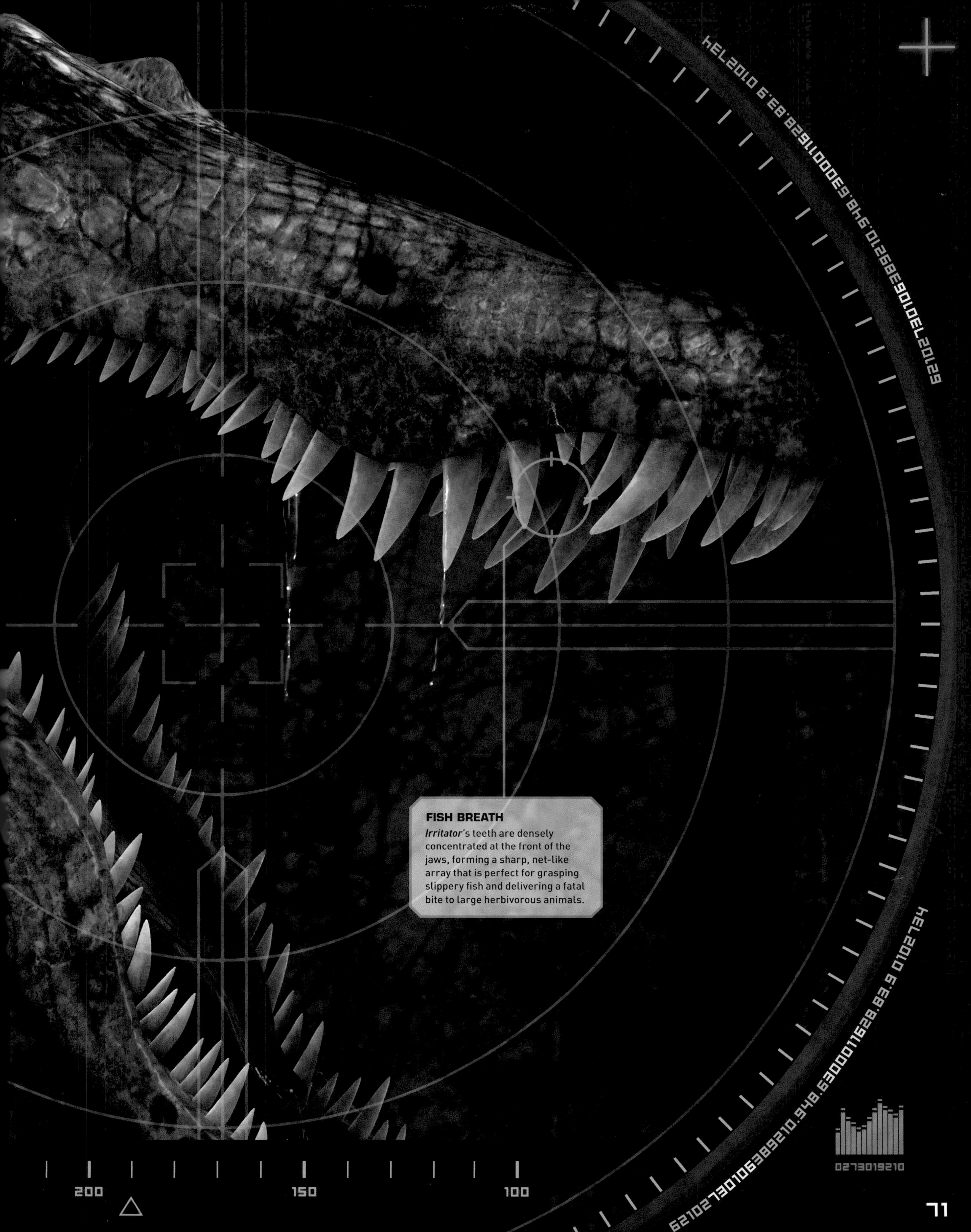

FISH BREATH

Irritator's teeth are densely concentrated at the front of the jaws, forming a sharp, net-like array that is perfect for grasping slippery fish and delivering a fatal bite to large herbivorous animals.

POTENTIAL RISK: **EXTREME**

Keen senses and a large, powerful bite make **Acrocanthosaurus** *a creature to avoid at all costs.*

HABITAT

NORTH AMERICA, EARLY CRETACEOUS

Acrocanthosaurus *preferred the wet and warm floodplains and river margins, where it could hunt its favourite prey: large sauropods.*

010273462102730106389210.948.6300011628.83.9

ACROCANTHOSAURUS

MEANING: 'high-spined lizard'

PRONUNCIATION: *ak-row-can-tho-SORE-uss*

Known as the 'terror of the south', ***Acrocanthosaurus*** reigns supreme in the lush southern river regions of North America. At 12 metres (40 ft) long, this predator is enormous – about the same size as ***Tyrannosaurus*** – and is distinguished by the high bump or sail along its spine.

250

0

TERROR OF THE SOUTH

Although ***Acrocanthosaurus*** looks similar to the spinosaurids and tyrannosaurids, it is actually a North American cousin of the carcharodontosaurids. Other members of this group, such as the African ***Carcharodontosaurus*** and the South American ***Giganotosaurus***, are among the largest predators ever to walk the Earth. Although slightly smaller, ***Acrocanthosaurus*** is also a terrifying hunter.

The back of ***Acrocanthosaurus*** *has a short sail along its length – probably a display device used to attract mates.*

0027301921000101510

00273019210

RANGE

14.1 METRES (46 FT) AND CLOSING
PROXIMITY ALERT
RETREAT IMMEDIATELY

TOP SPEED

23 KPH (14 MPH)

0102734621027301063 89

010273462102730106389210.948.6300011628.83.9 010273462102730106389210.948.6300011628.83.9 010273

FOSSIL FINDS

NORTH AMERICA, EARLY CRETACEOUS

Three good skeletons of **Acrocanthosaurus** *have been found in Texas and Oklahoma. This giant probably roamed across much of North America about 100 million years ago.*

LIGHT NECK

The neck of ***Acrocanthosaurus*** is both strong and light. Powerful muscles hold up the huge head and allow the skull to strike at prey with precision. However, the individual neck vertebrae are hollowed out in order to lighten the weight of the neck.

SIZE COMPARISON

A true terror that can tackle the largest prey imaginable.

LENGTH: 12 metres (40 ft)

HEIGHT: 1.8–2.5 metres (6–8 ft)

WEIGHT: 3–4 tonnes

CARCHARODONTOSAURUS

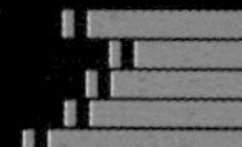

MEANING: 'shark-toothed lizard'

PRONUNCIATION: *car-car-o-don-to-SORE-uss*

The snarling ***Carcharodontosaurus*** is larger than ***Tyrannosaurus***, but has to share an ecosystem with a monster larger still – ***Spinosaurus***. However, ***Carcharodontosaurus***'s very strong bite and exceptional senses put it in a class above its rivals.

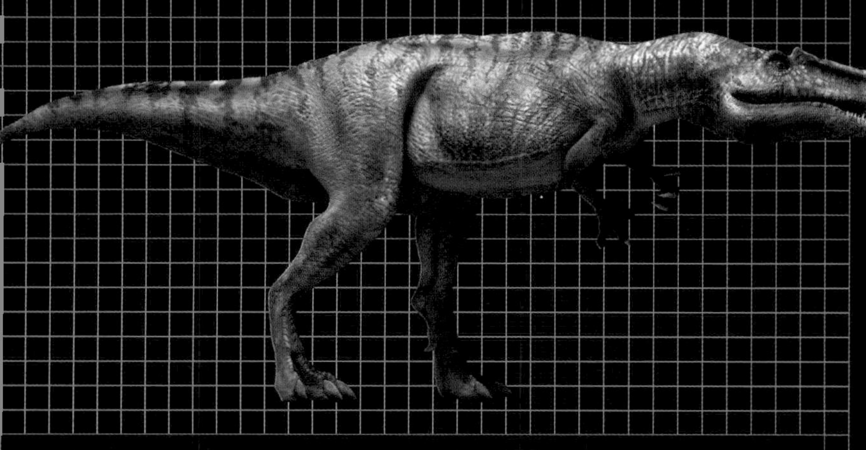

Carcharodontosaurus is a fine example of the carcharodontosaurid group, a collection of theropods that terrorizes much of the world, from Africa all the way to Asia. ***Carcharodontosaurus*** is one of the group's largest members. Its skull measures over 1.5 metres (5 ft), making it nearly as long as an average man is tall!

POTENTIAL RISK: EXTREME

Prey must be lucky enough to avoid both **Spinosaurus** *and the shark-toothed* **Carcharodontosaurus**. *This animal's teeth are unique among theropods – and lethal.*

SIZE COMPARISON

Larger than **Tyrannosaurus**, *but still smaller than the contemporary* **Spinosaurus**!

LENGTH: 12–14 metres (40–46 ft)

HEIGHT: 2.1–2.75 metres (7–9 ft)

WEIGHT: 6000–7500 kilograms (13200–16500 lb)

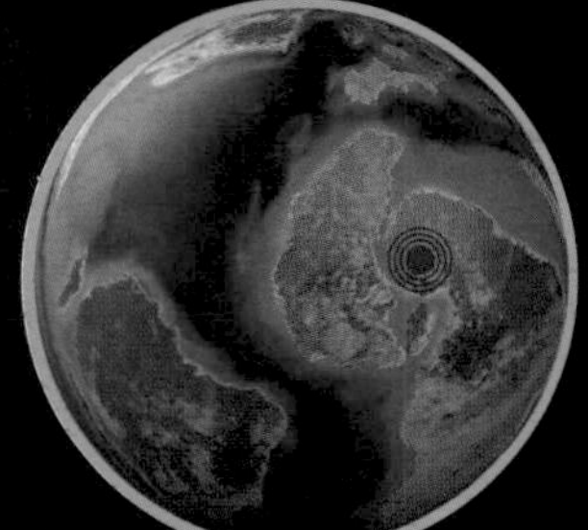

HABITAT

AFRICA, EARLY–MIDDLE CRETACEOUS

Northern Africa was home to **Carcharodontosaurus**, *about 100 million years ago. At that time the land was not desert, but wet and humid, and located near the tropics.*

FOSSIL FINDS

AFRICA, EARLY–MIDDLE CRETACEOUS

The bones and teeth of **Carcharodontosaurus** *are common finds in the Sahara Desert of North Africa, which was home to a lush ecosystem during the Early Cretaceous.*

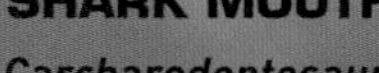

SHARK MOUTH

Carcharodontosaurus got its name 'shark-toothed lizard' because its teeth are thin, sharp and serrated, much like those of the great white shark – only much larger!

200
150
100
0273019210

GIGANOTOSAURUS

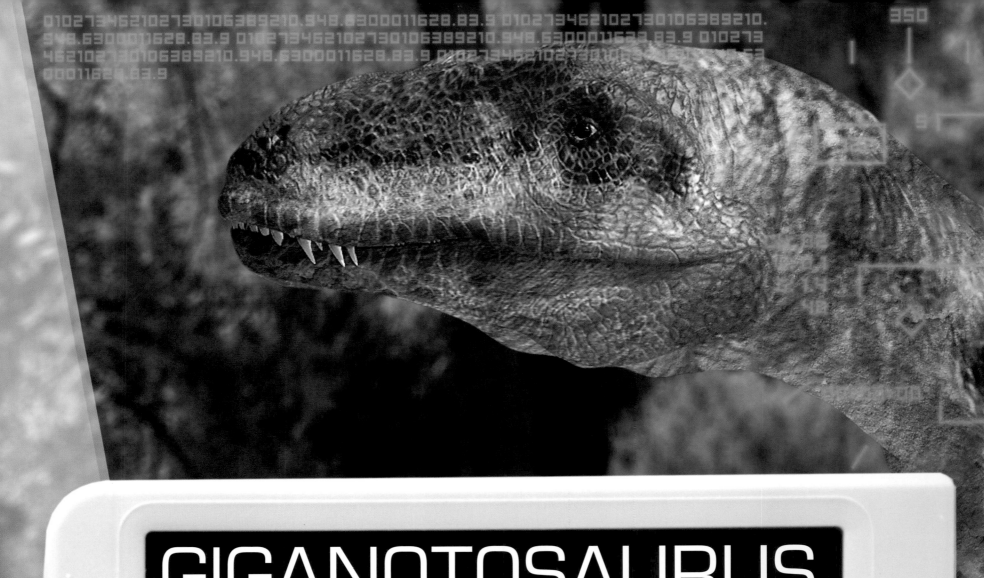

MEANING: 'giant southern lizard'

PRONUNCIATION: *ji-gan-ote-o-SORE-uss*

Large, long-necked sauropods gather in herds across South America to protect themselves from ***Giganotosaurus***. This carcharodontosaurid theropod is one of the most menacing carnivores of the dinosaur world, and one of the largest predators in the history of the Earth.

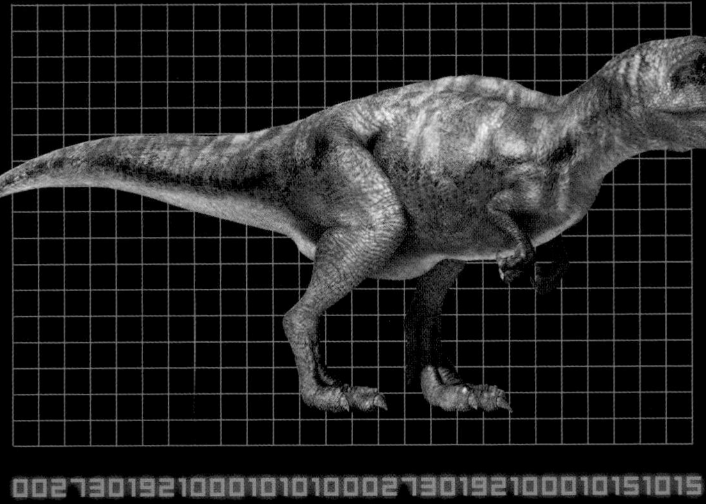

The largest individuals of ***Giganotosaurus*** are over 14 metres (45 ft) in length, much smaller than the enormous titanosaurian sauropods that form their primary source of food. However, ***Giganotosaurus*** can compete with much larger rivals by virtue of its strength, speed and, most importantly, 1.5-metre (5-ft) long skull, which is studded with shark-like teeth.

POTENTIAL RISK: EXTREME

This megapredator can take down the largest prey imaginable. It should be avoided on sight.

SIZE COMPARISON

The largest predator in its ecosystem, and a threat to all it encounters.

LENGTH: 12–14 metres (40–46 ft)

HEIGHT: 2.1–2.75 metres (7–9 ft)

WEIGHT: 6000–7000 kilograms (13200–15400 lb)

LIGHT FOR SPEED

Giganotosaurus is so large that its skeleton must be lightened in any way possible, otherwise this giant predator will not run fast enough to chase its prey! Weight is saved by the hollowed-out vertebrae in its back. Cavities (holes) help make the vertebrae light, while still keeping the bones strong enough to hold the animal's weight.

FOSSIL FINDS

SOUTH AMERICA, EARLY–MID CRETACEOUS

One good skeleton, as well as some fragmentary bones of **Giganotosaurus**, *have been found in the dry, rocky plains of Argentina.*

HABITAT

SOUTH AMERICA, EARLY–MID CRETACEOUS

Giganotosaurus *stalked the Argentine plains about 100 million years ago. At that time they were a lush ecosystem, teeming with life, and much warmer and wetter than they are today.*

RANGE

6.4 METRES (21 FT) AND CLOSING
PROXIMITY ALERT
WITHDRAW IMMEDIATELY

TOP SPEED

23 KPH (14 MPH)

WEAPONRY: FULLY ARMED

Any herbivore lucky enough to escape the jaws of **Giganotosaurus** *still has to avoid the sharp hand claws.*

POTENTIAL RISK: **MEDIUM**

The diminutive **Microraptor** *is only a risk to small animals, but its teeth and claws look pretty terrifying as it swoops out of trees.*

HABITAT

CHINA, EARLY CRETACEOUS

The Liaoning 'feathered dinosaurs' lived about 125 million years ago in a warm, rainy region of China that was frequently buried by volcanic eruptions.

MICRORAPTOR

MEANING: 'small thief'

PRONUNCIATION: *my-krow-rap-TOR*

The tiny theropod ***Microraptor*** looks more like a bird than a ferocious predatory raptor. However, this feathered and winged creature is a close relative of ***Deinonychus*** and ***Velociraptor***, and is one of the most bird-like dinosaurs in the entire dinosaur kingdom.

250

0

LITTLE TERROR

Microraptor is the smallest dinosaur in the world. It is less than 1 metre (3 ft) long and weighs less than 4 kilograms (9 lb), only slightly larger than a newborn human child. Unlike most dinosaurs, which make their living on the ground, ***Microraptor*** glides from tree to tree, using its sharp teeth and puncturing claws to catch insects and small mammals. It is easy to miss ***Microraptor***, as it is camouflaged by the trees it hides in.

The long, stiff tail of **Microraptor** *provides balance as it glides from branch to branch.*

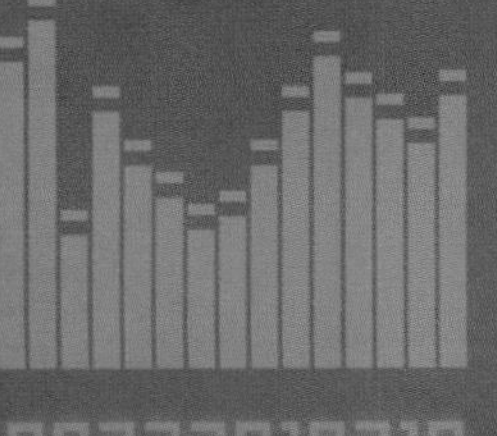

RANGE

4.6 METRES (15 FT) AND CLOSING
PROXIMITY ALERT
APPROACH WITH CAUTION

TOP SPEED

40 KPH (25 MPH)

01027346210273010б389

0102734621027301063892 10.948.6300011628.83.9 0102734621027301063892 10.948.6300011628.83.9 01027

FOSSIL FINDS
CHINA, EARLY CRETACEOUS
Microraptor is one of many 'feathered dinosaurs' known from Liaoning Province, China. These specimens preserve spectacular details of the skeleton, including beautiful feathers.
WARM COAT
The back of Microraptor, and that of many other feathered dinosaurs, is covered by a coat of downy feathers that resemble hair. These help keep it warm and dry.
FLYING LEGS
Microraptor is unique in possessing wings both on its arms (like modern birds) and on its legs (never seen in any birds today). These wings enable Microraptor to fly like a biplane, with one set of wings positioned above the body and the set other below!
SIZE COMPARISON
The smallest dinosaur in the world.
LENGTH: 45–75 centimetres (18–29 in)
HEIGHT: 22–36 centimetres (9–14 in)
WEIGHT: 2–4 kilograms (4–9 lb)

FOSSIL FINDS

NORTH AMERICA, EARLY CRETACEOUS

Fossils of **Deinonychus** *have been found in the western United States. Many of these, especially shed teeth, are found alongside the larger herbivorous ornithischian* **Tenontosaurus,** *which* **Deinonychus** *might have hunted.*

HABITAT

NORTH AMERICA, EARLY CRETACEOUS

The region inhabited by **Deinonychus** *looked very much like modern-day Louisiana in the United States – hot and humid with stagnant pools, estuaries and cypress swamps. In the south of its range were well-drained floodplains.*

POTENTIAL RISK: EXTREME

Deinonychus *is more dangerous than its size suggests, seizing prey in its sharp claws and ripping it to death. It sometimes hunts in packs, bringing down much larger prey.*

SIZE COMPARISON

A medium-sized dinosaur that is light and nimble for its size.

LENGTH: 3–3.5 metres (10–11 ft)

HEIGHT: 1 metre (36–42 in)

WEIGHT: 80–100 kilograms (176–220 lb)

USING ITS HEAD

The skull of *Deinonychus* is streamlined and lightweight, but strong and filled with a battery of razor-like teeth. It has massive eyes and a large brain, perfect weapons for outsensing and outsmarting prey.

DEINONYCHUS

MEANING: 'terrible claw'

PRONUNCIATION: *die-NON-e-kus*

Deinonychus is a bird-like theropod and one of the most fascinating dinosaurs in palaeontology. In the past we thought of dinosaurs as dim-witted, sluggish creatures, but ***Deinonychus*** changed that view. It is a smart, agile and ferocious raptor that terrorizes its ecosystem.

The forelimb is long and all three fingers are crowned with menacing claws. A mobile shoulder joint allows the arm to swing in a wide arc, an ideal technique for slashing and grasping prey. The tail is long, stiffened and sticks out straight. This greatly helps the animal's balance and agility.

RANGE

2 METRES (6.5 FT) AND CLOSING
PROXIMITY ALERT
URGENT EVASION RECOMMENDED

TOP SPEED

35 KPH (22 MPH)

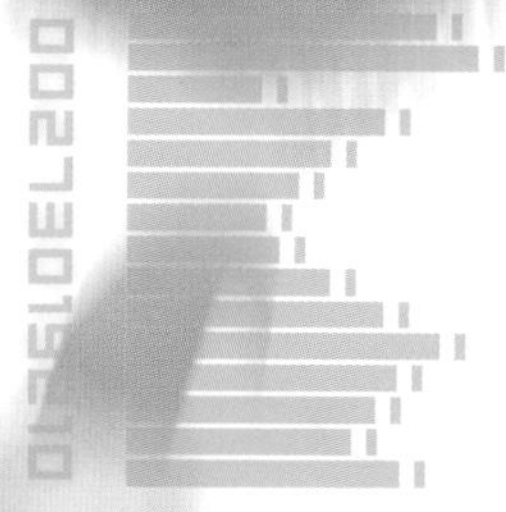

WEAPONRY: FULLY ARMED

Deinonychus *is armed with three claws on each forelimb and a set of sharp teeth for slashing and biting. It can also hold the sides of its prey with huge claws on the second toe of each hindlimb.*

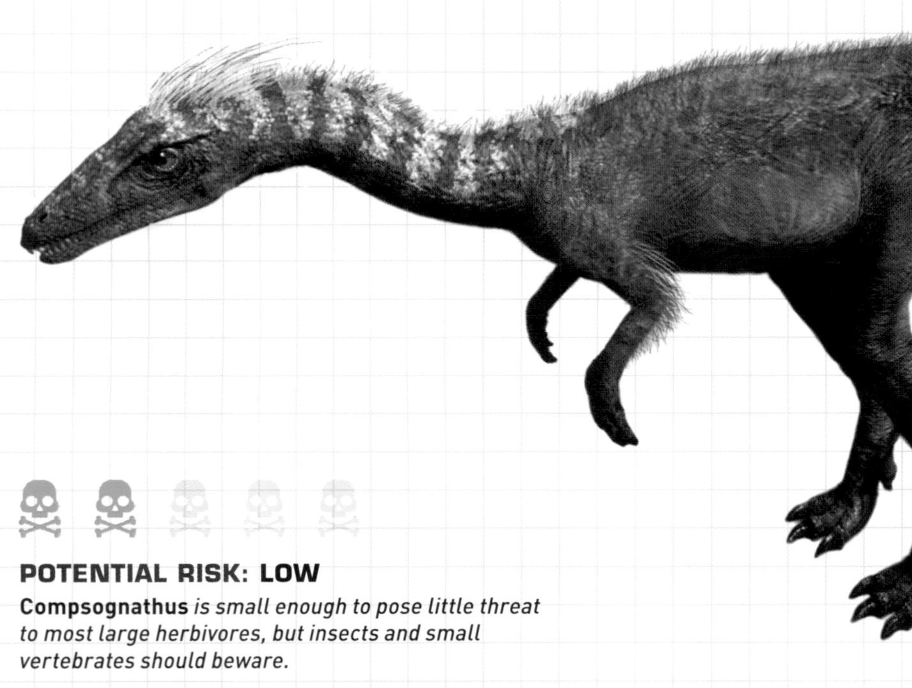

SIZE COMPARISON

LENGTH: 1–1.5 metres (3–5 ft)

HEIGHT: 25–60 centimetres (1–2 ft)

WEIGHT: 5–10 kilograms (11–22 lb)

This is one of the smallest dinosaurs that ever lived.

FOSSIL FINDS

EUROPE, LATE JURASSIC

Fossils of **Compsognathus** *have been found in Germany and France, where it lived about 150 million years ago. At this time, Europe was warm, wet and humid, and little more than a series of small flooded islands. Living alongside was* **Archaeopteryx**, *the first bird.*

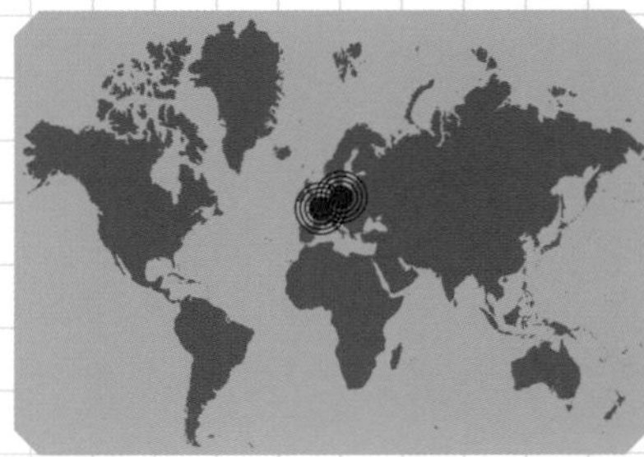

POTENTIAL RISK: LOW

Compsognathus *is small enough to pose little threat to most large herbivores, but insects and small vertebrates should beware.*

COMPSOGNATHUS

MEANING: 'elegant form'

PRONUNCIATION: *komp-sog-NAY-thuss*

Compsognathus is one of the smallest, sleekest and lightest members of the dinosaur kingdom. What it lacks in size it makes up for in speed and intelligence. In fact, it can run faster than any dinosaur and can even catch small insects on the fly.

POTENTIAL RISK: HIGH

Ornitholestes *is risky because its looks are deceiving. Don't dismiss this theropod because of its small weight and size: it will slash with its claws and rip flesh with its teeth.*

FOSSIL FINDS

NORTH AMERICA, LATE JURASSIC

Ornitholestes *is one of many theropods that lived in the wet floodplains of North America 150 million years ago. It is known from only one fossil, a nearly complete skeleton, found at Como Bluff in Wyoming.*

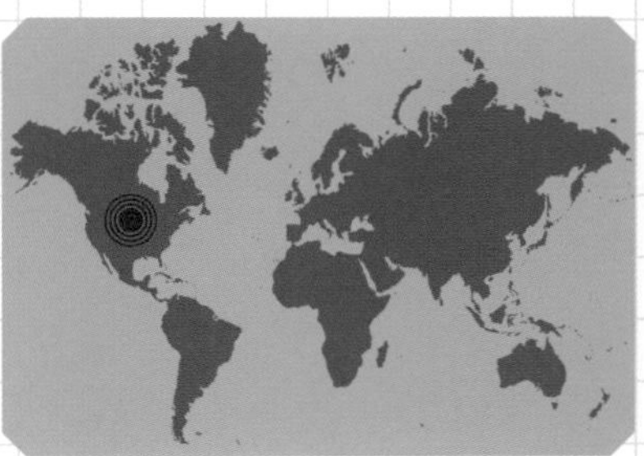

ORNITHOLESTES

MEANING: 'bird robber'

PRONUNCIATION: *or-nith-o-LESS-tees*

Ornitholestes might look small and skinny, but its battery of teeth and large hands are enough to finish off any prey that underestimates it. The hands of ***Ornitholestes*** are especially distinctive and perfect for dismembering. The fingers are very long, incredibly mobile and topped with massive, flexible claws.

SIZE COMPARISON

LENGTH: 2 metres (7 ft)

HEIGHT: 0.5–1 metre (2–3 ft)

WEIGHT: 15–20 kilograms (33–44 lb)

A sleek dinosaur that is slightly longer than a small car.

FEATHERS

Like many theropods, ***Ornitholestes*** has feathers. These keep the body warm during the winter and are also modified into colourful and fanciful displays used to attract mates and ward off rivals.

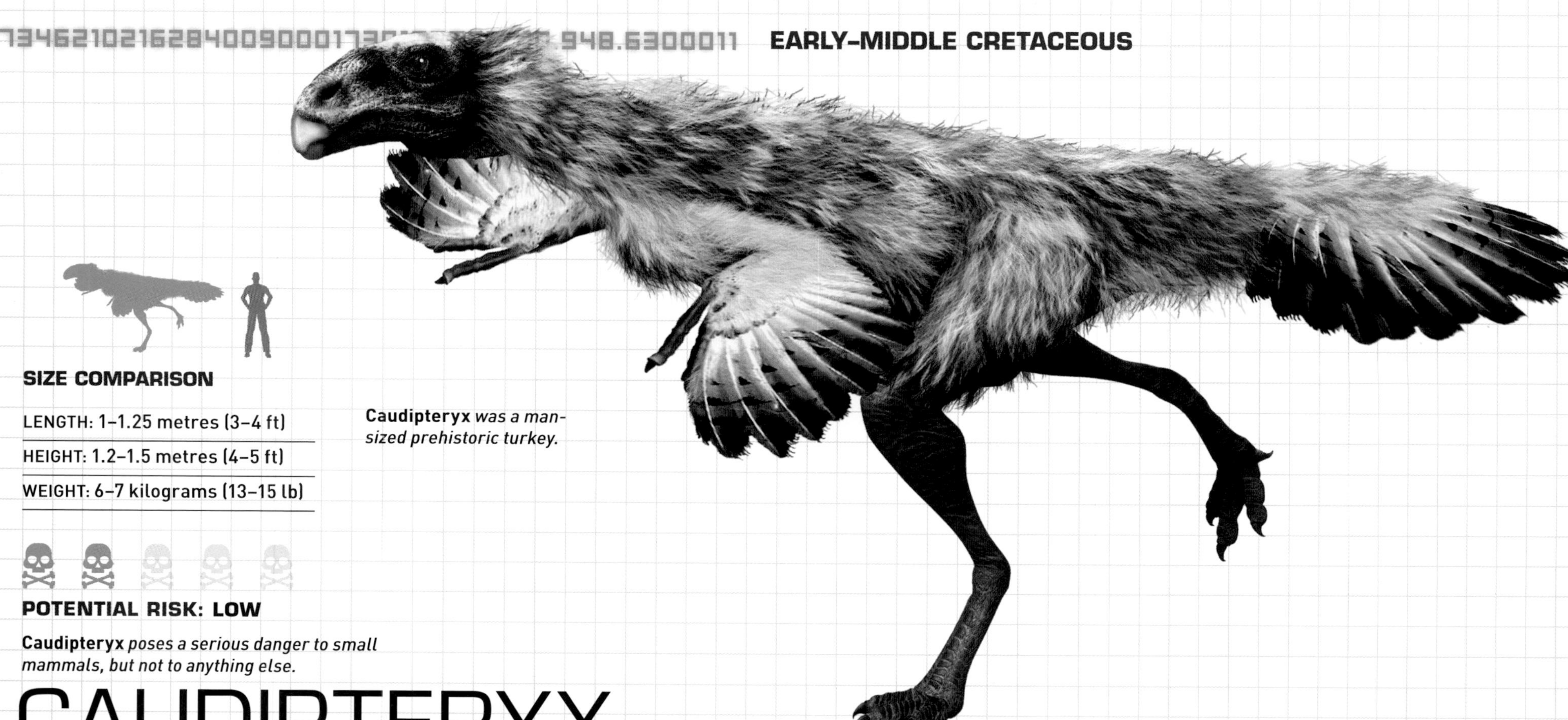

SIZE COMPARISON

LENGTH: 1–1.25 metres (3–4 ft)
HEIGHT: 1.2–1.5 metres (4–5 ft)
WEIGHT: 6–7 kilograms (13–15 lb)

Caudipteryx *was a man-sized prehistoric turkey.*

POTENTIAL RISK: LOW

Caudipteryx *poses a serious danger to small mammals, but not to anything else.*

CAUDIPTERYX

MEANING: 'tail feather'

PRONUNCIATION: *kaw-DIP-ter-icks*

The turkey of the Mesozoic, ***Caudipteryx*** is a fast runner that uses its speed to catch small mammals and lizards. Its bright, feathery plumage attracts mates and warns off rivals.

FOSSIL FINDS

ASIA, EARLY CRETACEOUS

Caudipteryx *lived alongside about 50 other species of dinosaurs in northeastern Asia about 125 million years ago. It was one of the first feathered dinosaurs to be unearthed in China.*

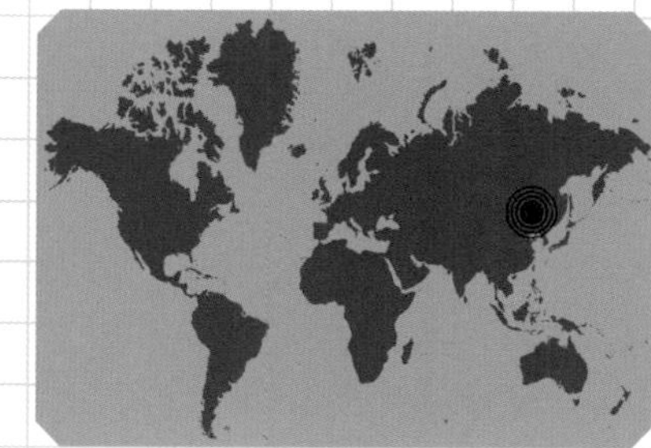

POTENTIAL RISK: LOW

Incisivosaurus *uses its teeth to take down both small and large prey.*

SIZE COMPARISON

LENGTH: 1–1.25 metres (3–4 ft)
HEIGHT: 1.2–1.5 metres (4–5 ft)
WEIGHT: 6–7 kilograms (13–15 lb)

This dinosaur is a large prehistoric bird – with teeth!

INCISIVOSAURUS

MEANING: 'incisor-toothed lizard'

PRONUNCIATION: *in-sice-i-vo-SORE-uss*

A close relative of ***Caudipteryx***, ***Incisivosaurus*** differs from its cousin in one important feature: teeth. While ***Caudipteryx*** only has a few teeth, the nutcracker jaws of ***Incisivosaurus*** contain a full array of small, sharp and pointed teeth used to spear small prey.

FOSSIL FINDS

ASIA, EARLY CRETACEOUS

Incisivosaurus, *like* **Caudipteryx**, *enjoyed the lush landscape of northeastern Asia 125 million years ago. Fragments of its skull and vertebrae have been found there.*

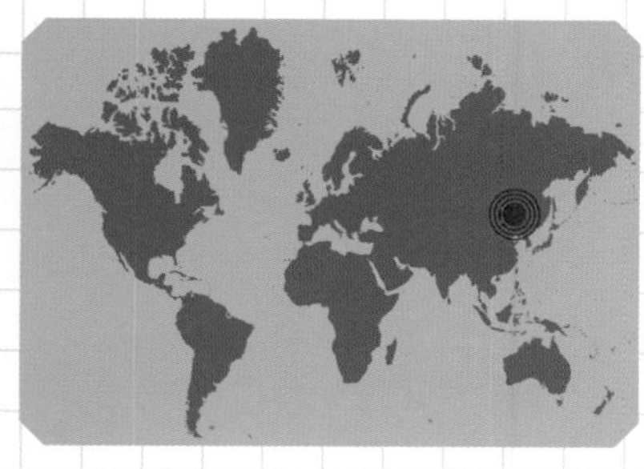

FEATHERED ARMS

The arms of ***Incisivosaurus*** and other small, bird-like theropods are used both for balance and to catch prey. They are large, adorned with feathers, and have a wide range of motion, just as they do in birds.

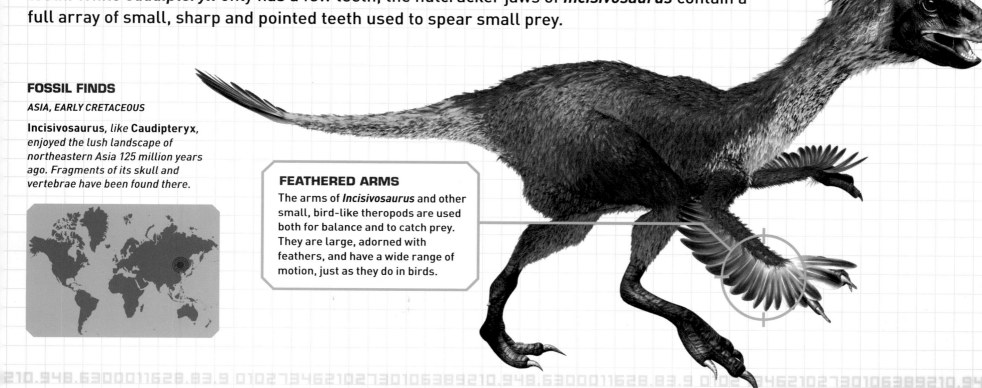

POTENTIAL RISK: **EXTREME**

Possesses all the typical raptor weapons – only in a larger size. A threat to avoid by any means necessary.

HABITAT

NORTH AMERICA, EARLY CRETACEOUS

Utahraptor *was certainly the top carnivore in its ecosystem. It lived about 125 million years ago, when western North America was warm and wet.*

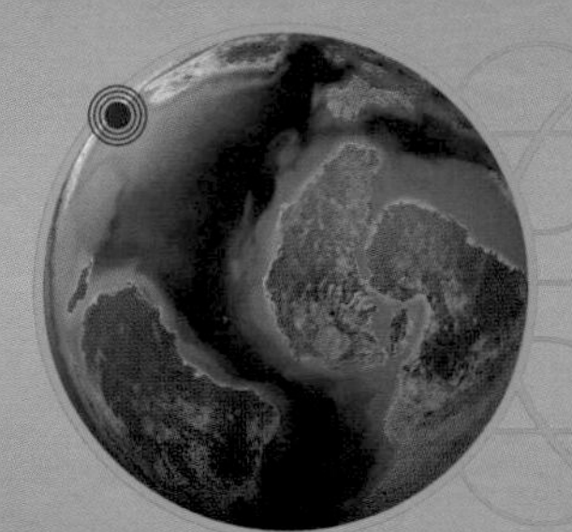

01027346210273010638921 0.948.6300011628.83.9

UTAHRAPTOR

MEANING: 'thief from Utah'

PRONUNCIATION: *you-taw-rap-TOR*

Most dromaeosaurs (raptors) are cunning and dangerous, but also very small. ***Utahraptor***, like its relatives, has heavy-duty weapons, such as a large foot claw, and keen intelligence, but is large in size, too. It is one of the true terrors of the dinosaur world.

250

0

COMPLETE KILLER KIT

Classic raptors, such as ***Velociraptor***, are no bigger than a large dog, but ***Utahraptor*** is nearly the size of ***Allosaurus***. This sickle-clawed predator grows up to 7 metres (23 ft) in length and weighs ten times as much as an average man. The puncturing claw on the second toe is as long as a man's arm! The claws and teeth combine with the intelligence and keen senses common to all raptors to make ***Utahraptor*** a real killing machine.

The tail of **Utahraptor** *and other dromaeosaurs is long and stiff, which provides balance as the animal chases and leaps after prey.*

0027301921000101 51015

RANGE

200 METRES (650 FT) AND CLOSING
PROXIMITY ALERT
RETREAT IMMEDIATELY

TOP SPEED

30 KPH (20 MPH)

0102734621027301 06389

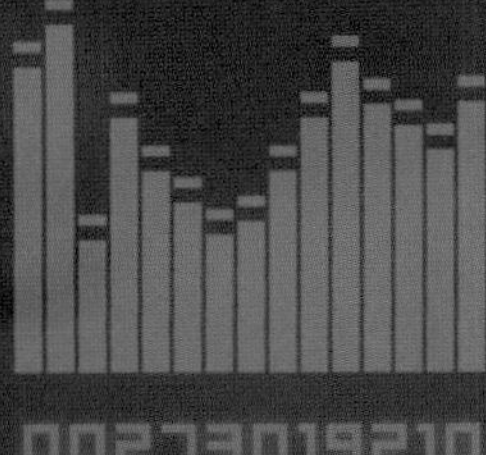

00273019210

01027346210273010638921 0.948.6300011628.83.9 01027346210273010638921 0.948.6300011628.83.9 01027

FOSSIL FINDS

NORTH AMERICA, EARLY CRETACEOUS

Utahraptor *is one of the oldest and most primitive raptors. It is known from one good fossil found in the state of Utah, hence its name.*

SMART HUNTER

Dromaeosaurs such as ***Utahraptor*** are feared predators because they are among the smartest of all dinosaurs. Their senses and intelligence allow them to outwit prey, and this enables ***Utahraptor*** to attack and snare herbivorous sauropods much larger than itself.

SIZE COMPARISON

A mid-sized predator that packed a mean punch with its foot claws.

LENGTH: 6–7 metres (20–23 ft)

HEIGHT: 1.8 metres (6 ft)

WEIGHT: 700–850 kilograms (1540–1875 lb)

AMARGASAURUS

MEANING: named after its discovery site in Argentina

PRONUNCIATION: *ah-mar-ga-SORE-uss*

Amargasaurus has a most unusual appearance, even among strange-looking dinosaurs. This plant-guzzler has the long neck and column-like limbs of all sauropods, but is much smaller than most of its huge relatives. Most bizarrely, its neck and back are ornamented with a fantastic fan of long, twig-like spines.

The neck and back spines of *Amargasaurus* are strange, almost space-alien features. What purpose do they serve? They are too thin and weak to offer protection against large theropod predators. Instead, they support a colourful, fleshy membrane that is used to attract mates and warn off other rival males in the herd.

00273019210001010100027301921000101510 15

LEAF RAKER

Like its close sauropod relatives, *Amargasaurus* has an array cf peg-like teeth at the front of its jaws. These teeth are not used for chewing plants, but rather are used like a rake to strip leaves and branches from trees.

POTENTIAL RISK: VERY LOW

Amargasaurus *is a peaceful plant-eater that occasionally becomes aggressive when a rival causes trouble in the herd.*

SIZE COMPARISON

One of the smallest known long-necked sauropods.

LENGTH: 8–9 metres (26–30 ft)

HEIGHT: 3–3.7 metres (10–12 ft)

WEIGHT: 3–4.7 tonnes

FOSSIL FINDS

ARGENTINA, EARLY CRETACEOUS

Amargasaurus *is known from a single incomplete skeleton, found in a 125-million-year-old rock unit near the town of La Amarga, Argentina.*

HABITAT

ARGENTINA, EARLY CRETACEOUS

Amargasaurus *lived alongside many other sauropods, as well as the small but cunning theropod* **Ligabueino**. *This diminutive meat-eater had to hunt in packs if it wanted to take down an* **Amargasaurus**.

RANGE

2.9 METRES (9.5 FT) AND CLOSING
PROXIMITY ALERT
APPROACH WITH CAUTION

TOP SPEED

8 KPH (5 MPH)

WEAPONRY: NONE

Although still large compared to most dinosaurs, **Amargasaurus** *is a small sauropod without any handy weapons such as claws or spikes.*

ARGENTINOSAURUS

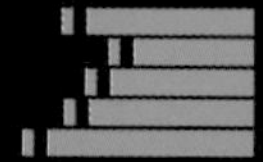

MEANING: 'Argentina lizard'

PRONUNCIATION: *ar-jen-TEE-no-sore-uss*

Of all the dinosaurs in the world, the noodle-necked ***Argentinosaurus*** is the largest. This record-holding sauropod reaches lengths of 41 metres (135 ft), about half the length of a football pitch.

CANOPY BROWSER

At its longest extent, the neck of ***Argentinosaurus*** can snake its way into the highest reaches of the forest canopy. No other sauropods can reach so far, giving *Argentinosaurus* a great advantage over its competitors.

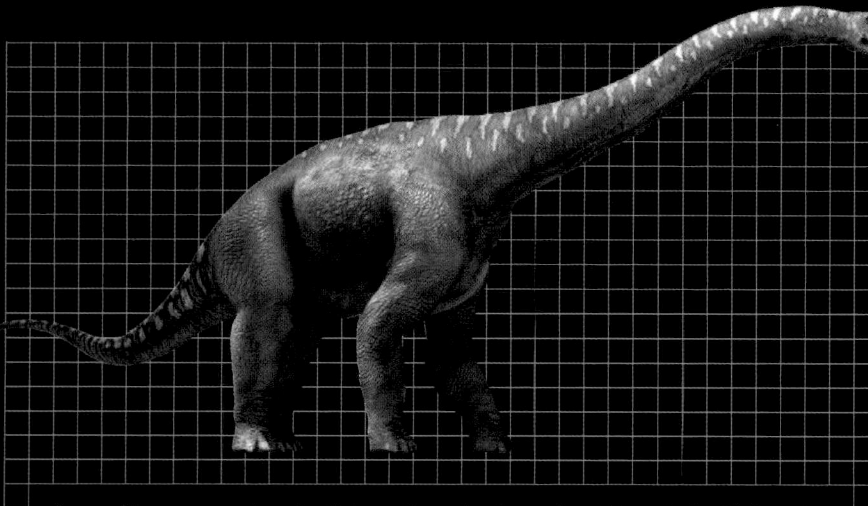

Argentinosaurus is a hulking, thundering giant that is both long and bulky. Its neck stretches high into the treetops, giving it a choice of plants that are not accessible to smaller sauropods. ***Argentinosaurus*** shares its ecosystem with ***Giganotosaurus***, one of the largest predators in the dinosaur kingdom.

POTENTIAL RISK: MEDIUM

Sauropods usually pose little risk, but **Argentinosaurus** *can scare away even the meanest predators with its incredible bulk. Any animal venturing too close risks being swept away by its heavy tail.*

SIZE COMPARISON

The largest dinosaur ever to live!

LENGTH: 33–41 metres (108–135 ft)

HEIGHT: 6–7.3 metres (20–24 ft)

WEIGHT: 75–90 tonnes

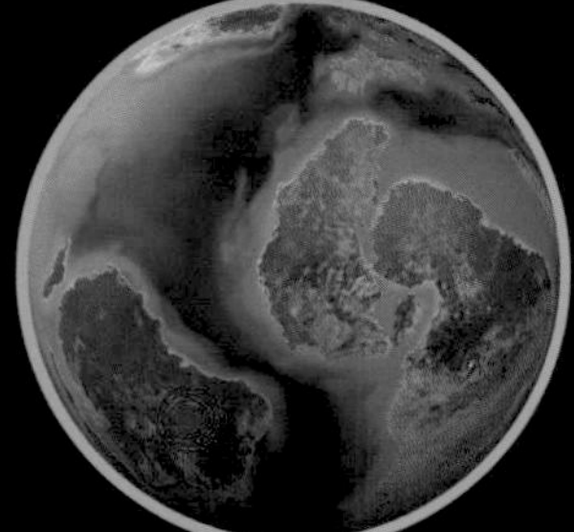

HABITAT

ARGENTINA, EARLY–MID CRETACEOUS

Argentinosaurus, *along with* **Giganotosaurus** *and a variety of other dinosaurs, populated the Argentine plains about 95 million years ago, when this region was wet and warm.*

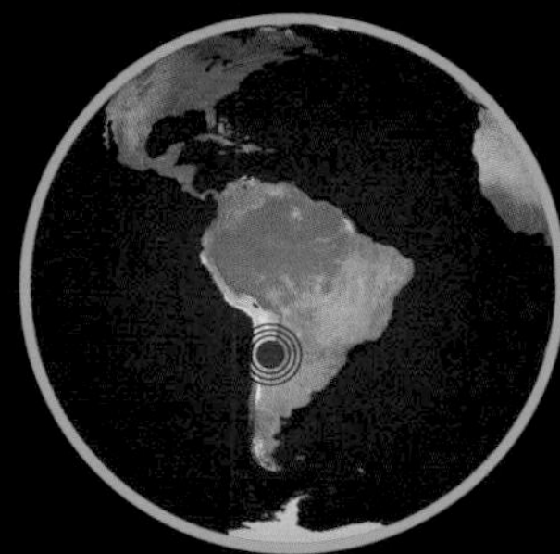

FOSSIL FINDS

ARGENTINA, EARLY–MID CRETACEOUS

Argentinosaurus *is known from just a fragmentary set of vertebrae and limb bones. Scientists are keen to find more fossils of this remarkable beast.*

200
150
100
0273019210

POTENTIAL RISK: **MEDIUM**

Leave **Sauropelta** *alone and there is nothing to fear. Provoke it and risk being impaled on a sharp shoulder spike!*

HABITAT

NORTH AMERICA, EARLY CRETACEOUS

Sauropelta *was one of the most common dinosaurs in the Early Cretaceous of North America. It fed on a range of plants that grew low to the ground.*

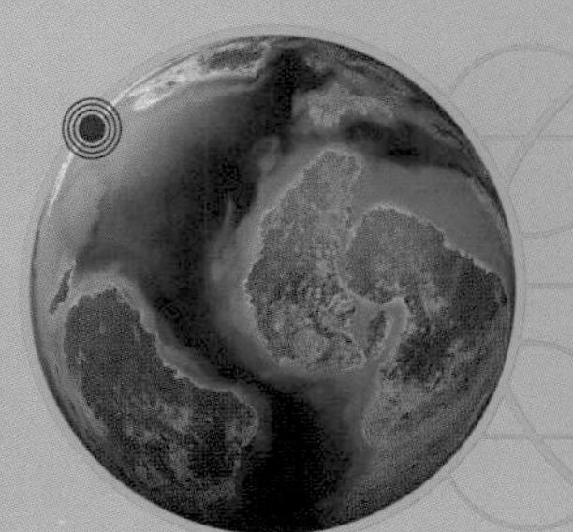

SAUROPELTA

MEANING: 'shield lizard'

PRONUNCIATION: *sore-oh-PEL-ta*

The spine-studded ***Sauropelta*** is an expert at avoiding predatory raptors. This tank-like creature moves at a slow crawl, but hides behind its armour and wields its thick neck spines whenever it is threatened.

ANTI-RAPTOR DEFENCE

The neck and shoulders sport a series of heavy spikes. The largest of these is longer than the neck itself! The spikes are powerful weapons that can easily wound attacking predators.

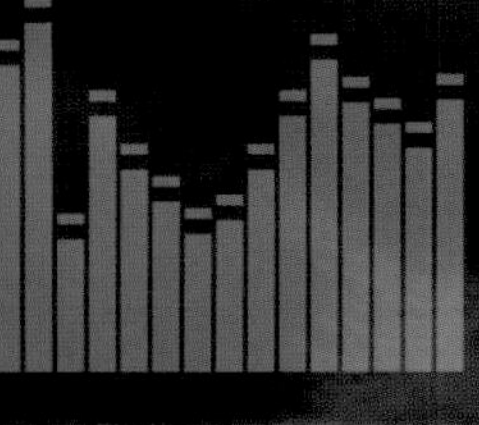

RANGE

4.3 METRES (14.1 FT) AND CLOSING
PROXIMITY ALERT
MAINTAIN SAFE DISTANCE

TOP SPEED

8 KPH (5 MPH)

FOSSIL FINDS

NORTH AMERICA, EARLY CRETACEOUS

Fossils of **Sauropelta** *have been dug up across the western United States, particularly in Wyoming and Montana. They are commonly found alongside the teeth of* **Deinonychus**.

PLATE ARMOUR

The armour pattern of ***Sauropelta*** is distinctive. Two rows of domed scutes (horny plates) shield the top of the neck, and a more random array of plates and smaller bony bits sheath the back and tail.

TANK TRAP

Sauropelta is one of the best-known ankylosaurs, and like all other members of this group, it is a lumbering plant-eater that walks on four legs. It can withstand attacks from the vicious raptor ***Deinonychus***, and the two dinosaurs routinely clash violently on the lush floodplains of North America, with the raptor pitting its claws against the ankylosaur's spikes.

Sauropelta *is a sturdy, strong animal that is difficult to budge, due to its powerful limbs and the strong muscles in its back.*

002730192100010151015

SIZE COMPARISON

A plodding tank of an animal, with hefty armour and a bulky frame.

LENGTH: 5–8 metres (16–26 ft)

HEIGHT: 0.67–1.5 metres (2–5 ft)

WEIGHT: 2.6–2.8 tonnes

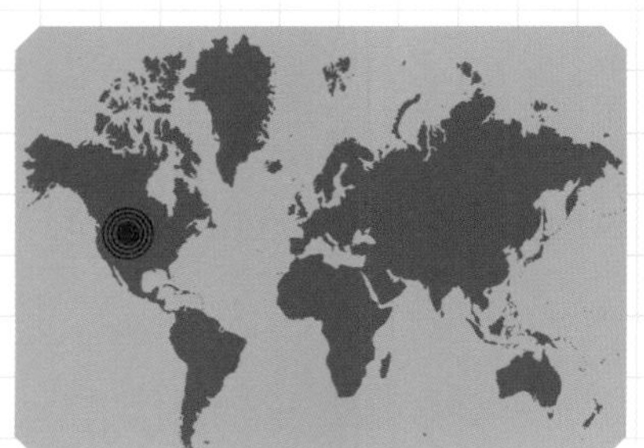

FOSSIL FINDS

NORTH AMERICA, EARLY CRETACEOUS

Gastonia *and* **Utahraptor** *lived in the American west more than 90 million years ago. Several well-preserved skeletons of* **Gastonia** *have been found here.*

SIZE COMPARISON

LENGTH: 2.5–4.5 metres (8–15 ft)

HEIGHT: 0.6–1.25 metres (2–4 ft)

WEIGHT: 1.5–3.7 tonnes

Gastonia *was a mid-sized armoured ankylosaur. Its heavy defences were necessary to survive attacks by packs of raptors.*

POTENTIAL RISK: LOW

Normally, **Gastonia** *is a placid herbivore, but when attacked it can use its huge spikes as deadly weapons.*

GASTONIA

MEANING: named after Rob Gaston (US palaeontologist)

PRONUNCIATION: *gas-TONE-ee-ah*

The tank-like ***Gastonia*** lives in constant fear of its main enemy, the large predator ***Utahraptor***. ***Gastonia***'s thick armour and sharp spikes are defensive adaptations. Most predatory attacks end in one way: with ***Utahraptor*** breaking its teeth on ***Gastonia's*** bony carapace and stumbling away wounded after a blow from one of the spikes.

SIMPLE DEFENCE

Minmi is a bizarre ankylosaur. Unlike most other ankylosaurs, it has little armour on its skull. The armour on its back is simple, giving it the look of a giant reptilian hedgehog.

POTENTIAL RISK: VERY LOW

Only the most aggressive predators can expect **Minmi** *to attack.*

MINMI

MEANING: named after a place near its Australian discovery site

PRONUNCIATION: *min-ME*

One of the smallest ankylosaurs that ever lived, ***Minmi*** stays active during the dark polar nights of Australia. It is slender but not particularly fast, and feeds on a diverse range of low-lying bushes, shrubs and ferns.

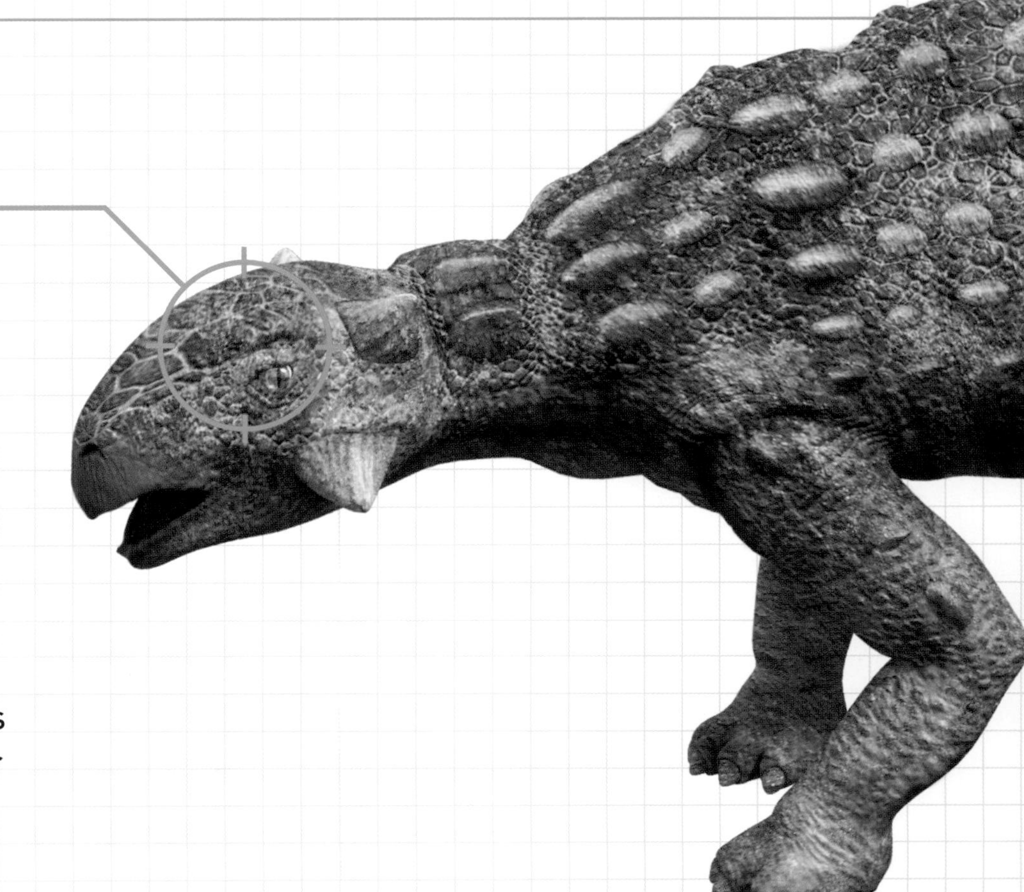

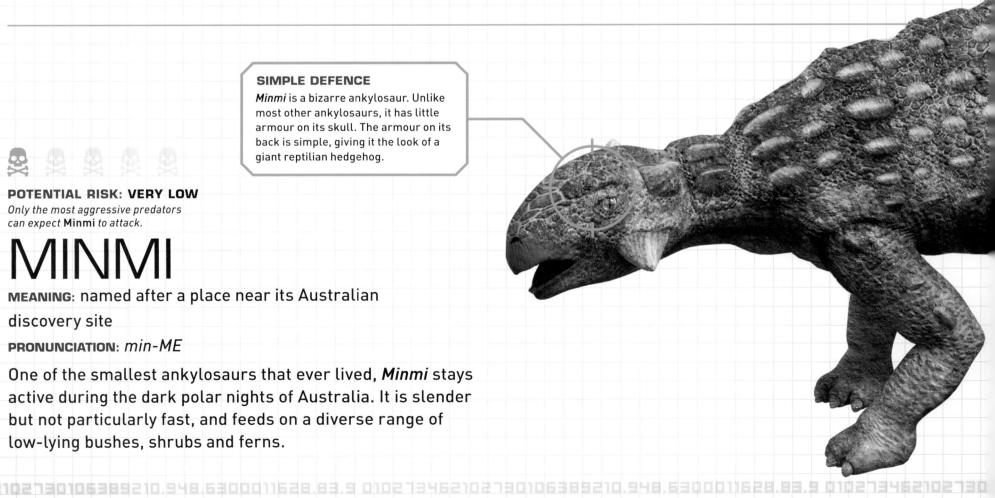

POTENTIAL RISK: LOW
Caution needed: spikes on the neck and sides can be turned against any animal **Hylaeosaurus** *sees as a threat.*

HYLAEOSAURUS

MEANING: 'forest lizard'

PRONUNCIATION: *hy-lay-e-oh-SORE-uss*

SIZE COMPARISON

LENGTH: 3–6 metres (10–20 ft)

HEIGHT: 0.67–1 metre (2–3 ft)

WEIGHT: 900–1100 kilograms (1985–2425 lb)

Hylaeosaurus *is a large but slender ankylosaur.*

The armour and spikes of ***Hylaeosaurus*** are quite simple compared with those of close cousins such as ***Gastonia***. However, they help this sleek and slender herbivore to avoid the deadly teeth and claws of raptors and other carnivorous predators.

FOSSIL FINDS

EUROPE, EARLY CRETACEOUS

Hylaeosaurus *was the third dinosaur ever discovered. It was found in 1832 in the Tilgate Forest of Sussex, England, and ate low-growing plants.*

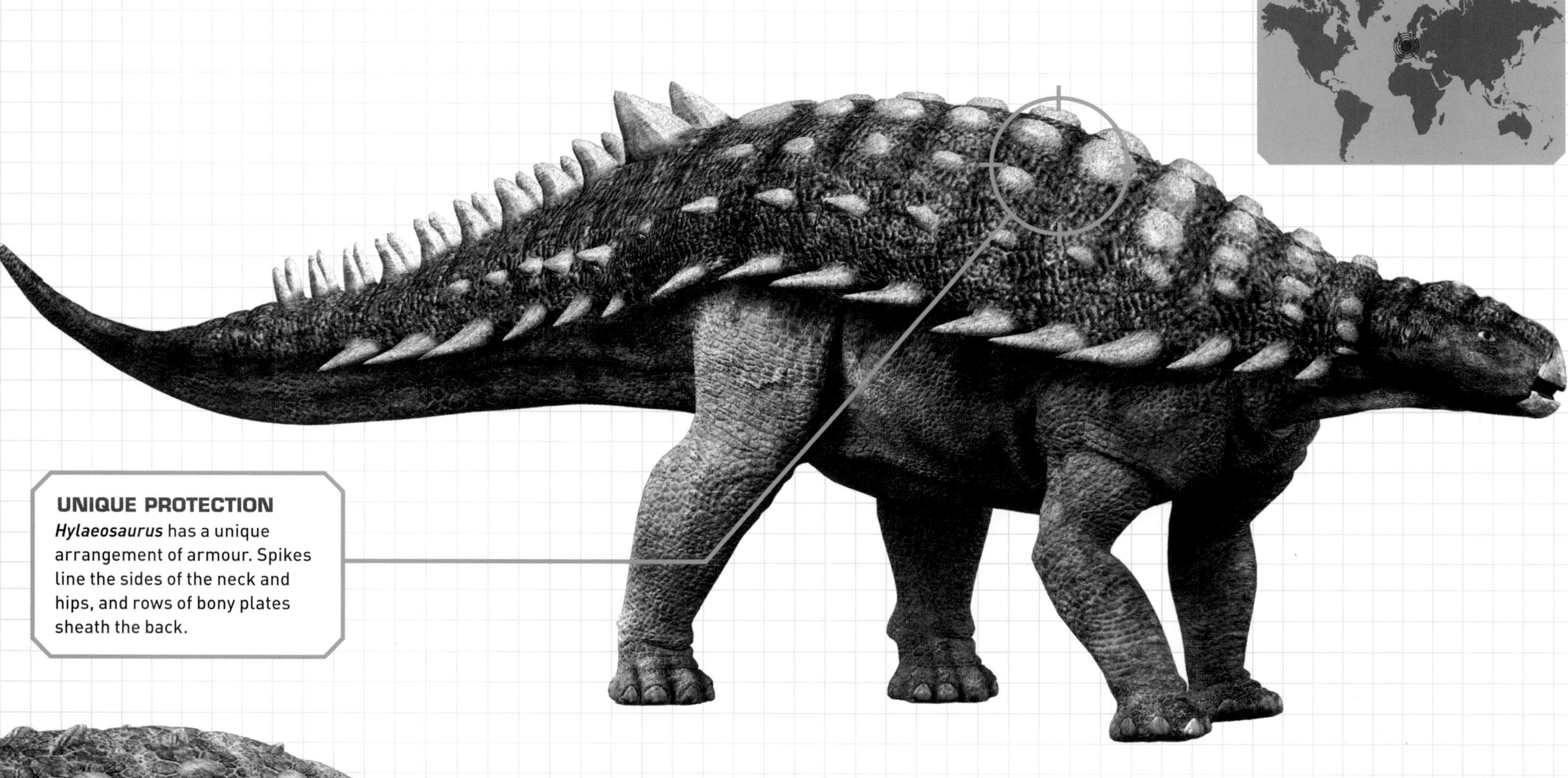

UNIQUE PROTECTION

Hylaeosaurus has a unique arrangement of armour. Spikes line the sides of the neck and hips, and rows of bony plates sheath the back.

FOSSIL FINDS

AUSTRALIA, EARLY CRETACEOUS

Dinosaurs were rare in Australia, but **Minmi** *is one of the more common Early Cretaceous fossils found down under. Australia lay within the polar region at that time.*

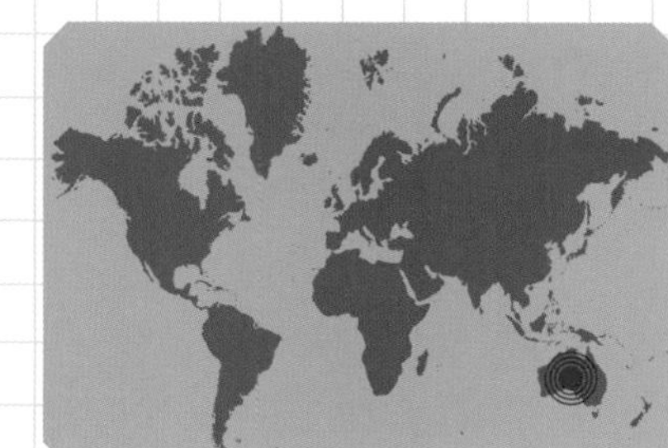

SIZE COMPARISON

LENGTH: 3 metres (10 ft)

HEIGHT: 0.67–1 metre (2–3 ft)

WEIGHT: 200–210 kilograms (440–463 lb)

Minmi *was one of the smallest ankylosaurs.*

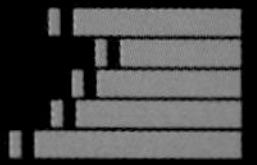

IGUANODON

MEANING: 'iguana tooth'

PRONUNCIATION: *ig-WAN-oh-don*

The 'cow' of the Cretaceous, ***Iguanodon*** is a common herbivore that ranges all across Europe and North America. A diet of low-growing and taller plants, as well as an advanced ability to chew, allow ***Iguanodon*** to prosper successfully in many ecosystems.

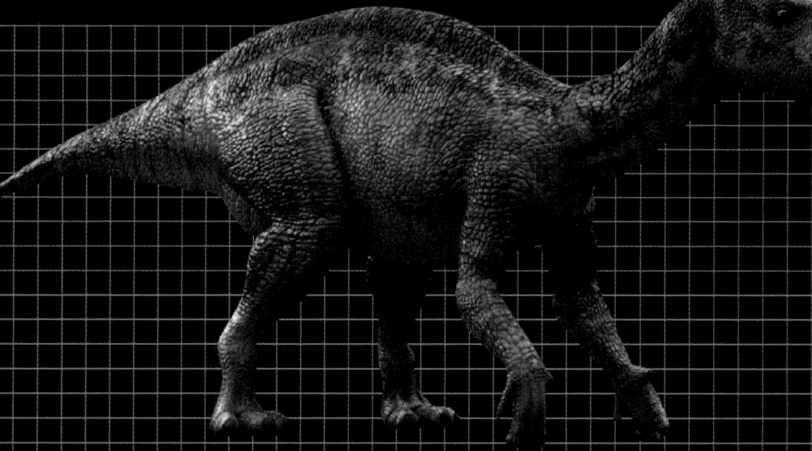

Iguanodon is the dominant herbivore in many Early–Mid Cretaceous ecosystems. The largest are slightly larger than some sauropods. ***Iguanodon*** walks on two legs most of the time, and rears back on its hind limbs to reach into the trees. However, it can run on all fours if it needs to escape a predator.

POTENTIAL RISK: LOW

Iguanodon *will stick its thumb spike into the flesh of attacking predators when provoked, but is otherwise peaceful.*

SIZE COMPARISON

An elephant-sized plant vacuum.

LENGTH: 6–11 metres (20–36 ft)

HEIGHT: 1.8–3.3 metres (6–11 ft)

WEIGHT: 3–6 tonnes

LEAF CROPPER

Iguanodon has a long and narrow skull, much like that of a horse, with a sharp beak at the front for cropping vegetation. Rows of leaf-like teeth crush and chew plant matter, an advanced feature that many other herbivores do not possess.

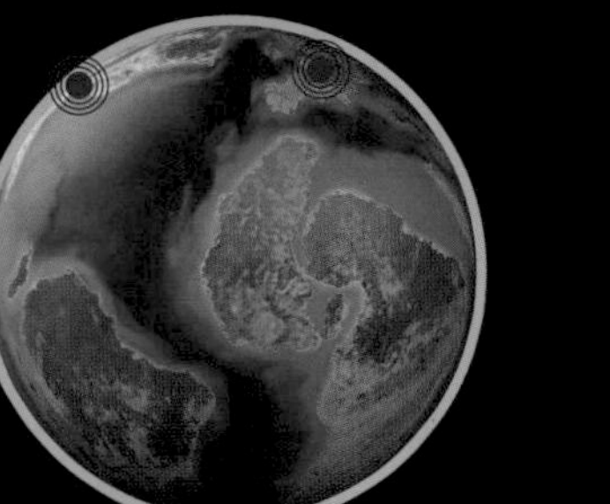

HABITAT

EUROPE AND NORTH AMERICA, EARLY-MID CRETACEOUS

Iguanodon *preferred lush, warm and wet environments that bordered lakes and rivers. Here it could find all sorts of vegetation to fuel its plant-eating lifestyle.*

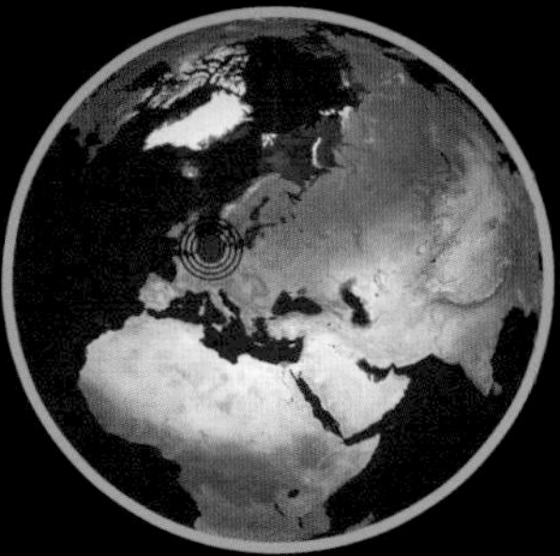

FOSSIL FINDS

EUROPE AND NORTH AMERICA, EARLY-MID CRETACEOUS

Iguanodon *was one of the first dinosaurs ever found by scientists. It was uncovered by English palaeontologist Gideon Mantell in 1825 and became the second dinosaur ever named.*

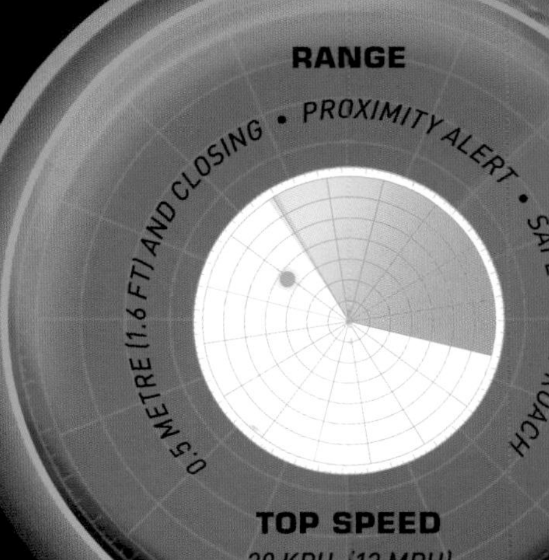

COOLING SYSTEM

The back vertebrae expand into long, thin spines to support a sail that stands more than 1 metre (3 ft) high. The sail is used to help ***Ouranosaurus*** keep cool during the humid days of summer.

FOSSIL FINDS

AFRICA, EARLY–MID CRETACEOUS

***Ouranosaurus** is the most common herbivorous dinosaur found in the sandstone rocks of northern Africa. Its fossils are known from across the Sahara Desert.*

HABITAT

AFRICA, EARLY–MID CRETACEOUS

***Ouranosaurus** lived alongside **Spinosaurus** and **Carcharodontosaurus** in the green river deltas of northern Africa 95 million years ago.*

POTENTIAL RISK: LOW

***Ouranosaurus** is no threat whatsoever unless it feels threatened. A frightened herd of them will break into a stampede and mow down anything in its path.*

SIZE COMPARISON

*A sail-backed creature slightly smaller than **Iguanodon**.*

LENGTH: 7 metres (23 ft)

HEIGHT: 2 metres (7 ft)

WEIGHT: 2.7–2.9 tonnes

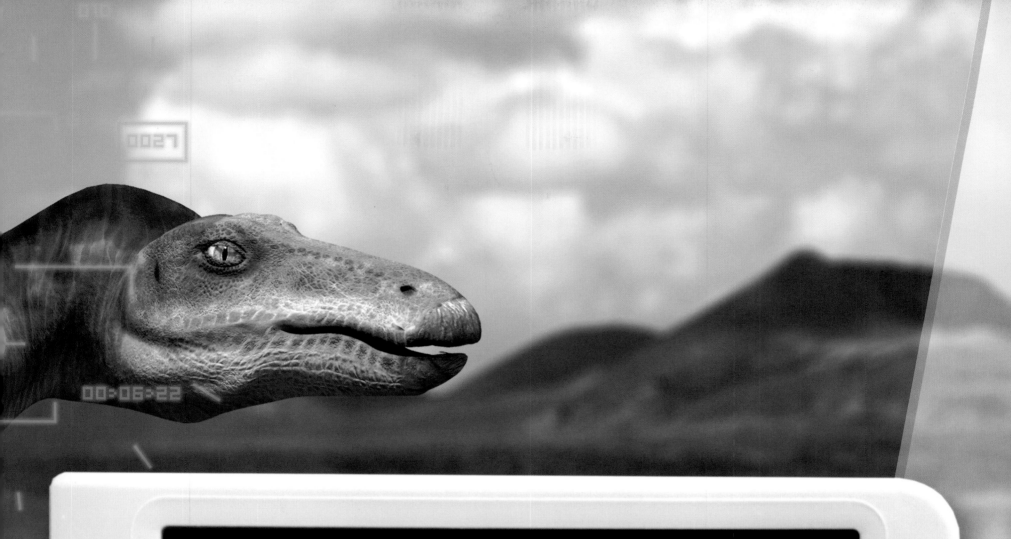

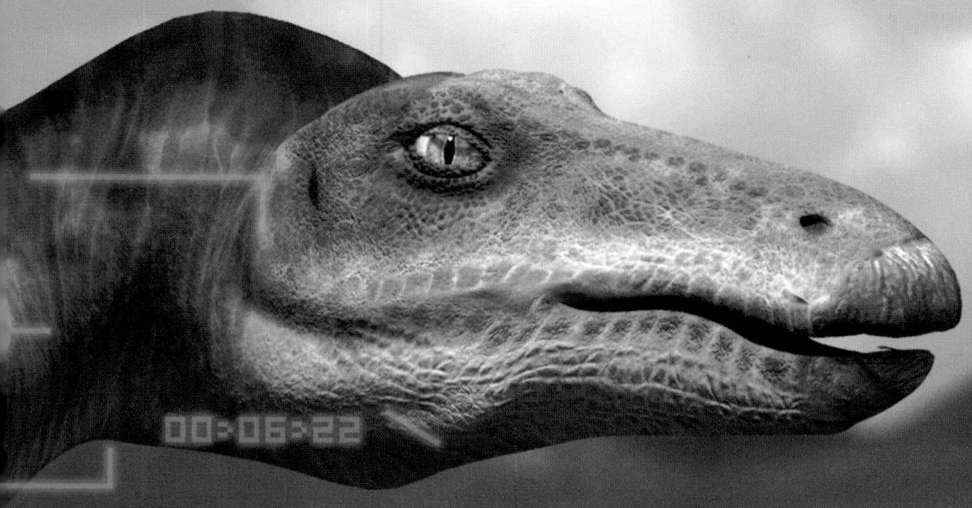

OURANOSAURUS

MEANING: 'brave lizard'

PRONUNCIATION: *oo-ran-o-SORE-uss*

One of the oddest and most recognizable dinosaurs is ***Ouranosaurus***, a peaceful plant-eater with a deep and colourful sail on its back. ***Ouranosaurus*** scurries around the deltas of northern Africa, chomping vegetation while trying to avoid the jaws of ***Spinosaurus***.

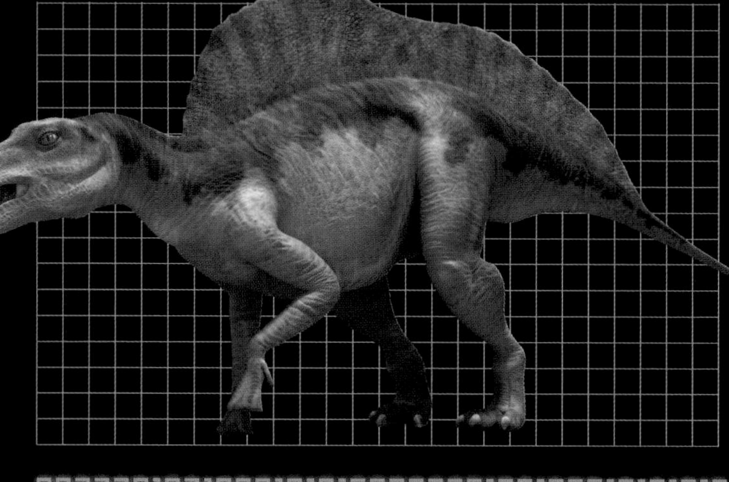

A close cousin of ***Iguanodon***, ***Ouranosaurus*** is also a large plant-eater that can feed on both short shrubs and taller trees. Most of the characteristic features of ***Iguanodon*** are also seen in ***Ouranosaurus***, including a horse-like skull that can crop and chew vegetation, an ability to walk on two or four legs, and a large thumb spike for warding off predators.

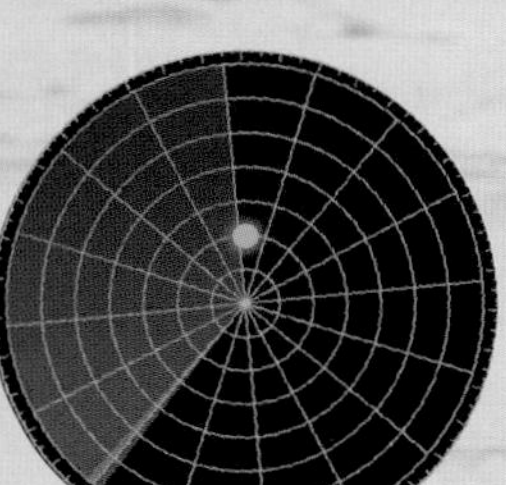

RANGE
5.2 METRES (17 FT) AND CLOSING
PROXIMITY ALERT
SAFE TO APPROACH

TOP SPEED
20 KPH (12 MPH)

WEAPONRY: LIGHTLY ARMED

Only the thumb spike is a dangerous tool, and this is employed just when a predator attacks.

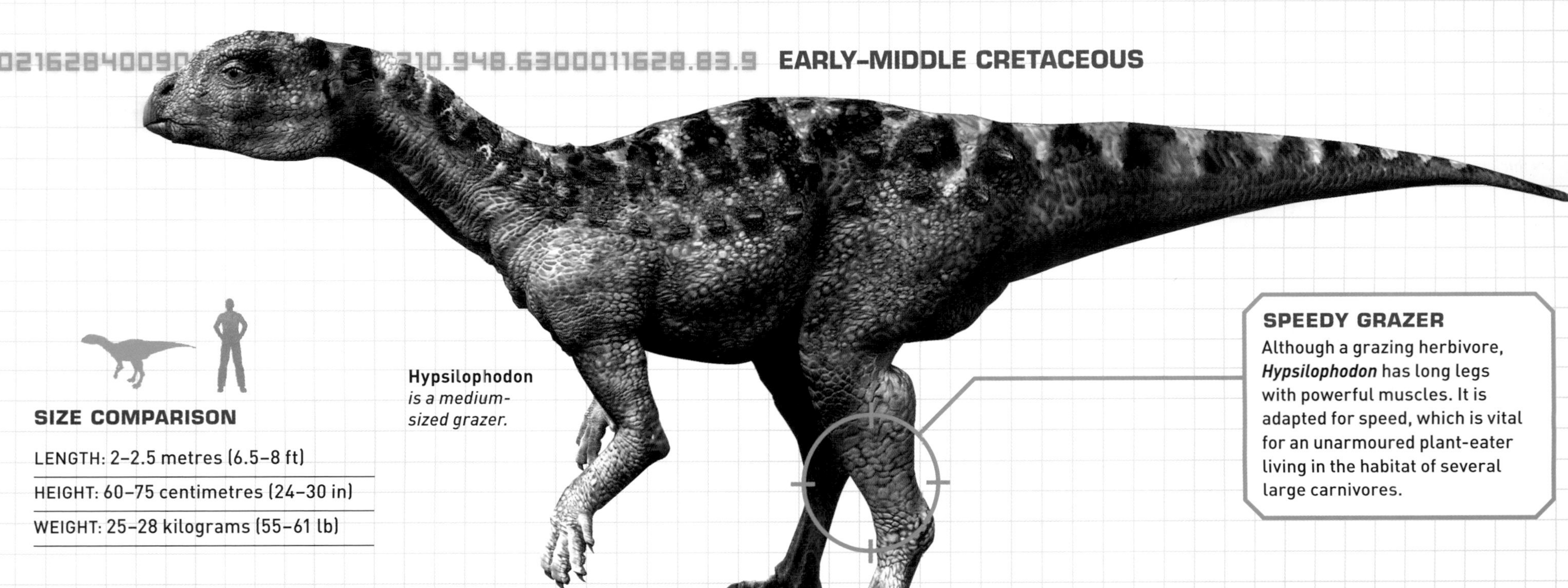

Hypsilophodon *is a medium-sized grazer.*

SIZE COMPARISON

LENGTH: 2–2.5 metres (6.5–8 ft)
HEIGHT: 60–75 centimetres (24–30 in)
WEIGHT: 25–28 kilograms (55–61 lb)

SPEEDY GRAZER

Although a grazing herbivore, ***Hypsilophodon*** has long legs with powerful muscles. It is adapted for speed, which is vital for an unarmoured plant-eater living in the habitat of several large carnivores.

POTENTIAL RISK: VERY LOW

Hypsilophodon *is the meekest and quietest dinosaur that ever lived.*

HYPSILOPHODON

MEANING: 'high-crested tooth'

PRONUNCIATION: *hip-SILL-oh-pho-don*

Hypsilophodon is a common sight along the English riverbanks. This small and skinny herbivore numbers in the millions, and munches ferns and other low-level vegetation. ***Hypsilophodon*** lives in herds for protection from large, menacing predators, such as ***Neovenator***.

FOSSIL FINDS

EUROPE, EARLY CRETACEOUS

Fossils of **Hypsilophodon** *were first found in southern England, where it lived about 125 million years ago. At first, scientists thought it lived in trees, but later studies showed that it was a very strong runner.*

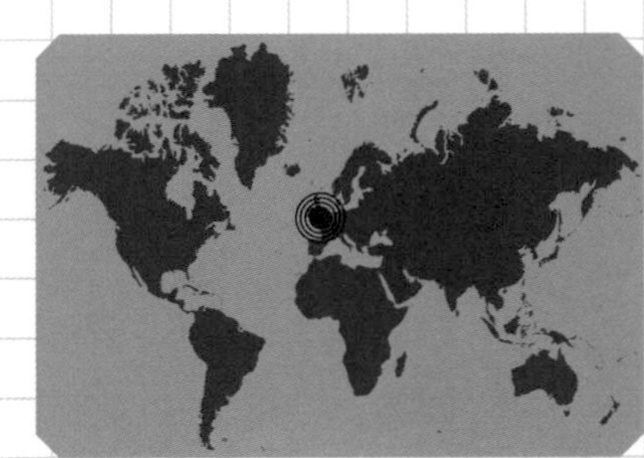

SIZE COMPARISON

LENGTH: 1–2 metres (38–77 in)
HEIGHT: 0.3–1 metre (1–3 ft)
WEIGHT: 7–16 kilograms (15–36 lb)

Leaellynasaura *is a small and peaceful herbivore.*

POTENTIAL RISK: VERY LOW

This is another meek and quiet dinosaur, much like **Hypsilophodon**.

LEAELLYNASAURA

MEANING: named after Leaellyn Rich (daughter of Australian palaeontologists Tom Rich and Patricia Vickers-Rich)

PRONUNCIATION: *lay-ell-in-uh-SORE-ah*

Even smaller than ***Hypsilophodon***, the herbivorous ***Leaellynasaura*** is well adapted for living in the dark, polar cold of Australia. Its eyes are enormous and its brain has enlarged optic lobes (the region controll ng vision). These combine to give ***Leaellynasaura*** a keen sense of sight, which it needs for survival in the long, dark nights.

FOSSIL FINDS

AUSTRALIA, EARLY CRETACEOUS

Abundant fossils of **Leaellynasaura**, *dating from 90–100 million years ago, have been found in southeastern Australia. In prehistoric times the landmass was largely cold and dark.*

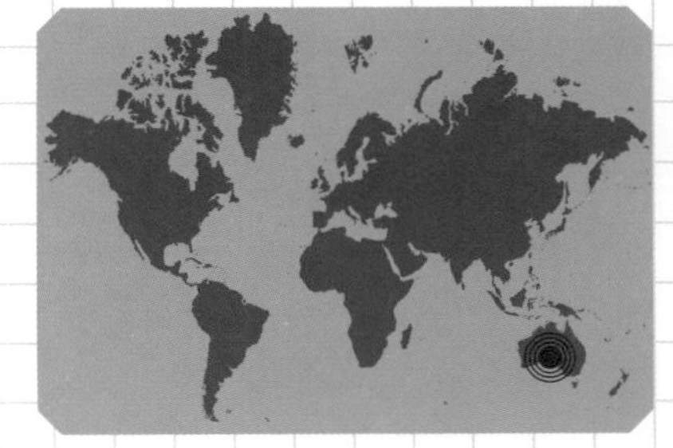

POTENTIAL RISK: LOW

Usually peaceful, **Muttaburrasaurus** *can use its thick thumb claw to fend off attackers.*

SIZE COMPARISON

LENGTH: 7–7.5 metres (23–25 ft)

HEIGHT: 2.2 metres (7–7.5 ft)

WEIGHT: 1.7–1.9 tonnes

A small and peaceful herbivore.

MUTTABURRASAURUS

MEANING: named after Muttaburra, a site in Australia

PRONUNCIATION: *mutt-a-burr-a-SORE-uss*

A contemporary of ***Leaellynasaura***, ***Muttaburrasaurus*** is a much larger, stronger and more common animal. It uses its long, narrow skull and leaf-shaped teeth to devour huge bunches of foliage.

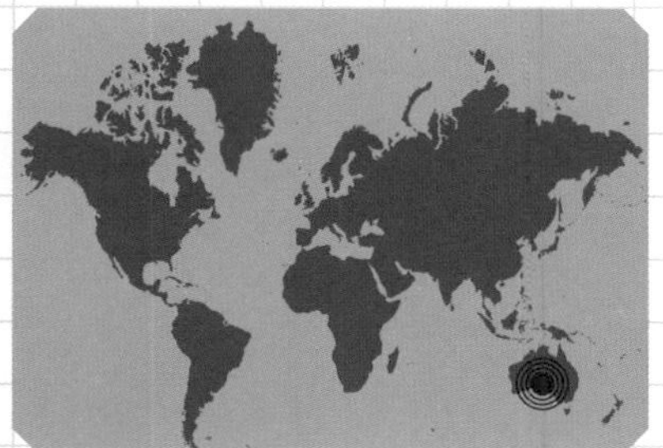

FOSSIL FINDS

AUSTRALIA, EARLY CRETACEOUS

Muttaburrasaurus *is among the most common dinosaur fossils found in Australia. It dominated the cold and dark polar environments of 90–100 million years ago.*

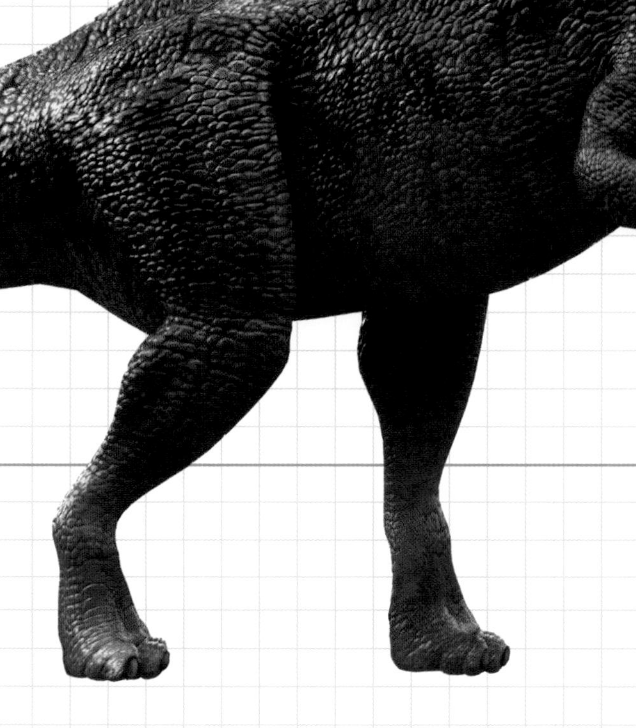

POTENTIAL RISK: LOW

Tenontosaurus *is accustomed to attacks from* **Deinonychus**, *and can use its large size as a defensive weapon.*

TENONTOSAURUS

MEANING: 'sinew lizard'

PRONUNCIATION: *ten-on-toe-SORE-uss*

The most common plant-eater in its environment, ***Tenontosaurus*** is a favoured prey of the agile raptor ***Deinonychus***. ***Deinonychus*** is especially fond of the muscular hindlimbs of ***Tenontosaurus***, which provide a tasty and nutritious meal.

FOSSIL FINDS

NORTH AMERICA, EARLY CRETACEOUS

Tenontosaurus *was incredibly common in North America about 80–90 million years ago. Its fossils are found in large numbers today.*

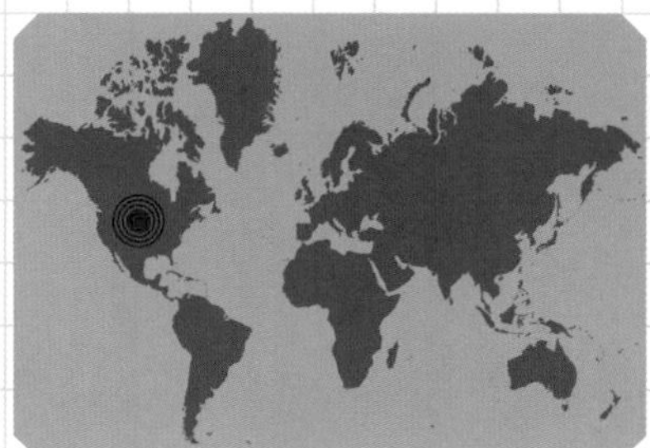

SNAKE TAIL

Tenontosaurus is different from most other dinosaurs in one feature. Its tail is snake-like and stiffened by bony tendons. It is used for balance.

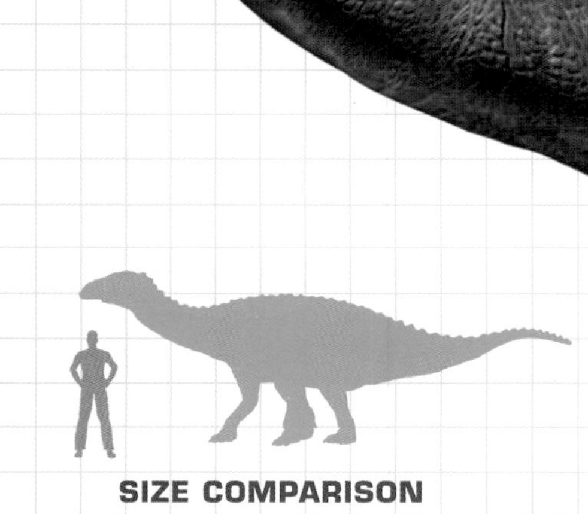

SIZE COMPARISON

LENGTH: 7–8 metres (23–26 ft)

HEIGHT: 1.7–2 metres (5.5–6.5 ft)

WEIGHT: 1000–1100 kilograms (2200–2425 lb)

Tenontosaurus *is one of the largest herbivores in its environment.*

DINOSAURS OF THE LATE CRETACEOUS

99.6–65.5 MILLION YEARS AGO

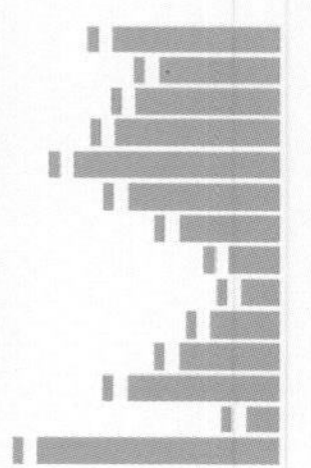

The dinosaurs were at their peak in the hot, wet and lush landscapes of the Late Cretaceous. By now the continents were separate, and the animals had evolved into astonishingly varied body forms and were living in distinct and complex communities. In Mongolia, for example, sleek hunters such as ***Velociraptor*** rubbed shoulders with the bird-like ***Oviraptor*** and the plant-eating ***Protoceratops***, but the southern continents had entirely different kinds of animals. While ***Tyrannosaurus***, for example, terrorized the north, peculiar abelisaurid theropods, such as ***Carnotaurus*** and ***Majungasaurus***, were ruling landmasses in the south. The evidence for this north–south divide comes from the fossil record, and one of the richest sources is the Hell Creek formation in Montana and the Dakotas in the United States. The animals it contains were to be wiped out by the effects of a giant asteroid hitting the Earth, but until that fateful day they confidently ruled the world.

CARNOTAURUS

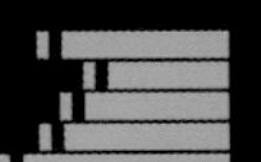

MEANING: 'carnivorous bull'

PRONUNCIATION: *car-no-TORE-uss*

The bull-horned ***Carnotaurus*** is the king of South America. While ***Tyrannosaurus*** and its relatives terrorize herbivores across the northern continents, ***Carnotaurus*** is the undisputed top predator of the south.

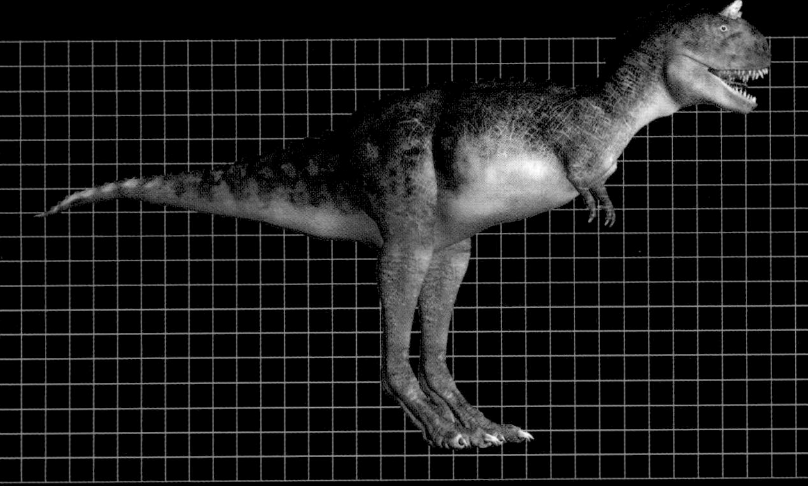

Carnotaurus is a close relative of ***Ceratosaurus*** but looks very little like its cousin. The most distinctive feature of ***Carnotaurus*** is its unusual skull, which is short and deep, has a rough bony texture that supports sandpaper-like skin, and sprouts two large, menacing horns over the eyes.

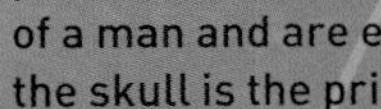

SMALL ARMS

The arms of *Carnotaurus* are comically puny. They are even smaller than the arms of a man and are essentially useless, so the skull is the primary weapon to catch and kill prey.

POTENTIAL RISK: EXTREME

Although peculiar-looking, **Carnotaurus** *is large, fast, heavy and mean, and can tackle any prey.*

SIZE COMPARISON

A bizarre large carnivore.

LENGTH: 7–9 metres (23–30 ft)

HEIGHT: 3–3.75 metres (9.5–12 ft)

WEIGHT: 2.1–2.3 tonnes

HABITAT

ARGENTINA, LATE CRETACEOUS

Carnotaurus *lived alongside a range of sauropod and ornithopod dinosaurs, and might have hunted in packs to take down large prey.*

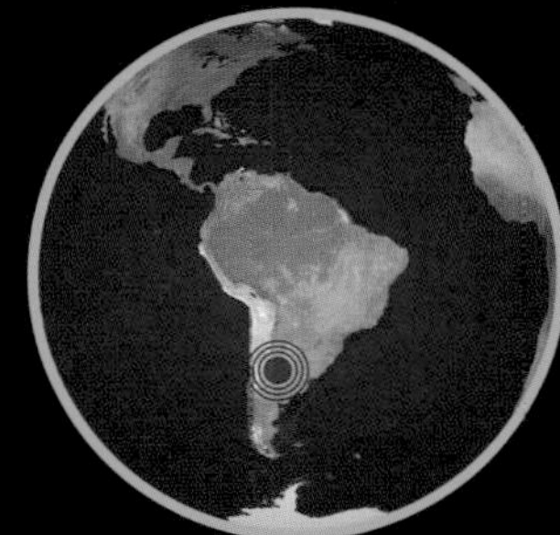

FOSSIL FINDS

ARGENTINA, LATE CRETACEOUS

Carnotaurus *is known from an exceptional skeleton found in the very Late Cretaceous rocks of Argentina. It is one of the best-known southern theropods.*

ATTRACT AND REPEL

What is the purpose of the bull-like horns of ***Carnotaurus***? They have a dual purpose, being used to attract mates and also to head-butt prey!

MAJUNGASAURUS

MEANING: named after a province in Madagascar

PRONUNCIATION: *mah-jung-o-SORE-uss*

The champion predator of its ecosystem, ***Majungasaurus*** is the terror of prehistoric Madagascar. This monstrous meat-eater is a close relative of ***Carnotaurus*** and, like the 'horned bull', uses its massive skull to knock out and kill prey.

Majungasaurus and ***Carnotaurus*** are members of the abelisaurid group, a subgroup of theropods that roam across the southern continents while tyrannosaurs dominate the north. Abelisaurids are some of the largest and most fearsome predators in the dinosaur world, and their short skulls and strong necks can choke large sauropods.

POTENTIAL RISK: EXTREME

Majungasaurus *is the most feared creature in prehistoric Madagascar.*

SIZE COMPARISON

An agile and muscular predator that also engages in cannibalism.

LENGTH: 7–9 metres (23–30 ft)

HEIGHT: 3–3.75 metres (9.5–12 ft)

WEIGHT: 2.1–2.3 tonnes

THUNDER THIGHS
Like all theropods, Majungasaurus walks on two legs. The hindlimbs are especially strong, packed full of muscle, allowing it to outrun and overpower its prey.
FOSSIL FINDS
MADAGASCAR, LATE CRETACEOUS
Majungasaurus is known from hundreds of fossils, including some remarkably complete skeletons, from the island of Madagascar.
HABITAT
MADAGASCAR, LATE CRETACEOUS
Majungasaurus shared the wet river bottoms of Late Cretaceous Madagascar with a variety of large sauropods, which were a favourite prey.
RANGE
7.8 METRES (25.5 FT) AND CLOSING
PROXIMITY ALERT
TAKE URGENT EVASIVE ACTION
TOP SPEED
23 KPH (14 MPH)
WEAPONRY: FULLY ARMED
The array of small but sharp teeth and long, clawed arms are enough to dispatch even the largest sauropods.

TYRANNOSAURUS

MEANING: 'tyrant lizard'

PRONUNCIATION: *ty-ran-o-SORE-uss*

Tyrannosaurus is the undisputed king of the Late Cretaceous. This 'tyrant lizard' is the top predator of the food chain, a carnivorous monster so large that herbivores are terrorized by the approaching thud of its footsteps.

It is difficult to exaggerate the strength and power of ***Tyrannosaurus***, the ultimate dinosaur predator. The enormous skull measures nearly 1.5 metres (5 ft) in length, almost as long as an average man is tall. The jaws are packed with more than 50 banana-sized teeth, and the brain is large and well developed.

JAWS OF DEATH

The largest teeth in the jaw measure over 30 centimetres (1 ft) in length. These teeth are thick, strong and serrated, and are powerful enough to crack through thick bones!

POTENTIAL RISK: EXTREME

No land creature that has ever existed can match the power and strength of **Tyrannosaurus**. *Its speed and intelligence add to the danger. Prey animals take every precaution not to get too close.*

SIZE COMPARISON

The most feared large carnivore of all time.

LENGTH: 12–13 metres (40–43 ft)

HEIGHT: 4–4.3 metres (13–14 ft)

WEIGHT: 6–7 tonnes

HABITAT

NORTH AMERICA, LATE CRETACEOUS

Tyrannosaurus, *along with* **Ankylosaurus**, **Triceratops** *and other creatures of the Hell Creek ecosystem, lived on a lush floodplain choked by rivers and streams.*

FOSSIL FINDS

NORTH AMERICA, LATE CRETACEOUS

Skeletons of **Tyrannosaurus** *are among the most common fossils in the 66-million-year-old Hell Creek Formation of the western United States. It was clearly a dominant predator.*

RANGE

2.1 METRES (6.8 FT) AND CLOSING • PROXIMITY ALERT • WITHDRAW IMMEDIATELY

TOP SPEED

23 KPH (14 MPH)

FEATHER HEAD
Tyrannosaurus, like most theropods, is feathered. Its neck is covered with a colourful mane of feathers, which are used to attract mates and scare off other tyrannosaur rivals.
200
150
100
0273019210

POTENTIAL RISK: **EXTREME**

Only **Tarbosaurus** *approaches the feared power and strength of* **Tyrannosaurus**.

HABITAT

ASIA, LATE CRETACEOUS

Tarbosaurus *hunted sauropods and large ornithopods across Asia during the Late Cretaceous, about 66 million years ago. Mongolia was not covered by desert at this time, but was home to a wide array of species that thrived in its warm and wet climate.*

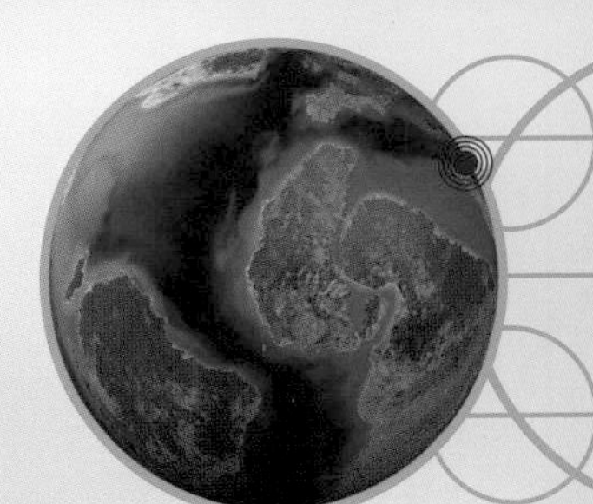

TARBOSAURUS

MEANING: 'alarming lizard'

PRONUNCIATION: tar-bo-SORE-uss

Tarbosaurus is the Asian cousin of ***Tyrannosaurus***. This horrifying meat-eater terrorizes its ecosystems and devours any prey it can find. At a length of more than 12 metres (40 ft) and a weight of more than 7 tonnes, it is truly enormous.

BONE CRUNCHER

Tarbosaurus and ***Tyrannosaurus*** are very similar animals, much as a lion and a tiger are. Like its famous cousin, ***Tarbosaurus*** has a skull about as long as a man, and crunches the bones of prey with its banana-sized teeth. But while ***Tyrannosaurus*** hunts its rival ***Triceratops***, ***Tarbosaurus*** has an appetite for large sauropods, such as ***Nemegtosaurus***.

Tarbosaurus *is so large that it cannot run, but it is still faster than the prey it hunts.*

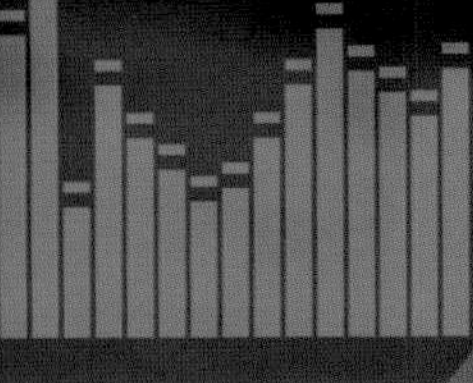

RANGE

6.3 METRES (20.6 FT) AND CLOSING
PROXIMITY ALERT
STAY CONCEALED AND DO NOT MOVE

TOP SPEED

23 KPH (14 MPH)

FOSSIL FINDS

ASIA, LATE CRETACEOUS

Fossils of **Tarbosaurus** *are found all across the Late Cretaceous rocks of Mongolia and China. Even small juveniles have been found.*

GRAPPLING ARMS

The arms of ***Tarbosaurus***, like those of ***Tyrannosaurus***, are absurdly tiny. However, they are sheathed in dense muscles and are actually quite powerful. They are used to hold struggling prey near the mouth so that the teeth can deliver a final killing blow.

POWER BITE

Tarbosaurus has the strongest bite-force in the dinosaur kingdom. Its robust teeth and massive jaw muscles allow it to rip through flesh and bone like a hyena.

SIZE COMPARISON

A close cousin of the most feared carnivore in history.

LENGTH: 12–13 metres (40–43 ft)

HEIGHT: 4–4.3 metres (13–14 ft)

WEIGHT: 6–7 tonnes

BARK STRIPPERS

Alxasaurus is immediately recognizable by its distinctive claws. These bizarre extremities are used for two things: to scare off large predators and to strip the bark from trees – a surprisingly rich source of nutrients inaccessible to most dinosaur herbivores that don't possess claws as large as these.

FOSSIL FINDS

ASIA, MID-CRETACEOUS

***Alxasaurus** was the first member of its subgroup, the therizinosaurs, to be known from a reasonably complete fossil. This skeleton was found in Inner Mongolia, China, in 1993.*

HABITAT

ASIA, MID-CRETACEOUS

***Alxasaurus** lived about 105 million years ago, soon after Asia collided with North America and Europe after a long period of isolation.*

POTENTIAL RISK: MEDIUM

*Usually a gentle herbivore, **Alxasaurus** can turn its scythe-like claws on attacking predators or any animal that ventures too close.*

SIZE COMPARISON

A clawed freak that dwarfs a man.

LENGTH: 3.5–4 metres (11–13 ft)

HEIGHT: 1.75–2 metres (5.5–6.5 ft)

WEIGHT: 350–400 kilograms (772–880 lb)

REACHING FOR THE BEST
The neck of *Alxasaurus* is remarkably long for a theropod. It is an adaptation for reaching the nourishing leaves and stems of tall trees, something that an average carnivorous theropod doesn't have to worry about.

ALXASAURUS

MEANING: named after the Alxa Desert, Mongolia

PRONUNCIATION: *al-ksa-SORE-uss*

Is any dinosaur more weird-looking than ***Alxasaurus***? This pot-bellied plant-eater looks like a cross between a sloth and turkey, but it is actually a member of the mainly carnivorous theropod group.

Alxasaurus has several bizarre features. Its skull is small and full of leaf-like teeth for chewing plants. Its hindlimbs are long and support the entire weight of the animal, including its massive gut. Perhaps most strangely of all, each finger sports a long, wispy claw that reaches up to 1 metre (3 ft) in length!

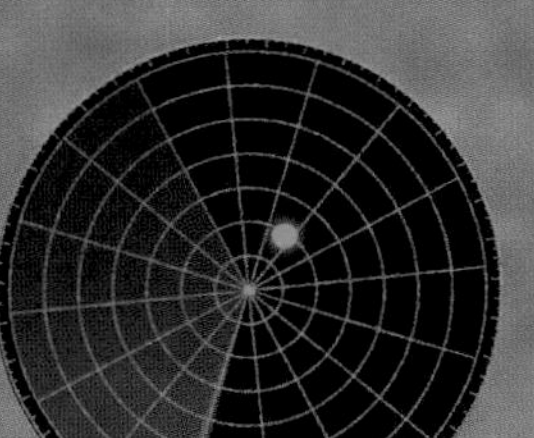

RANGE
4.1 METRES (13.5 FT) AND CLOSING
PROXIMITY ALERT
APPROACH WITH CAUTION

TOP SPEED
30 KPH (20 MPH)

WEAPONRY: ARMED
The claws of this animal should be avoided, but the lack of sharp teeth and a strong bite make this herbivore relatively harmless.

POTENTIAL RISK: **HIGH**

Pity the herbivores that have to live in fear of both tyrannosaurids and dromaeosaurs. **Dromaeosaurus***'s small size poses little risk to some individuals, but the pack is powerful.*

HABITAT

NORTH AMERICA, LATE CRETACEOUS

Dromaeosaurus *lived in the stifling conditions of the Late Cretaceous, when sea levels were high, rain was constant, and heatwaves parched the land.*

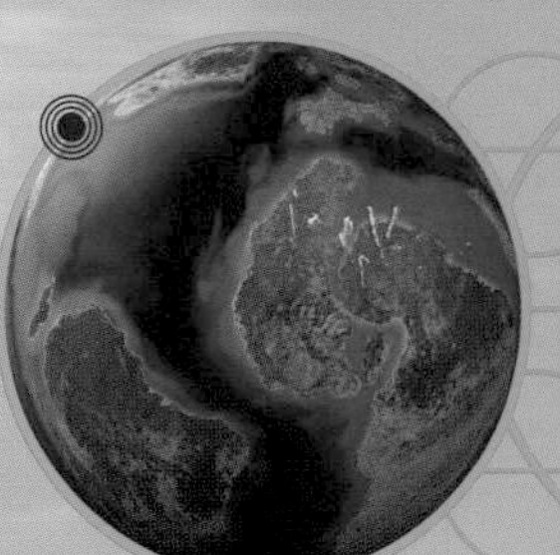

DROMAEOSAURUS

MEANING: 'running lizard'

PRONUNCIATION: *dro-me-oh-SORE-uss*

The pack-hunting ***Dromaeosaurus*** lives in the shadow of the monstrous tyrannosaurs, but is able to feed on smaller prey by using its cunning senses and deadly arsenal of weapons, especially the enlarged claw on the second toe, which is used for slashing and ripping.

POWER IN NUMBERS

Dromaeosaurus is the prime member of the dromaeosaurid group of theropods, commonly known as 'raptors'. ***Dromaeosaurus*** is only slightly larger than a large dog, and comes up just to hip- or chest-level on a man. However, by hunting in packs, ***Dromaeosaurus*** can subdue animals much larger than itself. Usually, a team of dromaeosaurs will stalk, surround, then leap onto the flanks of its prey.

Muscular hips and a stiff tail allow **Dromaeosaurus** *to run fast and pounce on its prey.*

HUNTER-SCAVENGER

The skull of ***Dromaeosaurus*** is long, with thick bones and tough teeth. It has one of the strongest skulls of any raptor, which allows it to tackle large prey and to scavenge on carcasses when a free meal presents itself.

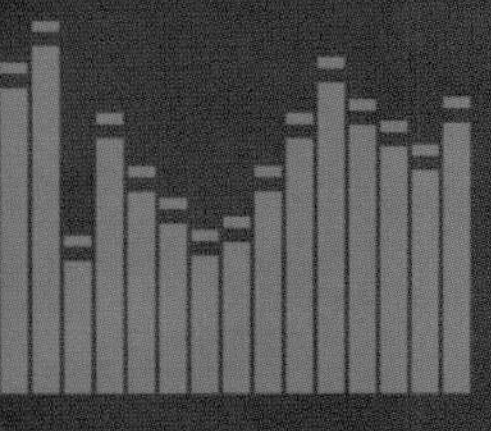

RANGE

5 METRES (16.4 FT) AND CLOSING
PROXIMITY ALERT
EVASIVE ACTION RECOMMENDED

TOP SPEED

35 KPH (22 MPH)

FOSSIL FINDS

NORTH AMERICA, LATE CRETACEOUS

Dromaeosaurus *fossils, especially shed teeth, are common in the 76-million-year-old rocks of Canada and the United States. Often the teeth are found mixed up with the bones of prey species.*

SIZE COMPARISON

A small predator that packs a mean bite.

LENGTH: 1.5–2 metres (5–6.5 ft)

HEIGHT: 46–70 centimetres (18–28 in)

WEIGHT: 15–35 kilograms (33–77 lb)

VELOCIRAPTOR

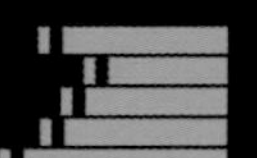

MEANING: 'speedy thief'

PRONUNCIATION: *vel-oss-ih-rap-TOR*

Velociraptor is the cleverest and most cunning of all the dinosaurs. Although only slightly bigger than a large dog, ***Velociraptor*** uses its keen senses and pack-hunting abilities to overcome prey ten times bigger than itself.

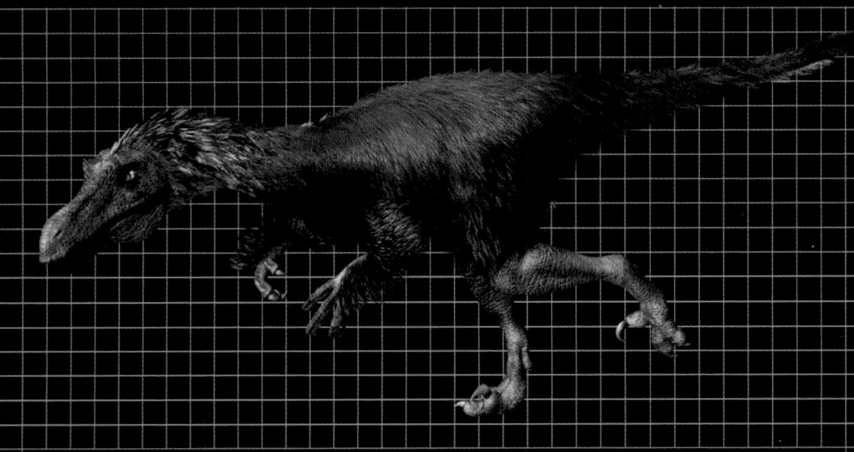

The intelligence and agility of ***Velociraptor*** recall the sharp senses and movements of a bird, so perhaps it's no surprise that they are closely related. ***Velociraptor's*** arms support strong feathers, like those of birds, and although it cannot actually fly, it uses these feathers to help it manoeuvre while chasing prey.

AGILE ARMS

The arms of ***Velociraptor*** can fold against the body, just like the wings of birds. The wrist is incredibly mobile and the arm can swing in a wide arc, allowing ***Velociraptor*** to attack its prey from all angles.

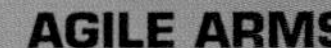

POTENTIAL RISK: EXTREME

Velociraptor *is a predator of the highest power, since it uses both physical weapons and sharp intelligence to overpower and outwit prey.*

SIZE COMPARISON

A small predator whose intelligence compensates for its small size.

LENGTH: 1.5–2 metres (5–6.5 ft)

HEIGHT: 46–70 centimetres (18–28 in)

WEIGHT: 15–18 kilograms (33–39 lb)

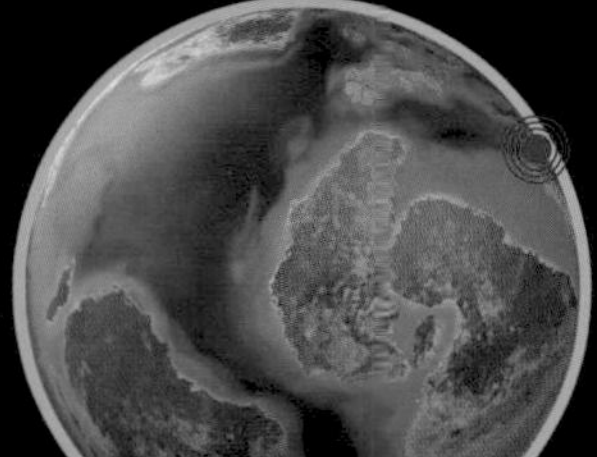

HABITAT

ASIA, LATE CRETACEOUS

Velociraptor *lived alongside many dinosaurs, including its favourite prey* **Protoceratops**, *in a sandy dune field that was often inundated by flash floods.*

FOSSIL FINDS

ASIA, LATE CRETACEOUS

Velociraptor *fossils are found in the Gobi Desert of Mongolia, a windy and dry landscape today populated by bands of nomadic sheep herders and little else.*

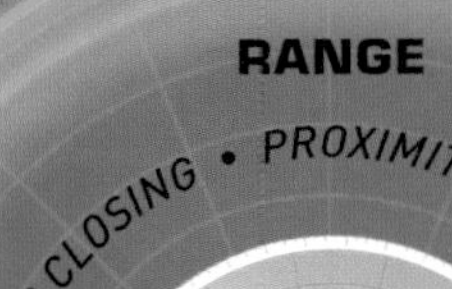

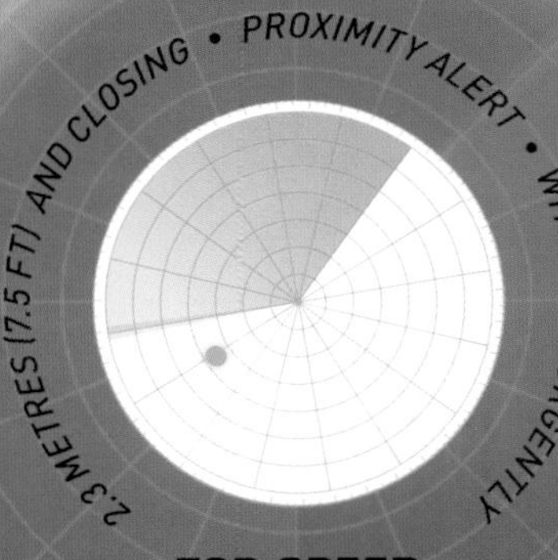

TOP SPEED

36 KPH (23 MPH)

TERROR TOES

The most characteristic weapon for all raptors is the enlarged claw on the second toe. The toe itself can move freely and easily, allowing the claw to latch onto the flanks of prey. Once attached, the claw is then used to sever the blood vessels and rip down through the flesh of the prey.

TROODON

MEANING: 'wounded tooth'

PRONUNCIATION: *TROO-o-don*

The sleek and slender ***Troodon*** is a predator well adapted for stealth hunting. This omnivore surprises its prey by approaching with a blazing show of speed and kills the shocked creature within seconds.

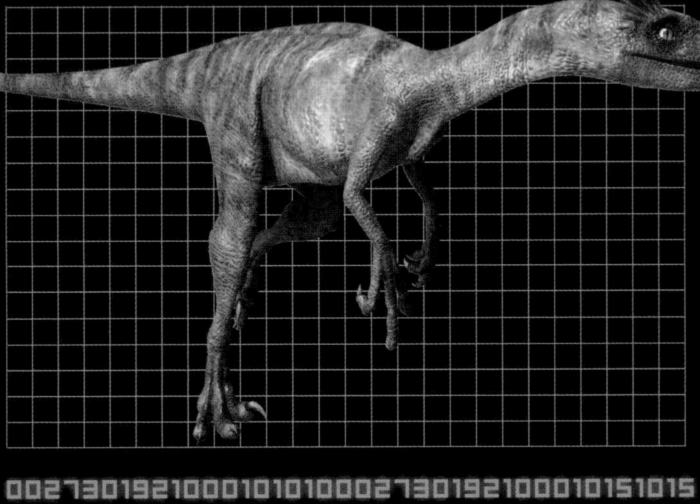

Troodon is a classic example of yet another group of small, bird-like theropods, the Troodontidae. These theropods are very similar to dromaeosaurs, and the two groups are closely related to each other and to birds. However, unlike dromaeosaurs, troodontids are also able to eat plants. Although well adapted for speed and hunting, ***Troodon*** can feed on leaves and stems if unable to find fresh meat.

POTENTIAL RISK: HIGH

Herbivorous dinosaurs and plants are keenly devoured by this strange omnivore. Beware its sharp senses and high speed.

SIZE COMPARISON

A small omnivore that can easily outrace large prey.

LENGTH: 1.5–2 metres (5–6.5 ft)

HEIGHT: 50–70 centimetres (20–28 in)

WEIGHT: 50 kilograms (110 lb)

NIFTY MOVER

Troodon is a lean and streamlined dinosaur. The thin body, hollowed-out bones and muscular legs allow *Troodon* to move quickly for long periods of time.

FOSSIL FINDS

NORTH AMERICA, LATE CRETACEOUS

***Troodon** was first found and named in 1856 from only a single tooth. Better fossils have been found since, but **Troodon** is still one of the rarest North American dinosaurs.*

HABITAT

NORTH AMERICA, LATE CRETACEOUS

***Troodon** lived in North America at a time when a vast inland sea stretching from the Arctic to the Gulf of Mexico divided the continent in two.*

RANGE

3.1 METRES (10.1 FT) AND CLOSING
PROXIMITY ALERT
EVASIVE ACTION RECOMMENDED

TOP SPEED

35 KPH (22 MPH)

WEAPONRY: FULLY ARMED

*Like **Velociraptor**, **Troodon** has that rare combination of first-rate intelligence and a physical arsenal of teeth, claws and speed.*

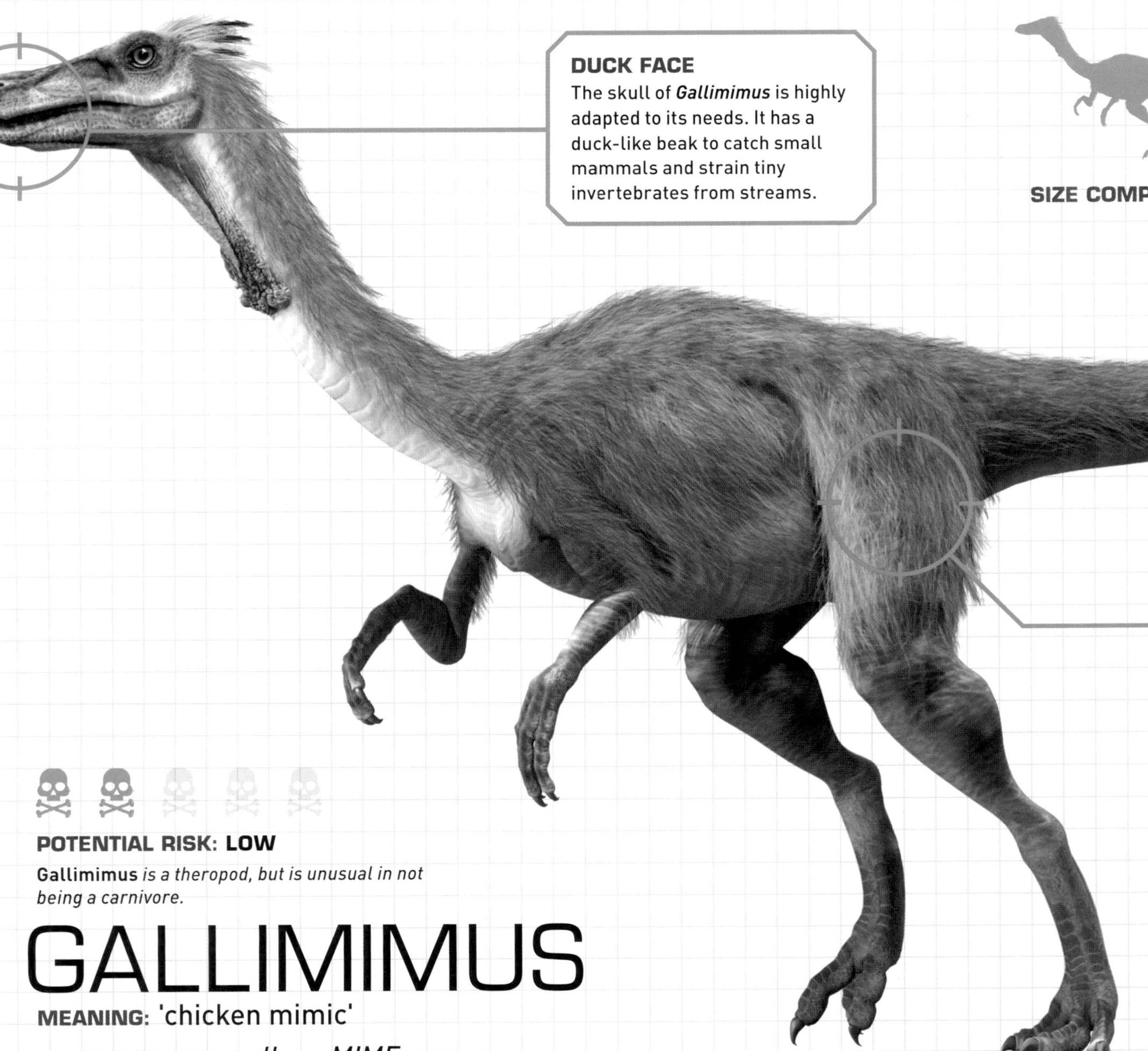

DUCK FACE
The skull of ***Gallimimus*** is highly adapted to its needs. It has a duck-like beak to catch small mammals and strain tiny invertebrates from streams.

SIZE COMPARISON

LENGTH: 5–6 metres (16–20 ft)
HEIGHT: 2.5–3 metres (8–10 ft)
WEIGHT: 160–220 kilograms (353–485 lb)

Gallimimus *looks rather like an overgrown chicken.*

STRONG SUPPORT
The elongated hindlimbs carry the entire weight of ***Gallimimus***, so they are very muscular.

POTENTIAL RISK: LOW
Gallimimus *is a theropod, but is unusual in not being a carnivore.*

GALLIMIMUS

MEANING: 'chicken mimic'

PRONUNCIATION: *gall-ee-MIME-uss*

Gallimimus is the ostrich of the Cretaceous. This theropod resembles a large, flightless bird: it is sheathed in feathers, has a beak and lacks teeth. It also has extremely long legs, which enable it to run quickly and escape aggressive predators, such as ***Tarbosaurus***.

FOSSIL FINDS
ASIA, LATE CRETACEOUS

Gallimimus *was a common animal in Late Cretaceous Mongolia about 65–70 million years ago. Its fossils are not well preserved, but they do show that it had many bird-like features.*

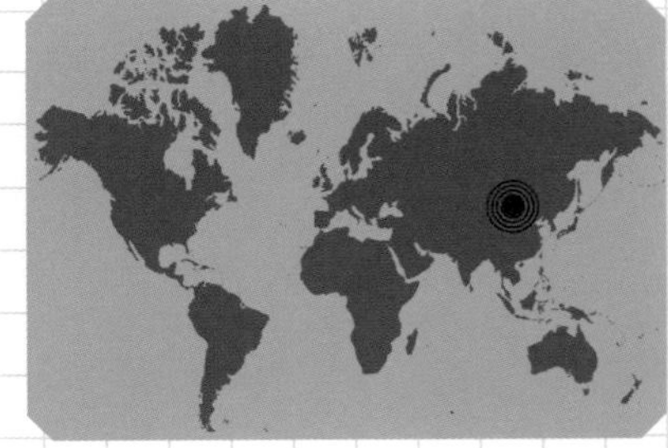

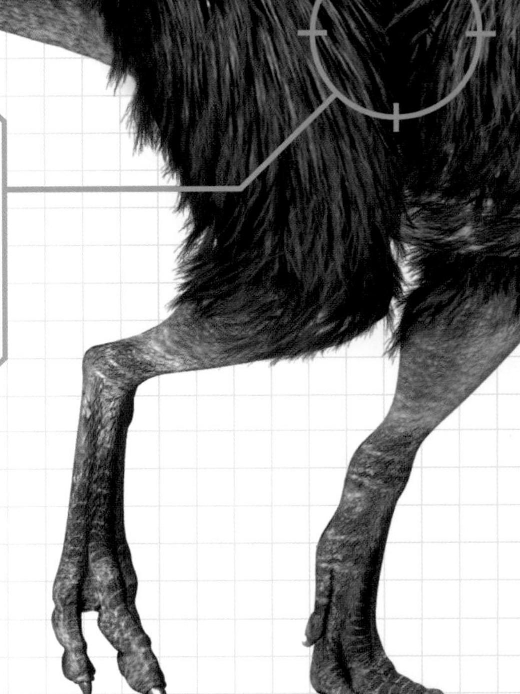

POTENTIAL RISK: VERY LOW
Oviraptor*'s strong beak is more probably used for cracking nuts than as a weapon.*

OVIRAPTOR

MEANING: 'egg thief'

PRONUNCIATION: *oh-vih-rap-TOR*

The freaky ***Oviraptor*** looks more like an alien life-form than a theropod dinosaur. It is one of the fastest, lightest and most bird-like of all the dinosaurs. Its skull is toothless and has a gaudy crest on top to attract mates.

FEATHERED FREAK
The entire body of ***Oviraptor*** is covered with dense feathers. These are not the flight feathers of birds, however, but simpler filaments that are used for warmth, display and to insulate nests of eggs.

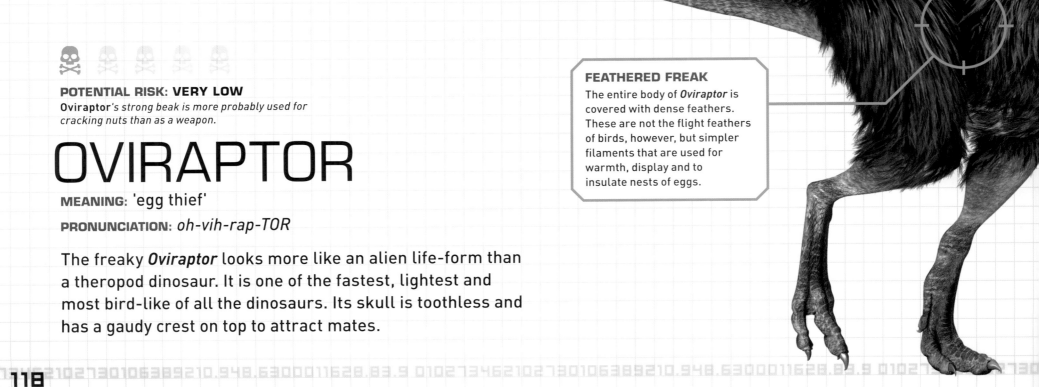

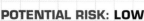

POTENTIAL RISK: LOW

Dangerous to small vertebrates, but harmless to others.

PELECANIMIMUS

MEANING: 'pelican mimic'

PRONUNCIATION: *pell-eh-can-ih-MIME-uss*

SIZE COMPARISON

LENGTH: 2–2.5 m (6.5–8 ft)

HEIGHT: 1–1.25 m (3–4 ft)

WEIGHT: 25–40 kg (55–88 lb)

Pelecanimimus is a smaller version of Gallimimus.

Pelecanimimus is a primitive cousin of ***Gallimimus***. Unlike its more famous relative, ***Pelecanimimus*** has a mouth full of hundreds of small teeth. In fact, it has more teeth than any other theropod dinosaur.

FOSSIL FINDS

EUROPE, EARLY CRETACEOUS

A single fossil of **Pelecanimimus** *is known from Cuenca, Spain. It was found alongside many exceptionally well-preserved bird skeletons.*

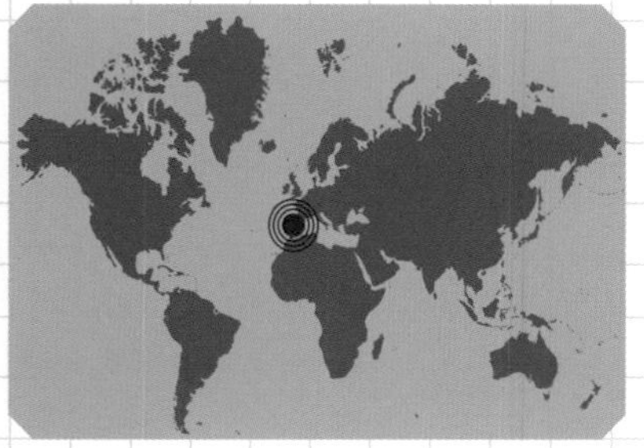

FOOD POUCH

Pelecanimimus has a pouch underneath its lower jaw. Many aquatic birds have a similar pouch to store fish.

BEAK HEAD

Oviraptor has a light skull with a toothless beak, which is used to crack nuts and shellfish.

SIZE COMPARISON

LENGTH: 2–2.5 metres (6.5–8 ft)

HEIGHT: 1–1.25 metres (3–4 ft)

WEIGHT: 35–40 kilograms (77–88 lb)

Shorter and lighter than a man.

FOSSIL FINDS

ASIA, LATE CRETACEOUS

Oviraptor *fossils unearthed in Mongolia during the 1990s show the creature protecting a nest of its own eggs, which puts paid to the idea that it merely stole eggs belonging to others.*

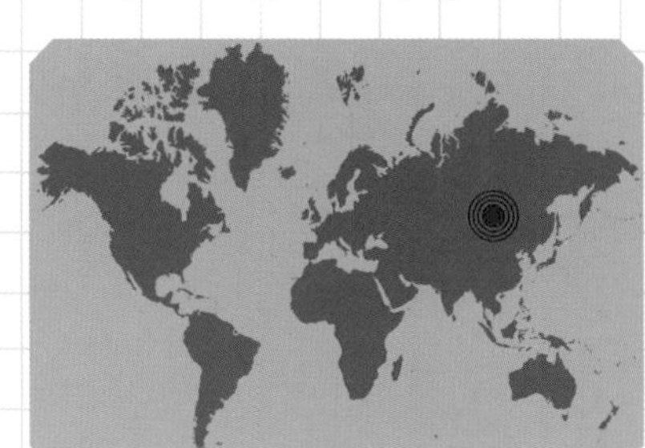

ANKYLOSAURUS

MEANING: 'stiffened lizard'

PRONUNCIATION: *ang-ki-lo-SORE-uss*

Living alongside *Tyrannosaurus*, the gentle herbivore *Ankylosaurus* is heavily armed with a swinging clubbed tail and a bristling array of spines, spikes and plates that not even the world's most feared and aggressive predator can penetrate.

Ankylosaurus is a large and slow-moving animal. It is slightly taller than a man but much longer than an elephant, and its heavy armour makes anything other than a slow waddle impossible. It is the most familiar member of the ornithischian subgroup that bears its name, the ankylosaurids.

BONE HEAD

The skull of *Ankylosaurus* is tiny in comparison to the rest of the body, measuring no more than 50 centimetres (20 in) long. Like all ankylosaur skulls, it is fused into a solid structure and is full of leaf-like teeth for chopping plants.

POTENTIAL RISK: MEDIUM

A placid herbivore most of the time, **Ankylosaurus** *can wield its bony tail club at threatening predators. The club can easily smash a carnivore's skull in a fatal blow.*

SIZE COMPARISON

A monstrous and heavy creature that resembles a giant armadillo.

LENGTH: 8–10 metres (26–33 ft)

HEIGHT: 2–2.75 metres (7–9 ft)

WEIGHT: 5.8–8 tonnes

RANGE

PROXIMITY ALERT • RETREAT CAUTIOUSLY • 3.3 METRES (10.8 FT) AND CLOSING

TOP SPEED

8 KPH (5 MPH)

HABITAT

NORTH AMERICA, LATE CRETACEOUS

Ankylosaurus, Tyrannosaurus *and* **Triceratops** *lived together on the floodplains of North America 65 million years ago, when the climate was much warmer and wetter than today.*

FOSSIL FINDS

NORTH AMERICA, LATE CRETACEOUS

Ankylosaurus *is known from many fossils, especially isolated plates and spikes from its armour coat that are found in the same rock units as* **Tyrannosaurus** *bones.*

200
150
100
0273019210

POTENTIAL RISK: LOW

Maiasaura *has no weapons of its own and must travel in herds to shield itself from predatory attacks.*

HABITAT

NORTH AMERICA, LATE CRETACEOUS

This large herbivore preferred to live and nest along the banks of rivers, even though the waters could occasionally flood the nesting grounds.

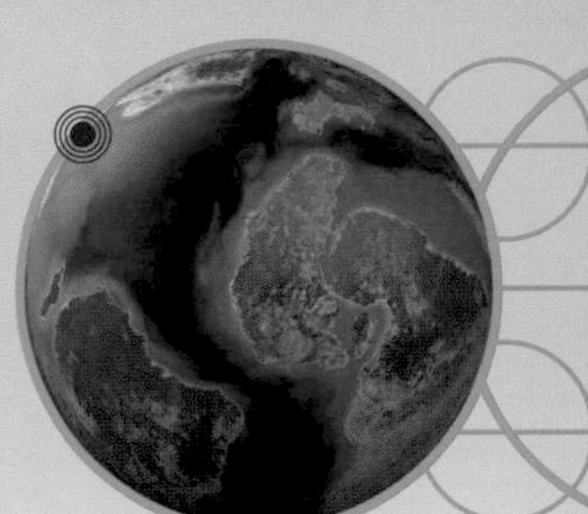

01027346210273010638921 0.948.6300011628.83.9

MAIASAURA

MEANING: 'good mother lizard'

PRONUNCIATION: *my-uh-SORE-uh*

250

0

A gentle giant, ***Maiasaura*** is one of the most familiar and successful of the hadrosaurid herbivores. This 'good mother lizard' carefully guards its nests and cares for its young until they are strong enough to survive on their own.

HANDY HOOF

The forelimbs of ***Maiasaura*** are multipurpose tools. They can grab vegetation, but are also capped with hooves, which help the animal to gallop away from predators.

RANGE

10.7 METRES (35 FT) AND CLOSING
PROXIMITY ALERT
APPROACH WITH CAUTION

TOP SPEED

20 KPH (12 MPH)

00273019210

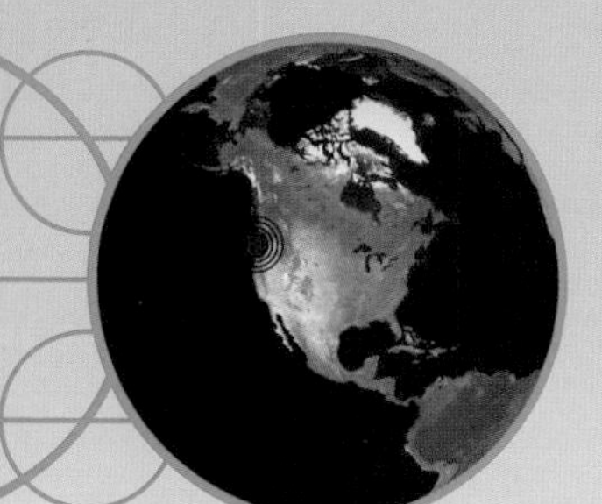

FOSSIL FINDS

NORTH AMERICA, LATE CRETACEOUS

One fossil site in Montana contains the remains of more than 10,000 individuals, ranging in size and age from large adults to tiny juveniles.

BIG BABIES

Maiasaura is a generalized hadrosaurid. It has a long skull capped with a downturned beak, which is used to shear plants. The jaws are packed with thousands of small teeth, perfect for grinding and chewing these plants into pieces. Its eggs are the size of a rugby ball, and it lays 30–40 of them at a time.

The centre of weight is over the hips, and **Maiasaura** *can rear up on two legs or stroll on all four.*

RAPID GROWERS

Maiasaura nests in large groups and lays several eggs at a time. The hatchlings are weak and must be fed by their parents before they can venture out of the nest. However, ***Maiasaura*** grows very quickly, so this feeding period lasts only a few months.

SIZE COMPARISON

A large herbivore that grows quickly.

LENGTH: 9 metres (30 ft)

HEIGHT: 3 metres (10 ft)

WEIGHT: 3 tonnes

FOSSIL FINDS

NORTH AMERICA, LATE CRETACEOUS

Edmontonia *shared the wet and humid floodplains of North America with giant predators, such as* **Albertosaurus**. *Both dinosaurs are common fossils today.*

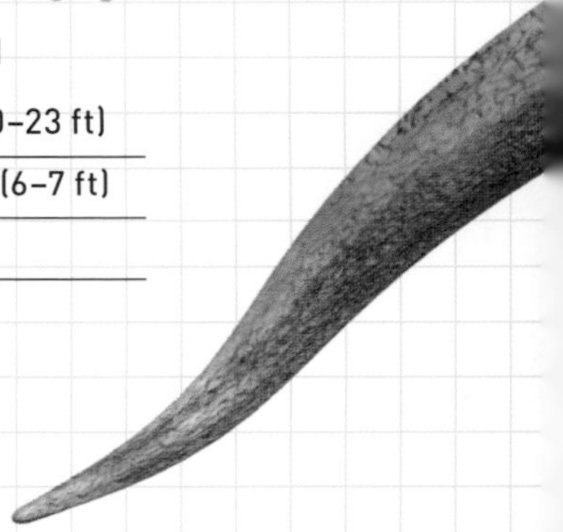

POTENTIAL RISK: LOW

Edmontonia *is a quiet and non-threatening herbivore. It only gets aggressive if attacked.*

SIZE COMPARISON

A massive, lumbering tank.

LENGTH: 6–7 metres (20–23 ft)

HEIGHT: 1.8–2.1 metres (6–7 ft)

WEIGHT: 4–5 tonnes

EDMONTONIA

MEANING: named after Edmonton, Alberta, in Canada

PRONUNCIATION: *ed-mon-TONE-e-uh*

Although at constant risk of tyrannosaur attacks, the ankylosaur ***Edmontonia*** is well protected by a coat of armour and several sharp, pointed spikes around its shoulders. Not a particularly fast animal, ***Edmontonia*** must stand its ground if confronted.

POTENTIAL RISK: LOW

This is one herbivore that all creatures, including predators, should keep away from.

SIZE COMPARISON

LENGTH: 5–6 metres (16–20 ft)

HEIGHT: 1.2–1.8 metres (4–6 ft)

WEIGHT: 2–4 tonnes

While **Euoplocephalus** *is smaller than* **Edmontonia**, *it is still a heavy, lumbering creature.*

EUOPLOCEPHALUS

MEANING: 'well-armed head'

PRONUNCIATION: *u-oh-plo-CEPH-uh-luss*

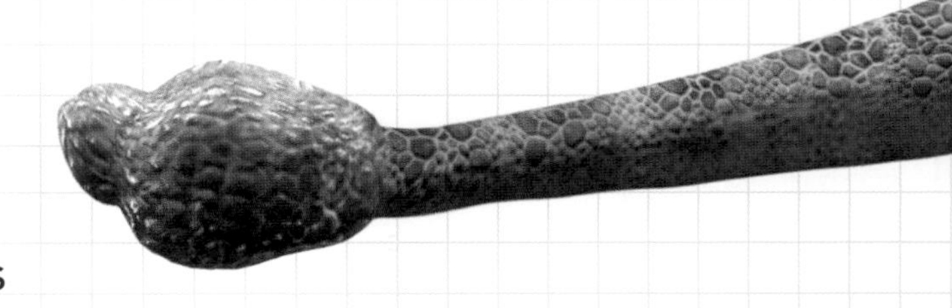

One of the most common ankylosaurs, ***Euoplocephalus*** is plentiful because of its effective arsenal of defensive weapons. It is difficult for predators such as ***Albertosaurus*** to puncture the thick armour coat of ***Euoplocephalus***. However, it is rare that predators even have the chance, as this ankylosaur will swing its bulbous tail club at the first sign of an attack.

POTENTIAL RISK: LOW
Only predatory attacks bring out any aggressive behaviour in **Saltasaurus**.

SALTASAURUS

MEANING: named after a site in Argentina

PRONUNCIATION: *sal-tah-SORE-uss*

Small by sauropod standards, ***Saltasaurus*** is one of the dominant herbivores of the South American ecosystem. It is immediately recognizable from afar due to its distinctive shield of body armour. This is a useful defence against the ferocious abelisaurid theropods, such as ***Carnotaurus***.

FOSSIL FINDS

SOUTH AMERICA, LATE CRETACEOUS

Saltasaurus *lived in Argentina about 65–70 million years ago, during the last days of the Cretaceous. Many of its eggs have been discovered in a vast nesting ground close to the banks of an ancient river.*

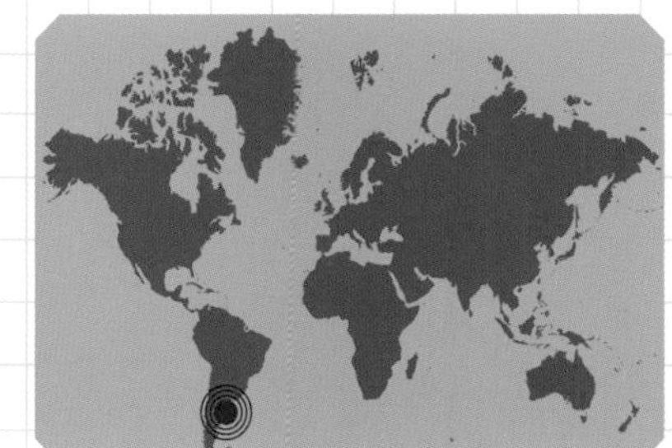

SIZE COMPARISON

LENGTH: 12 metres (40 ft)
HEIGHT: 3.3 metres (11 ft)
WEIGHT: 6–7 tonnes

Saltasaurus *is a small sauropod, but still huge compared to most dinosaurs.*

HEAVY ARMOUR

The armour of ***Saltasaurus*** is a unique feature. Its entire back is covered with large, oval plates, which can break even the largest abelisaurid teeth.

SHRUB FEEDER

The neck of ***Saltasaurus*** is not as long as those of other sauropods. It cannot reach high into trees, but is perfect for probing deep into shrubs and bushes.

FOSSIL FINDS

NORTH AMERICA, LATE CRETACEOUS

Euoplocephalus *lived about 70 million years ago on the broad, densely vegetated floodplains of western North America. Over 40 fossil specimens have been found in the rocks of that area.*

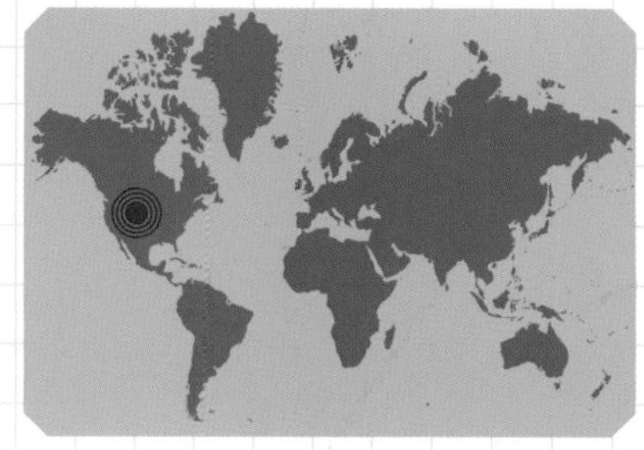

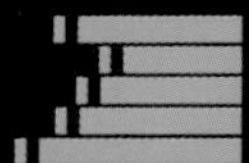

PARASAUROLOPHUS

MEANING: 'near crested lizard'
PRONUNCIATION: *par-ah-SORE-oh-loph-us*

The deep cry of ***Parasaurolophus*** can be heard booming across the landscapes of the Late Cretaceous. Enormous herds of these herbivores roam across the landscape, announcing their presence with a symphony of grunts and mating calls.

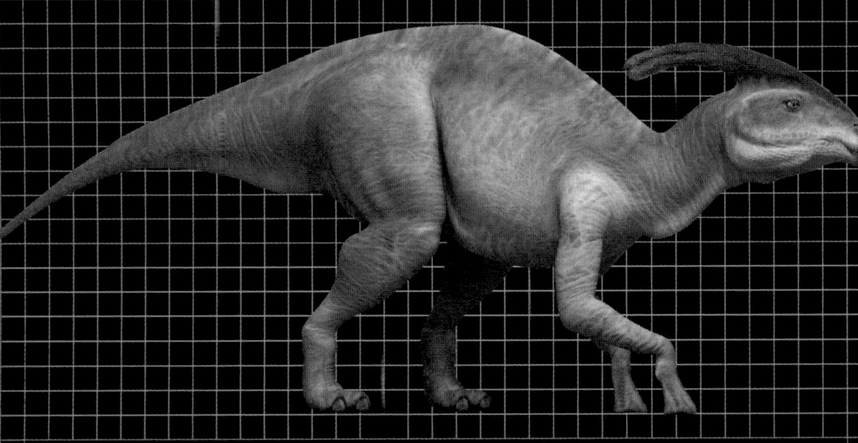

Parasaurolophus is a hadrosaurid, a member of the same group as ***Maiasaura*** and ***Edmontosaurus***. The curved tube on its head is about 1.25 metres (4 ft) long, which is longer than an average seven-year-old child! The crest is hollow and filled with a complex maze of sinuses that are connected to the nostrils.

POTENTIAL RISK: VERY LOW

Like other hadrosaurids, **Parasaurolophus** *has no defensive weapons, so relies on its bulk and fellow members of the herd for group protection.*

SIZE COMPARISON

A large plant-eater with a remarkable skull crest.

LENGTH: 7.8–10 metres (26–33 ft)
HEIGHT: 2.3–3 metres (7.5–10 ft)
WEIGHT: 4–6 tonnes

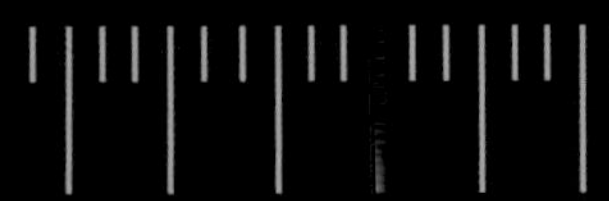

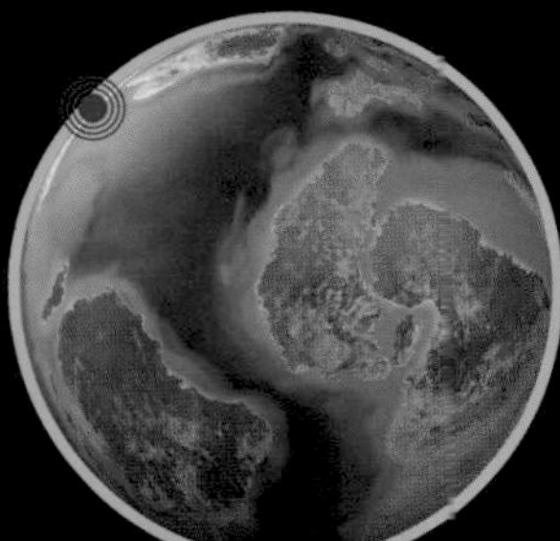

HABITAT

NORTH AMERICA, LATE CRETACEOUS

The colourful herds of **Parasaurolophus**, *some numbering in the thousands, roamed across the flat plains of North America about 75 million years ago.*

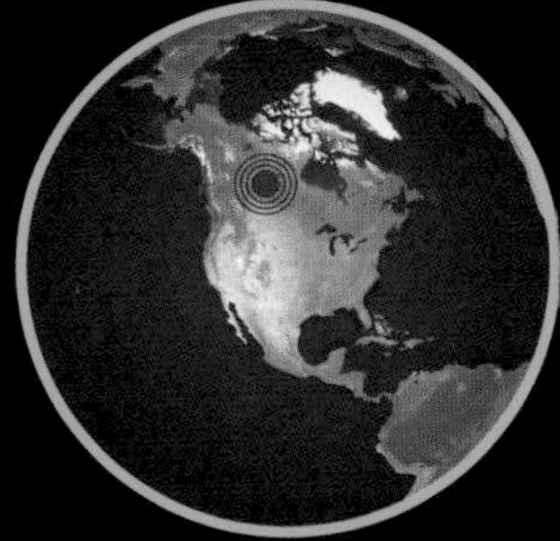

FOSSIL FINDS

NORTH AMERICA, LATE CRETACEOUS

Parasaurolophus *is commonly found in the picturesque Red Deer River badlands of Alberta, Canada, where millions of years of erosion have sculpted the landscape.*

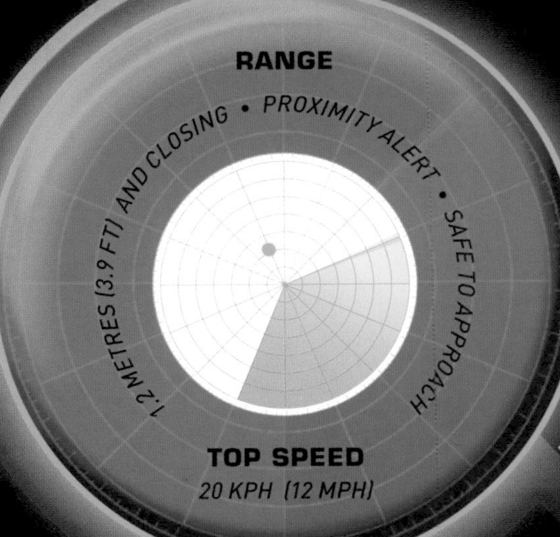

SOUND SYSTEM

What is the purpose of the spectacular skull crest? It serves three functions: as a display for attracting mates, as an instrument used to make the distinctive calls of the species, and as a device for keeping the animal cool.

SIZE COMPARISON

LENGTH: 10–12 metres (33–40 ft)

HEIGHT: 3–3.7 metres (10–12 ft)

WEIGHT: 3–5 tonnes

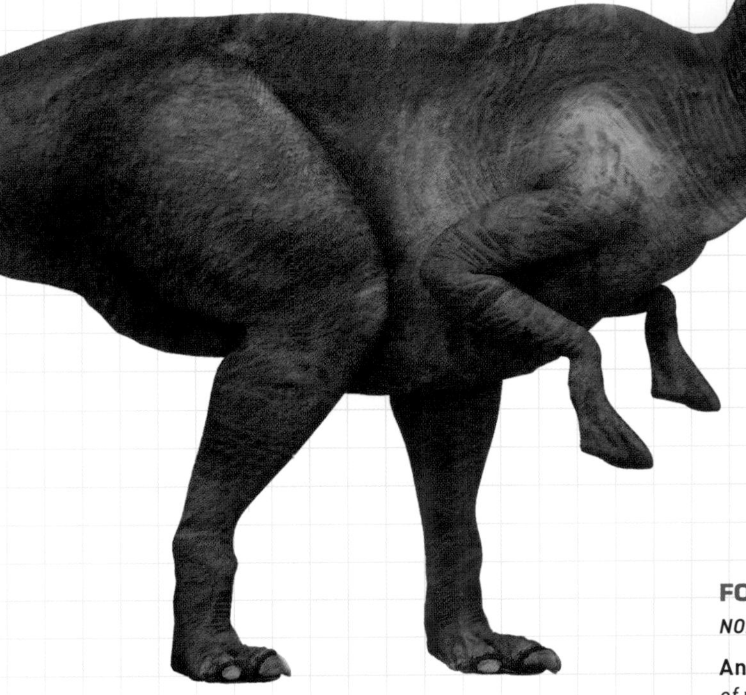

A mammoth, plant-munching dinosaur that lumbers across the plains.

POTENTIAL RISK: LOW

Even **Tyrannosaurus** *is afraid of angering the strong and hefty* **Anatotitan**.

ANATOTITAN

MEANING: 'duck titan'

PRONUNCIATION: *AN-at-oh-tit-an*

Anatotitan is one of the largest duck-billed hadrosaurs ever to live. It is a close relative of ***Edmontosaurus***, but grows to much larger sizes. The largest individuals reach lengths of 12 metres (40 ft), the same size as its enemy ***Tyrannosaurus***. Indeed, ***Anatotitan*** relies on its bulky frame to scare off hungry tyrannosaurs.

FOSSIL FINDS

NORTH AMERICA, LATE CRETACEOUS

Anatotitan *lived on the floodplains of western North America about 65 million years ago. Fossils of this dinosaur are relatively rare, but we have a good idea of what it looked like.*

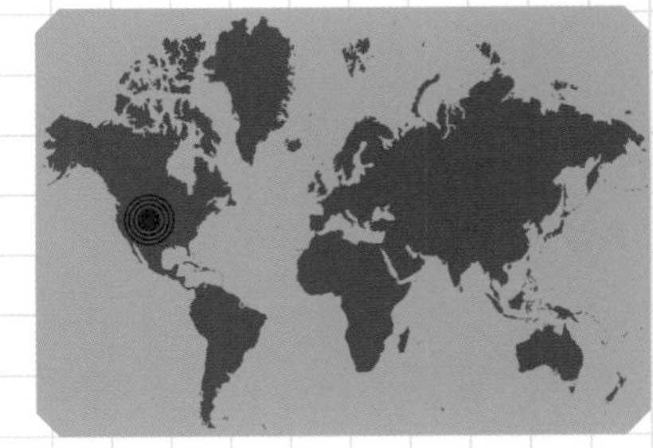

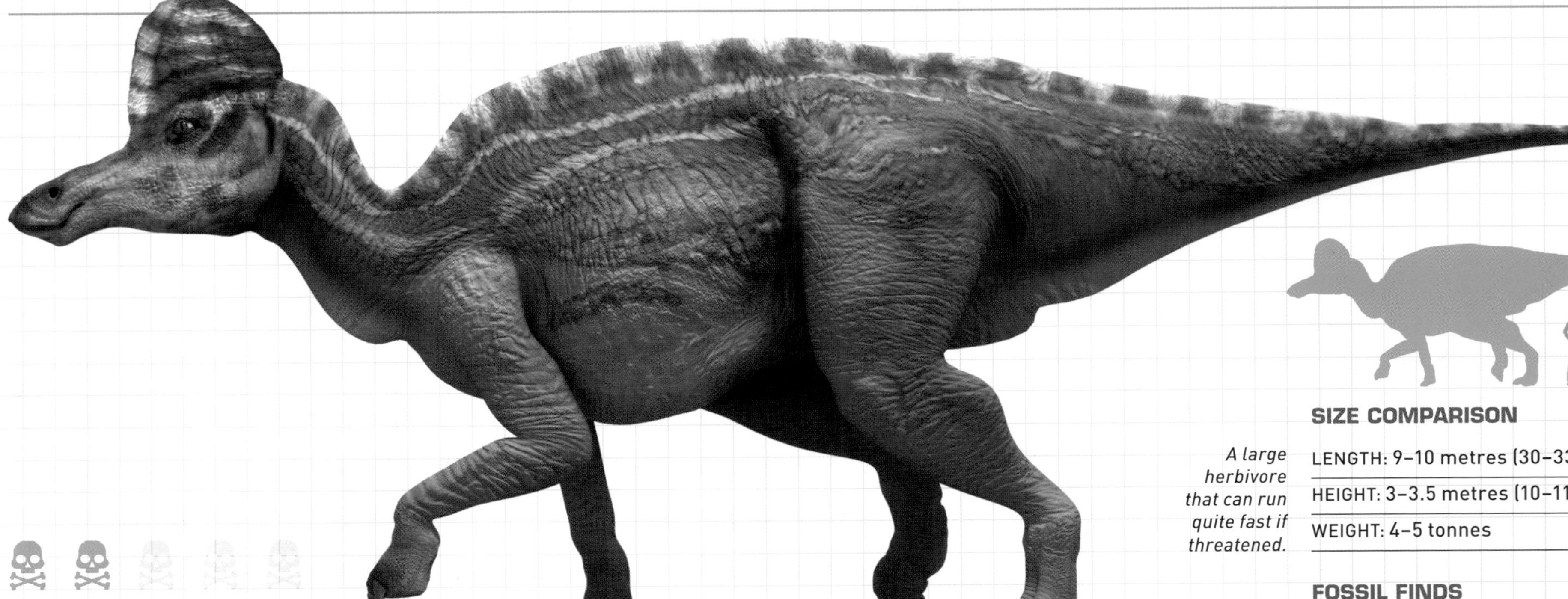

SIZE COMPARISON

LENGTH: 9–10 metres (30–33 ft)

HEIGHT: 3–3.5 metres (10–11 ft)

WEIGHT: 4–5 tonnes

A large herbivore that can run quite fast if threatened.

POTENTIAL RISK: LOW

Corythosaurus *is large but gentle, and its only defence against predators is running.*

CORYTHOSAURUS

MEANING: 'helmet lizard'

PRONUNCIATION: *co-rith-oh-SORE-uss*

The 'helmet-crested' herbivore ***Corythosaurus*** is a peculiar sight. This large duck-billed herbivore boasts one of the most unusual head crests of any dinosaur. Its ornament is gigantic, rounded and hollow, much like a pith helmet. It also stands straight upwards, a sign to potential mates that the individual is strong and fit.

FOSSIL FINDS

NORTH AMERICA, LATE CRETACEOUS

Corythosaurus *and its cousin* **Lambeosaurus** *are common fossils in 80-million-year-old rocks in Alberta, Canada. They lived at a time of warm temperatures and heavy rainfall.*

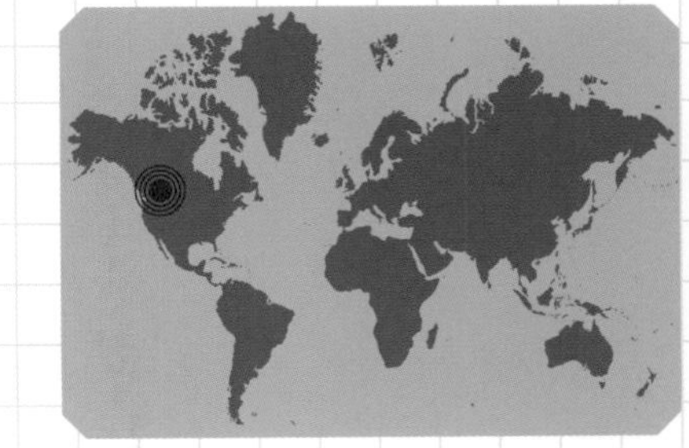

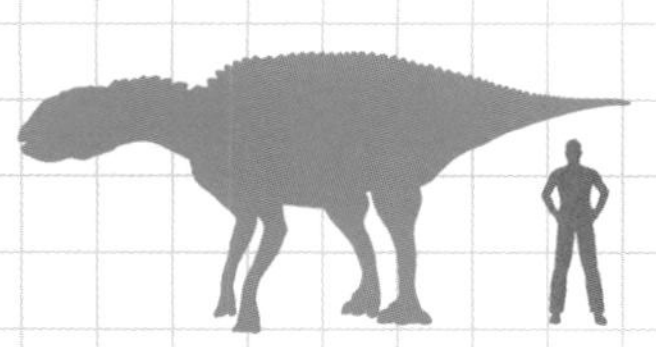

SIZE COMPARISON

LENGTH: 7–9 metres (23–30 ft)

HEIGHT: 2.5–3 metres (8–11 ft)

WEIGHT: 2–3 tonnes

A large herbivore with scaly skin.

BATTERING NOSE
The bizarre bony nostril bump of ***Gryposaurus*** is used both as a signal to potential mates and as a battering ram against predators.

POTENTIAL RISK: LOW

Gryposaurus, *like* **Corythosaurus**, *is a gentle beast that normally poses no threat.*

GRYPOSAURUS

MEANING: 'hook-nose lizard'

PRONUNCIATION: *gry-po-SORE-uss*

Gryposaurus is the most diverse and common of the duck-billed, plant-crunching hadrosaurs. It does not attract mates with a showy crest like many of its relatives, but does have an awkward-looking bump on its nose. Like most hadrosaurs, ***Gryposaurus*** alternates between walking on two or four legs, depending on whether it is feeding or running.

FOSSIL FINDS

NORTH AMERICA, LATE CRETACEOUS

Gryposaurus *ranged across North America during the Late Cretaceous. Its fossils have been found between Canada in the north and Mexico in the south to Utah in the west.*

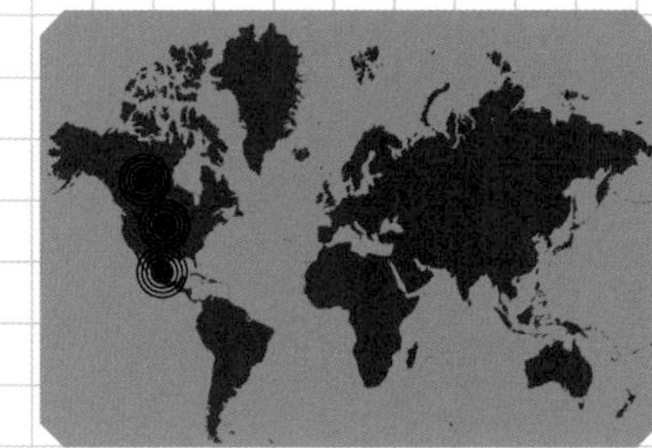

POTENTIAL RISK: LOW

Like most hadrosaurs, **Lambeosaurus** *only gets aggressive if provoked.*

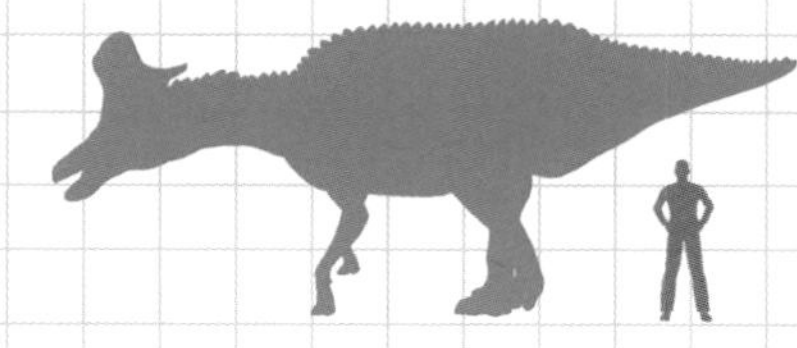

SIZE COMPARISON

LENGTH: 9–15 metres (30–50 ft)

HEIGHT: 3–4.5 metres (10–15 ft)

WEIGHT: 3–8.5 tonnes

A large hadrosaur with a crest that is almost half a man's height.

LAMBEOSAURUS

MEANING: named after palaeontologist Lawrence Lambe

PRONUNCIATION: *lam-bee-oh-SORE-uss*

Lambeosaurus is nearly identical in size and shape to its close cousin ***Corythosaurus***. However, the two are distinguished by their very different skull crests. The crest of ***Lambeosaurus*** is hatchet-shaped: the blade of the hatchet is a tall, arched hump above the eye, while the handle is a thin prong that extends backwards behind the skull.

FOSSIL FINDS

NORTH AMERICA, LATE CRETACEOUS

Lambeosaurus *is a common fossil in the Late Cretaceous rocks of Canada, but fossils have also been found as far south as Mexico. Both areas were wet and bordered by shallow seas when* **Lambeosaurus** *was alive.*

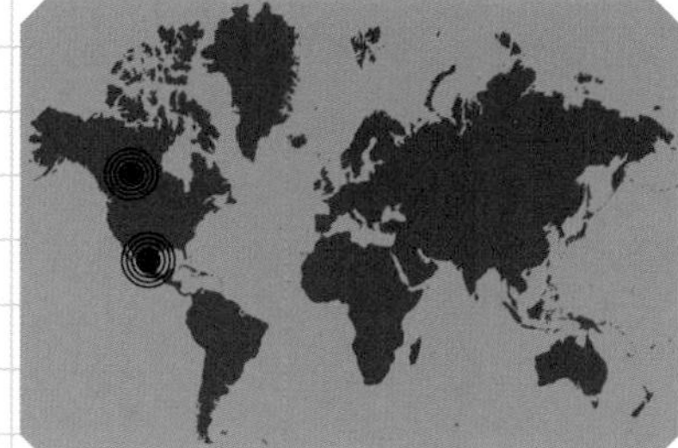

TAIL BALANCE
The tail of ***Lambeosaurus*** is extremely deep and muscular. It is used for balance while running. Hadrosaurs can usually outrun their predators.

FRILL SEEKER

Protoceratops, like all ceratopsians, has a long, thin frill extending from the back of its skull. This frill is both a display ornament used to attract mates, and a large, broad surface to which strong jaw muscles are attached. These power the animal's constant chewing.

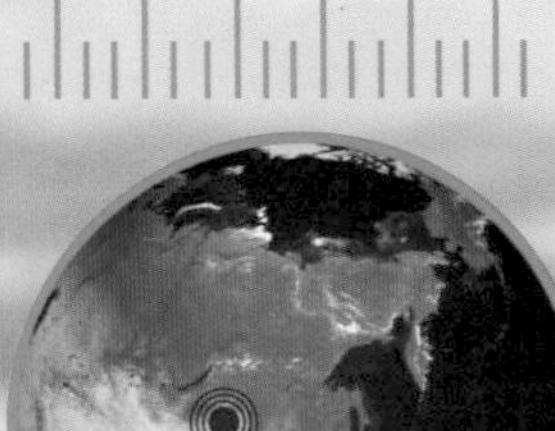

FOSSIL FINDS

ASIA, LATE CRETACEOUS

Protoceratops *is the most common fossil in the famous Late Cretaceous rocks of the Gobi Desert. Several thousand skeletons have been found.*

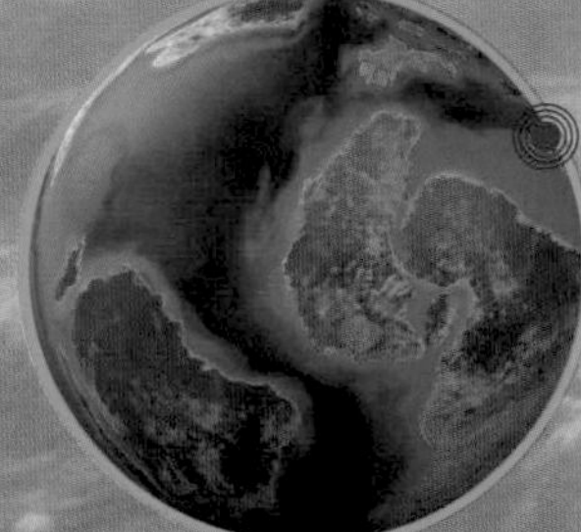

HABITAT

ASIA, LATE CRETACEOUS

Protoceratops *travelled in small herds through the dune fields of Late Cretaceous Asia, a dry environment that was occasionally hit by freak storms.*

POTENTIAL RISK: LOW

Protoceratops *is about the size of a sheep and just as meek.*

SIZE COMPARISON

A gentle herbivore, about knee-high to an average man.

LENGTH: 1.5–2 metres (5–6.5 ft)

HEIGHT: 50–67 centimetres (20–26 in)

WEIGHT: 240 kilograms (529 lb)

PROTOCERATOPS

MEANING: 'early horned face'

PRONUNCIATION: *pro-toe-SER-a-tops*

The beaked ***Protoceratops*** is a smaller and more primitive cousin of the familiar horned ***Triceratops***. ***Protoceratops*** is exceptionally common in the sandy dunes of Mongolia, where it munches on plants while on constant lookout for its greatest enemy, the highly dangerous ***Velociraptor***.

Although much smaller and more generalized than its more famous cousin, ***Protoceratops*** has many classic features of the ceratopsian group. It walks slowly on four legs and uses its parrot-like beak to graze on low shrubs and bushes. The jaws house a battery of small teeth that combine to form a scissor-like cutting surface. And, of course, ***Protoceratops*** has a large frill on the back of its skull.

00273019210001010100027301921000101510 15

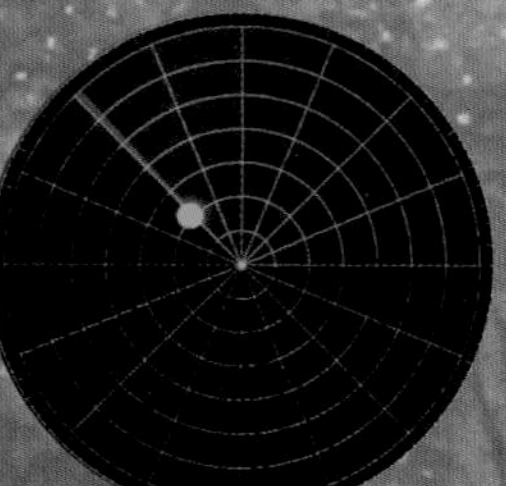

RANGE

2.3 METRES (7.5 FT) AND CLOSING
PROXIMITY ALERT
SAFE TO APPROACH

TOP SPEED

20 KPH (12 MPH)

WEAPONRY: UNARMED

If cornered, **Protoceratops** *can swipe at a predator with its cheek horns, but otherwise lacks specific weapons.*

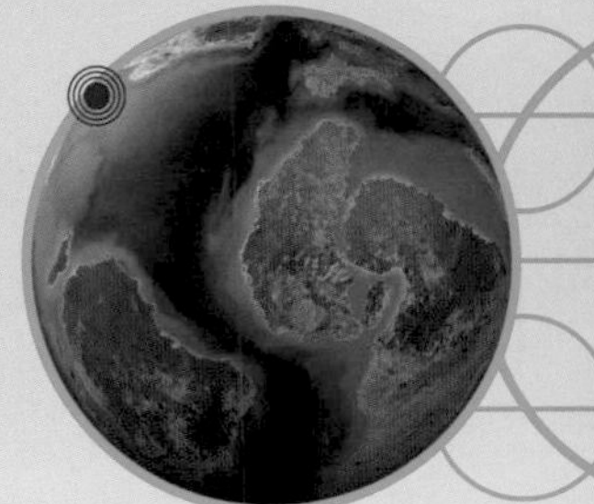

HABITAT

NORTH AMERICA, LATE CRETACEOUS

***Triceratops** adults are solitary animals, but smaller juveniles travel in packs along riverbanks for protection from the bone-crunching jaws of **Tyrannosaurus**.*

POTENTIAL RISK: EXTREME

*Not just any dinosaur can stand face-to-face with **Tyrannosaurus** and live to remember it. The sharp horns of **Triceratops** can be deadly.*

01027346210273010638921O.948.6300011628.83.9

TRICERATOPS

MEANING: 'three-horned face'

PRONUNCIATION: *try-SER-a-tops*

Along with its rival ***Tyrannosaurus***, ***Triceratops*** is one of the most recognizable of all dinosaurs. The three-horned face and shield-like skull frill are unmistakable features that distinguish ***Triceratops*** from all other creatures.

250 —

0 —

THREE-PRONGED ATTACK

Triceratops is one of the largest members of the ceratopsian group and a common sight along the rivers and floodplains of North America. The skull itself is more than 3 metres (10 ft) long, making it one of the largest ever seen on a land-living animal. Its long, deadly horns make tyrannosaurs think twice before attacking.

*The frill of **Triceratops** is larger than a billiard table and strong enough to withstand a bite from **Tyrannosaurus**.*

PRONGED ATTACK

Triceratops has a single, short horn on top of the nose, and a wider, stronger and longer horn extending from above each eye. These horns are used for protection from ***Tyrannosaurus***, as well as for wrestling matches with rival ***Triceratops***.

RANGE

71.3 METRES (235 FT) AND CLOSING
PROXIMITY ALERT
RETREAT IMMEDIATELY

TOP SPEED

15 KPH (10 MPH)

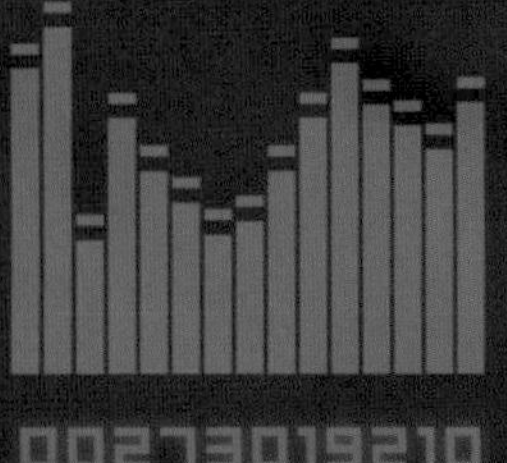

010273462102730106389

FOSSIL FINDS

NORTH AMERICA, LATE CRETACEOUS

Triceratops *fossils are exceptionally common in the Hell Creek Formation of the western USA. Several hundred fossils have been found, ranging from tiny juveniles to fully grown adults.*

SIZE COMPARISON

A three-horned giant whose skull is larger than an average man.

LENGTH: 8–9 metres (26–30 ft)

HEIGHT: 2.4–3 metres (8–10 ft)

WEIGHT: 8 tonnes

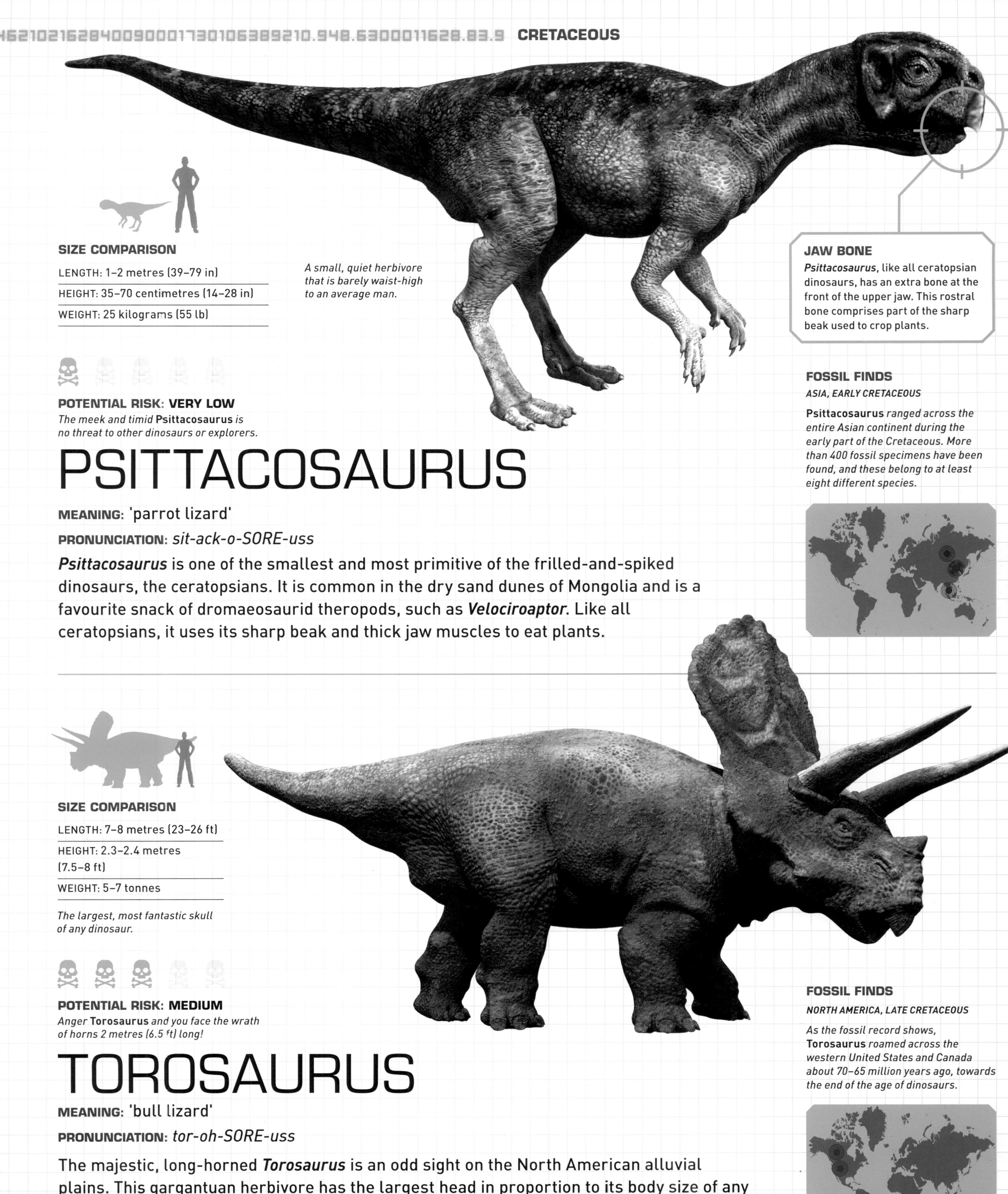

SIZE COMPARISON

LENGTH: 1–2 metres (39–79 in)

HEIGHT: 35–70 centimetres (14–28 in)

WEIGHT: 25 kilograms (55 lb)

A small, quiet herbivore that is barely waist-high to an average man.

JAW BONE

Psittacosaurus, like all ceratopsian dinosaurs, has an extra bone at the front of the upper jaw. This rostral bone comprises part of the sharp beak used to crop plants.

POTENTIAL RISK: VERY LOW

*The meek and timid **Psittacosaurus** is no threat to other dinosaurs or explorers.*

PSITTACOSAURUS

MEANING: 'parrot lizard'

PRONUNCIATION: *sit-ack-o-SORE-uss*

Psittacosaurus is one of the smallest and most primitive of the frilled-and-spiked dinosaurs, the ceratopsians. It is common in the dry sand dunes of Mongolia and is a favourite snack of dromaeosaurid theropods, such as ***Velociroaptor***. Like all ceratopsians, it uses its sharp beak and thick jaw muscles to eat plants.

FOSSIL FINDS

ASIA, EARLY CRETACEOUS

***Psittacosaurus** ranged across the entire Asian continent during the early part of the Cretaceous. More than 400 fossil specimens have been found, and these belong to at least eight different species.*

SIZE COMPARISON

LENGTH: 7–8 metres (23–26 ft)

HEIGHT: 2.3–2.4 metres (7.5–8 ft)

WEIGHT: 5–7 tonnes

The largest, most fantastic skull of any dinosaur.

POTENTIAL RISK: MEDIUM

*Anger **Torosaurus** and you face the wrath of horns 2 metres (6.5 ft) long!*

TOROSAURUS

MEANING: 'bull lizard'

PRONUNCIATION: *tor-oh-SORE-uss*

The majestic, long-horned ***Torosaurus*** is an odd sight on the North American alluvial plains. This gargantuan herbivore has the largest head in proportion to its body size of any dinosaur. Its colourful, frilled skull is 40 per cent of the length of the body. The huge horns ward off predators, and the decorative frill attracts mates.

FOSSIL FINDS

NORTH AMERICA, LATE CRETACEOUS

*As the fossil record shows, **Torosaurus** roamed across the western United States and Canada about 70–65 million years ago, towards the end of the age of dinosaurs.*

POTENTIAL RISK: MEDIUM

Provoking this usually quiet herbivore risks injury or death from nine sharp horns.

SIZE COMPARISON

LENGTH: 5–5.5 metres (16–18 ft)

HEIGHT: 1.5–1.65 metres (5–5.5 ft)

WEIGHT: 2–3 tonnes

A large herbivore that can hold its own against the more fearsome predators.

STYRACOSAURUS

MEANING: 'spiked lizard'

PRONUNCIATION: *sty-rack-o-SORE-uss*

Of all the ceratopsians, ***Styracosaurus*** boasts the most fantastic array of cranial ornamentation. A single large horn juts upwards above the nose, two horns protrude sideways from each cheek, and six horns surround the margin of the enormous frill. These nine horns mean that ***Styracosaurus*** is well prepared to handle large predators, such as the tyrannosaurs.

FRILLS AND SPIKES

The six horns circling the frill are used more for display than defence. However, the two centre horns are longer and sharper than the nasal horn, and can be turned on an attacking predator.

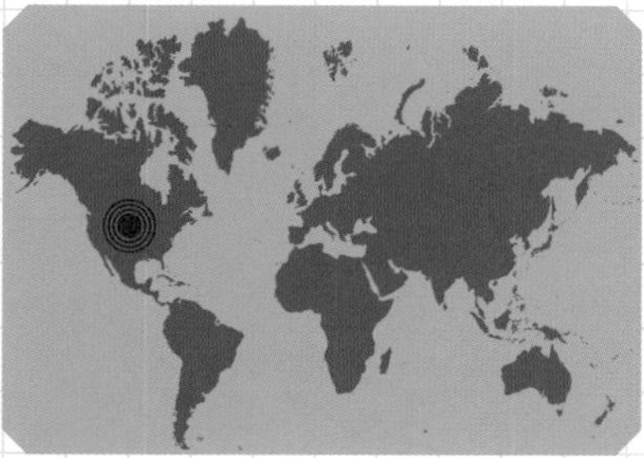

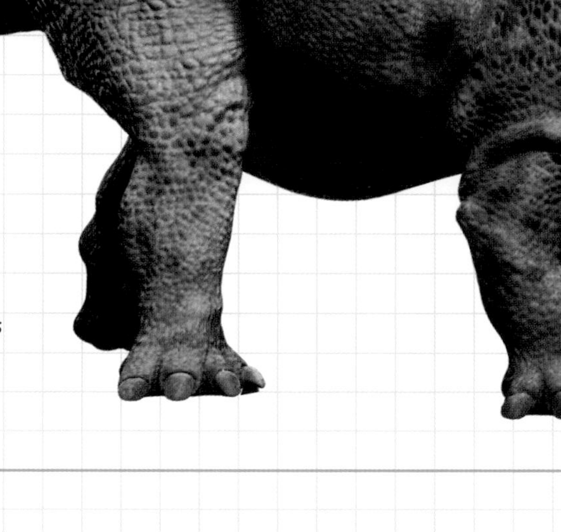

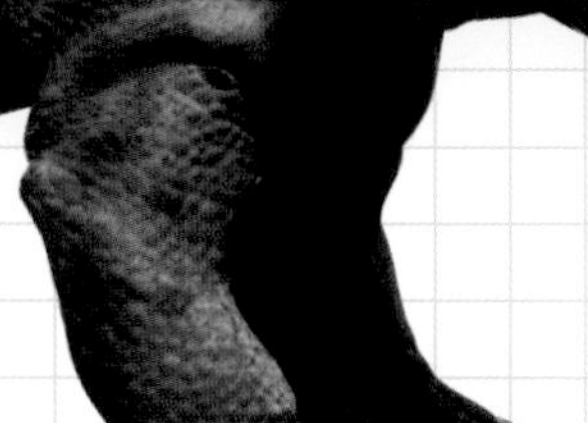

FOSSIL FINDS

NORTH AMERICA, LATE CRETACEOUS

Styracosaurus *is known from fossils found in 75-million-year-old rocks in Dinosaur Provincial Park, Alberta.*

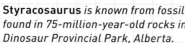

POTENTIAL RISK: MEDIUM

Large body size is the primary weapon this herbivore wealds when threatened.

EINIOSAURUS

MEANING: 'buffalo lizard'

PRONUNCIATION: *ie-nee-oh-SORE-uss*

The sound of roaring thunder echoing across the plains is likely to be an approaching herd of the frilled herbivore ***Einiosaurus***. This ceratopsian is distinguished from its cousins by one bizarre feature: a single short, fat spike over the nose that curves forwards, much like a can-opener.

SIZE COMPARISON

LENGTH: 7.2–7.6 metres (24–25 ft)

HEIGHT: 2.1–2.3 metres (7–7.5 ft)

WEIGHT: 4.5–5 tonnes

One of the larger ceratopsians, its can-opener nose can spear a man.

FOSSIL FINDS

NORTH AMERICA, LATE CRETACEOUS

Einiosaurus *is found in a 75-million-year-old area of rock in Montana called the Two Medicine Formation. At least 15 individuals have been found in two bonebeds.*

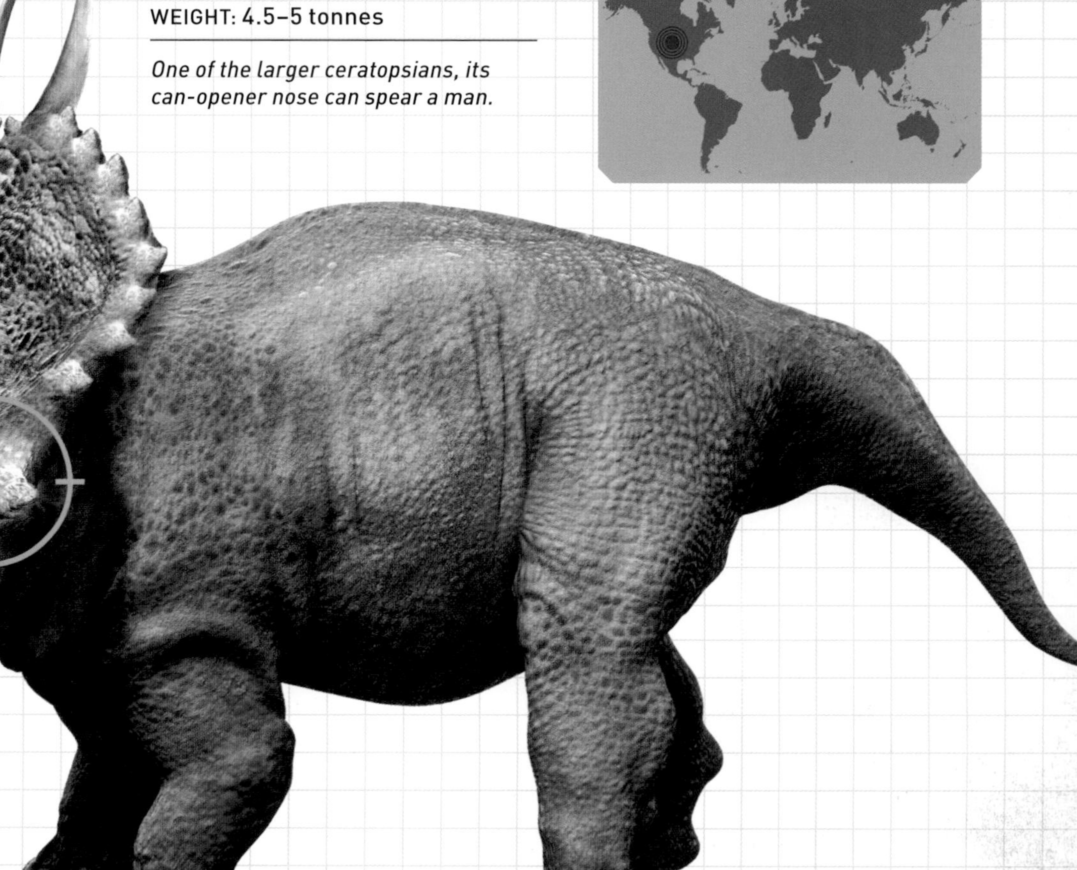

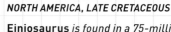

BONY GROWTHS

The skull of *Einiosaurus* is weird indeed. In addition to the truly bizarre nose, the frill is ornamented with two large spikes, and surrounded by numerous knobbly growths all around its edge.

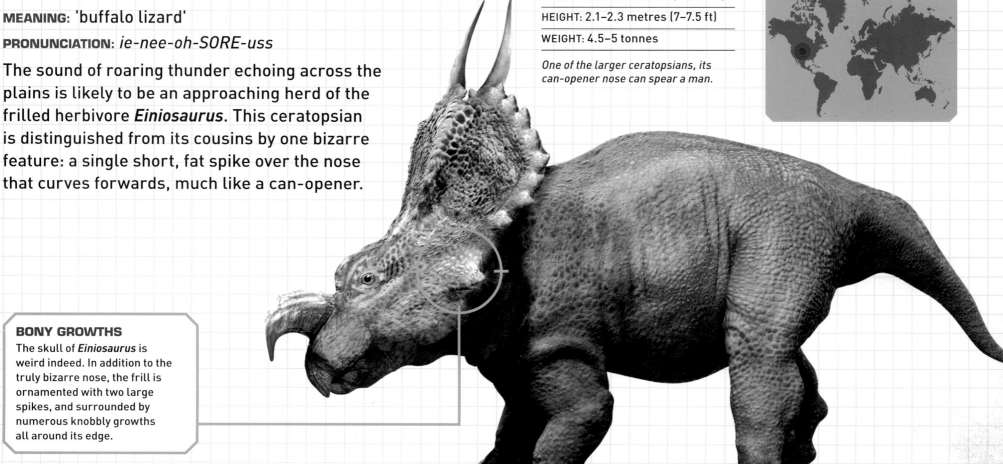

PACHYCEPHALOSAURUS

MEANING: 'thick-headed lizard'

PRONUNCIATION: *pack-ee-seph-uh-LOW-sore-uss*

Like something out of a science fiction movie, the dome-headed ***Pachycephalosaurus*** bounds across the North American floodplains on the lookout for plants to eat and rivals to fight.

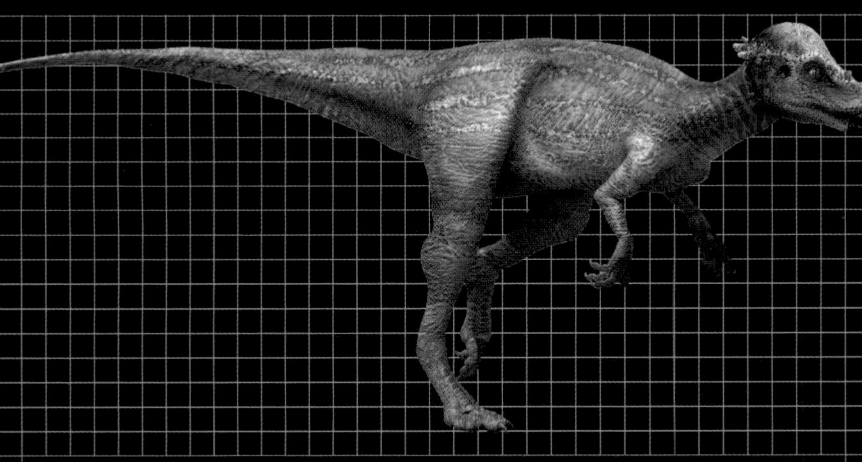

Pachycephalosaurus is the most typical member of a weird subgroup of ornithischians, the pachycephalosaurs. These plant-eaters are distinguished by a peculiar skull, which is thick and studded with a fabulous array of spikes, bumps and bony blisters. They walk on two legs and can run very fast.

002730192100010101000273019210001015101573019210001015

POTENTIAL RISK: MEDIUM

Any attacking predator, such as **Tyrannosaurus,** *has to risk a battering punch from the thick, powerful skull of* **Pachycephalosaurus.**

SIZE COMPARISON

A brute as tall as a man, but much longer.

LENGTH: 4–5 metres (13–16 ft)

HEIGHT: 1.6–1.8 metres (5–6 ft)

WEIGHT: 250–300 kilograms (550–660 lb)

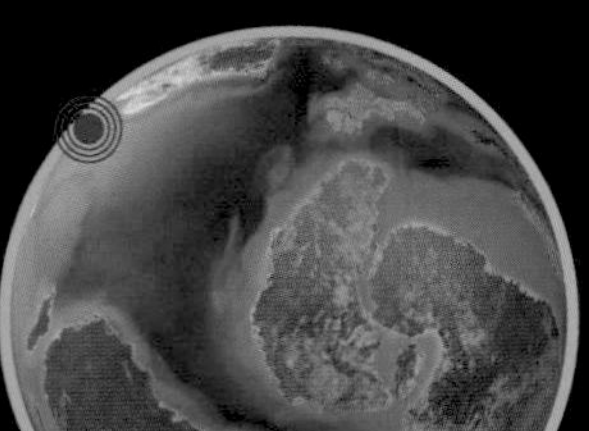

HABITAT

NORTH AMERICA, LATE CRETACEOUS

Pachycephalosaurus *is a rare fossil in the Hell Creek ecosystem of the United States, and is not as common as other herbivores, such as* **Triceratops** *and* **Edmontosaurus.**

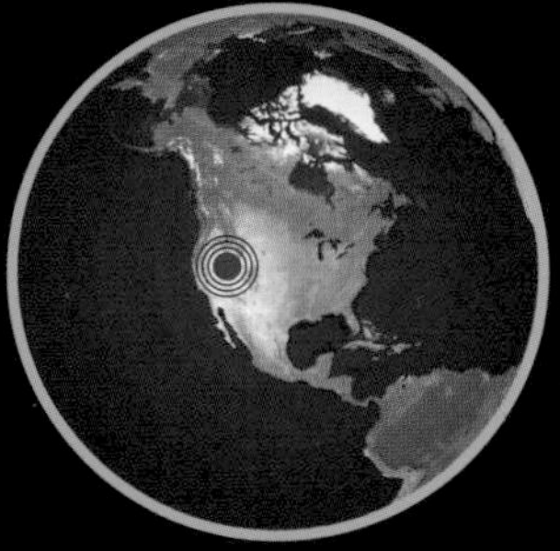

FOSSIL FINDS

NORTH AMERICA, LATE CRETACEOUS

Fossils of the thick, domed skull of **Pachycephalosaurus** *are common in the Hell Creek Formation, but complete skeletons have yet to be found.*

BONE HEAD

The skull roof of *Pachycephalosaurus* is amazingly thick – 25 centimetres (10 in) of solid bone. This region of the head is rounded into a dome, which is more of a display device than a battering ram.

RANGE

2.2 METRES (7.2 FT) AND CLOSING • PROXIMITY ALERT • RETREAT SLOWLY

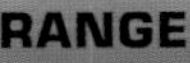

TOP SPEED

25 KPH (15 MPH)

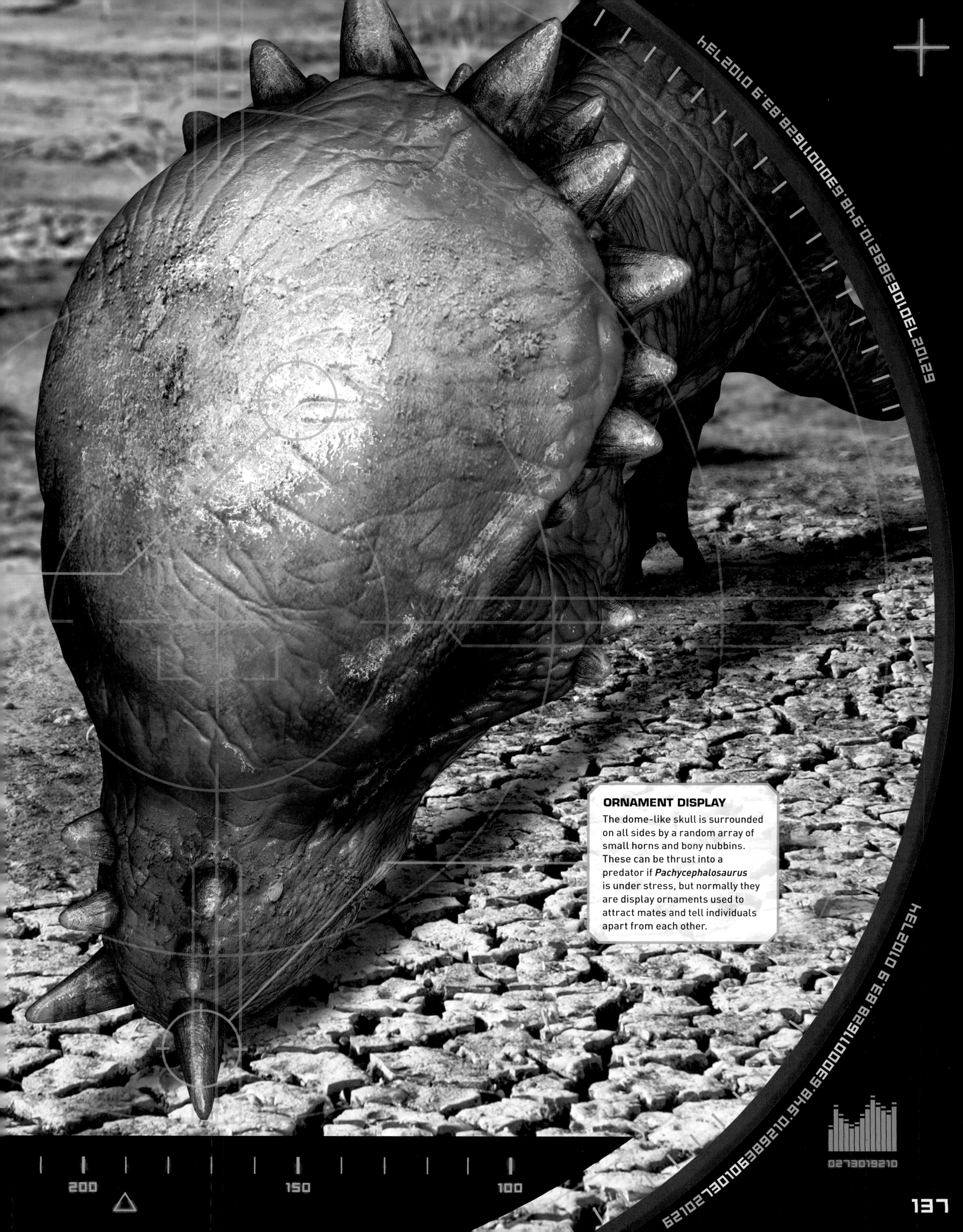

ORNAMENT DISPLAY

The dome-like skull is surrounded on all sides by a random array of small horns and bony nubbins. These can be thrust into a predator if *Pachycephalosaurus* is under stress, but normally they are display ornaments used to attract mates and tell individuals apart from each other.

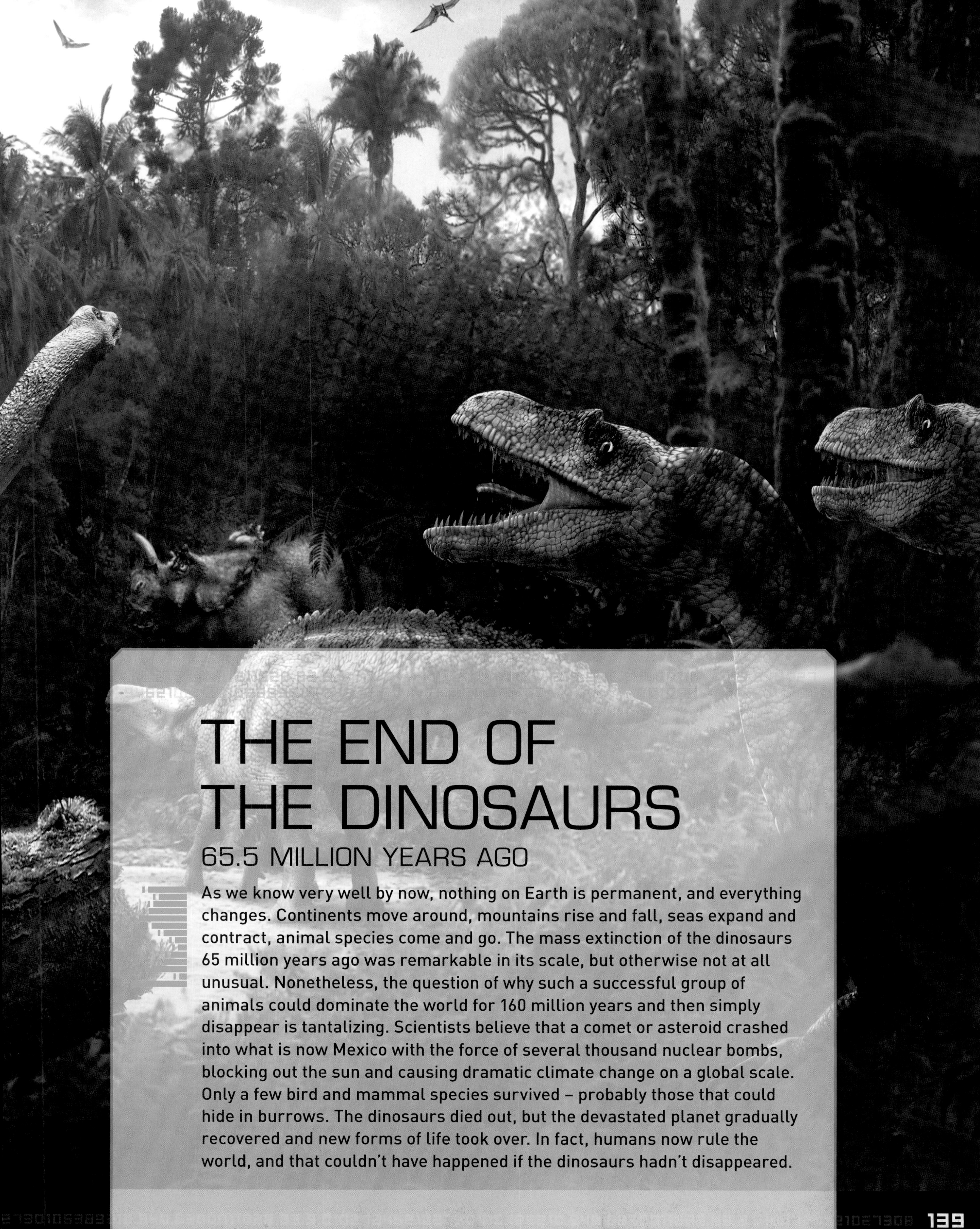

THE END OF THE DINOSAURS

65.5 MILLION YEARS AGO

As we know very well by now, nothing on Earth is permanent, and everything changes. Continents move around, mountains rise and fall, seas expand and contract, animal species come and go. The mass extinction of the dinosaurs 65 million years ago was remarkable in its scale, but otherwise not at all unusual. Nonetheless, the question of why such a successful group of animals could dominate the world for 160 million years and then simply disappear is tantalizing. Scientists believe that a comet or asteroid crashed into what is now Mexico with the force of several thousand nuclear bombs, blocking out the sun and causing dramatic climate change on a global scale. Only a few bird and mammal species survived – probably those that could hide in burrows. The dinosaurs died out, but the devastated planet gradually recovered and new forms of life took over. In fact, humans now rule the world, and that couldn't have happened if the dinosaurs hadn't disappeared.

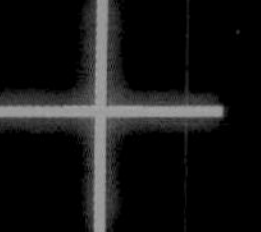

GLOSSARY

ABELISAURIDS: A subgroup of theropods (meat-eating dinosaurs) that primarily lived in the southern continents (Gondwana) during the Cretaceous; well-known examples include ***Abelisaurus*, *Carnotaurus*** and ***Majungasaurus***.

ADVANCED: A feature or characteristic of an animal that is new and inherited from more recent evolutionary ancestors.

ANKYLOSAURIDS: A subgroup of ankylosaurs (armoured, tank-like dinosaurs) characterized by a bony tail club; examples include ***Ankylosaurus*** and ***Euoplocephalus***.

ANKYLOSAURS: A group of ornithischian (bird-hipped) dinosaurs, characterized by a plant-eating diet and a tank-like body covered in armour shields, plates and spikes. Ankylosaurs are divided into two subgroups: ankylosaurids and nodosaurids.

ARCHOSAURS: The so-called 'ruling reptiles', a major group of reptiles that first evolved in the Triassic Period and includes dinosaurs, crocodiles, birds, pterosaurs and several extinct groups.

BIPEDAL: Walking on two legs.

CARCHARODONTOSAURIDS: A subgroup of tetanuran theropods, closely related to ***Allosaurus***, that includes some of the largest predators ever to live (***Carcharodontosaurus*** and ***Giganotosaurus***).

CARNIVORE: An animal that eats meat.

CERATOPSIANS: The 'horned dinosaurs', a subgroup of ornithischian (bird-hipped) dinosaurs, characterized by a plant-eating diet and a skull bearing horns and a frill (shield).

CERATOSAURS: A subgroup of theropods (meat-eating dinosaurs) with primitive features, including ***Ceratosaurus*** and the abelisaurids.

COELOPHYSOIDS: A subgroup of theropods (meat-eating dinosaurs) with primitive features that lived during the Triassic and Early Jurassic; examples include ***Coelophysis*** and ***Liliensternus***.

COELUROSAURS: A subgroup of theropods (meat-eating dinosaurs) with advanced features, including many bird-like characteristics; examples include tyrannosauroids, troodontids, dromaeosaurs and birds, which evolved from coelurosaurs.

CONTEMPORARY: Living at the same time. For example, ***Gasosaurus*** was a contemporary of ***Monolophosaurus***.

CRETACEOUS: The third and final period of the Mesozoic Era (also known as the Age of Dinosaurs). During this period, coelurosaurian predators, ornithischian herbivores (ornithopods, ceratopsians) and titanosaurid sauropod herbivores dominated ecosystems.

DERIVED: *See* Advanced.

DINOSAURS: The 'fearfully great reptiles', a subgroup of reptiles that dominated the Mesozoic world and evolved into modern birds.

DIPLODOCIDS: A subgroup of sauropod (long-necked) dinosaurs that includes ***Apatosaurus*** and ***Diplodocus***, which were common throughout the Jurassic Period.

DIVERSIFY: To evolve into a larger range of species.

DROMAEOSAURS: A subgroup of coelurosaurs (bird-like theropods), most of which were small- or medium-sized predators with enlarged claws on their feet; examples include ***Deinonychus*, *Dromaeosaurus*, *Microraptor*** and ***Velociraptor***.

ECOSYSTEM: All the biological and physical components that make up an environment.

ERA: *See* Period.

EVOLUTION: The change of plants and animals over time into new forms.

FOSSIL: A remnant of a plant or animal from a previous geological age.

GENERALIZED: Having a relatively simple body type without many distinctive weapons, crests, ornaments, or other features.

GENUS: A group of closely related species. For instance, 'Tyrannosaurus' is the genus name of the dinosaur species ***Tyrannosaurus rex***.

GONDWANA: A landmass that comprised modern-day Africa, South America, India, Australia and Madagascar. It split apart from the northern continents (Laurasia) during the break-up of the supercontinent known as Pangaea.

HABITAT: The natural home of a plant or animal.

HADROSAURS: The 'duck-billed dinosaurs', a subgroup of ornithopod (large plant-eating) dinosaurs characterized by hoof-like feet and a large beak at the front of the snout.

HERBIVORE: An animal that eats plants.

JURASSIC: The second period of the Mesozoic Era (the Age of Dinosaurs), during which large ceratosaur and tetanuran predators and sauropod herbivores dominated ecosystems.

LAURASIA: A large landmass that comprised modern-day North America, Europe and Asia. It split apart from the southern continents (Gondwana) during the break-up of Pangaea.

01027346210211628.83.9 01027346210273010638921O.948.63000116 28.83.9
010273462102730106389210.948.6300011628.83.9 0102734621027301063892 10

MESOZOIC ERA: The Age of Dinosaurs, an era of geological time subdivided into the Triassic, Jurassic and Cretaceous Periods, and ended with the extinction of all dinosaurs except for birds.

OMNIVORE: An animal that eats everything – both meat and plants.

ORNITHISCHIANS: The 'bird-hipped dinosaurs', one of the three major subgroups of the dinosaurs (along with theropods and sauropodomorphs), so named because part of the pelvis slants backwards, as in birds. This subgroup includes many plant-eating dinosaurs, such as the stegosaurs, ankylosaurs, ceratopsians and pachycephalosaurs.

ORNITHOPODS: A subgroup of ornithischians (bird-hipped) dinosaurs that ate plants and is divided into its own subgroups, such as *Iguanodon* and hadrosaurs.

PACHYCEPHALOSAURS: The 'domed dinosaurs', a subgroup of ornithischian (bird-hipped) dinosaurs characterized by an incredibly thick skull that is shaped like a rounded dome.

PALAEONTOLOGY: The scientific study of fossils and ancient life, including dinosaurs.

PANGAEA: A huge landmass comprising all the modern-day continents, which existed before the Age of Dinosaurs and began to break apart during the Triassic.

PERIOD: A span of geological time in the history of the Earth. Examples are the Triassic, Jurassic and Cretaceous: the three periods of the Age of Dinosaurs. Periods are subdivisions of eras, and can be further subdivided into epochs.

PREDATORS: Animals that hunt and eat other animals (meat-eaters).

PRIMITIVE: A feature or characteristic of an animal that is 'old-fashioned' and inherited from distant evolutionary ancestors.

PROSAUROPODS: A subgroup of sauropodomorphs that lived during the Triassic and Early Jurassic. They ate plants and are characterized by a mid-sized body with a long neck, small head with a beak, and may have walked on two or four legs.

PTEROSAURS: A subgroup of archosaurs, commonly known as pterodactyls, that was a major group of flying reptiles during the Age of Dinosaurs.

RAUISUCHIANS: A subgroup of archosaurs, closely related to crocodiles, which were large predators during the Triassic Period. Some resembled large meat-eating dinosaurs but are only distant cousins.

REPTILES: Vertebrate animals with scaly skin that lay eggs. Reptiles include crocodiles, snakes and dinosaurs. As birds evolved from dinosaurs, they are classified within the group Reptilia, even though they look very different.

SAUROPODS: The 'long-necked dinosaurs', a subgroup of sauropodomorphs, which arose during the Triassic and were the primary plant-eating dinosaurs during the Late Jurassic. They are characterized by a massive body with an extremely long neck and small head, and walk on four legs.

SPECIES: A group of living organisms that can breed together and reproduce offspring, but cannot breed with members of another species. For instance, '*rex*' is the species name of the dinosaur species *Tyrannosaurus rex*.

SPINOSAURIDS: A subgroup of tetanuran theropods characterized by a large sail on the back and possibly a fish-eating diet; examples include *Baryonyx*, *Irritator* and *Spinosaurus*.

STEGOSAURS: The 'plated dinosaurs', a subgroup of ornithischian (bird-hipped) dinosaurs, characterized by large plates that covered the back and massive spikes on the tail.

SUPERCONTINENT: A huge, ancient landmass, such as Pangaea, which eventually broke up into the smaller continents that we know today.

TETANURANS: A subgroup of theropods (meat-eating dinosaurs) with advanced features, such as a stiff tail and a hand reduced to three fingers; examples include *Allosaurus* and birds.

THERIZINOSAURS: A subgroup of coelurosaurs (bird-like theropods), characterized by a skull with a beak and teeth for eating plants, a large gut, enormous hand claws, and sturdy legs; an example is *Alxasaurus*.

THEROPODS: One of the three major subgroups of the dinosaurs (along with sauropodomorphs and ornithischians), which includes all the meat-eating dinosaurs. Subgroups of theropods include coelophysoids, ceratosaurs, tetanurans, coelurosaurs and birds.

TITANOSAURS: A subgroup of sauropod (long-necked) dinosaurs that includes *Argentinosaurus* and *Saltasaurus*, which were common in the Cretaceous Period and especially prevalent on Gondwana.

TRIASSIC: The first period of the Mesozoic Era (the Age of Dinosaurs), during which dinosaurs originated, diversified and spread across the globe.

TYRANNOSAUROIDS: A subgroup of coelurosaurs (bird-like theropods) that lived during the Jurassic and Cretaceous and includes monstrous carnivores, such as *Tyrannosaurus*.

VERTEBRATE: An animal with a backbone. The individual bones of the spine are called 'vertebrae'.

100

200

0273019210

948.63000116 28.83.9
273462102730106389210

INDEX

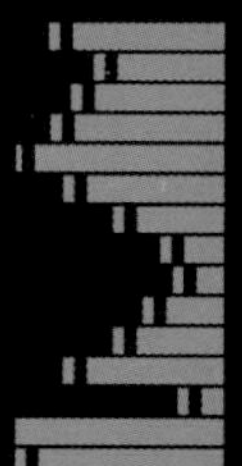

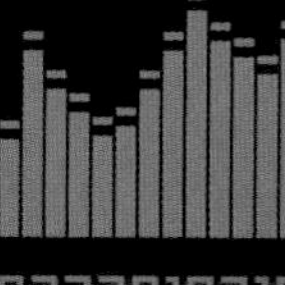
0273019210

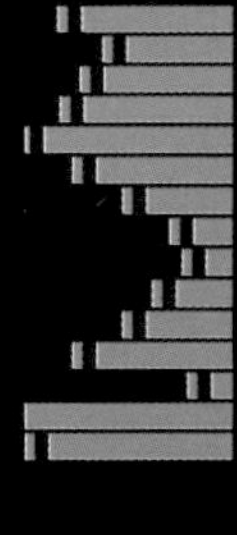

Quercus Publishing Plc
21 Bloomsbury Square
London
WC1A 2NS

First published in 2009

A catalogue record of this book is available from the British Library.

ISBN 13: 978 1 84916 006 3

Printed and bound in China

10 9 8 7 6 5 4 3 2

ARTWORK CREDITS
All artwork in this book has been supplied by Jon Hughes and Russell Gooday of Pixel-shack.com, except the habitat globes, which are © Quercus Publishing Plc.

ACKNOWLEDGEMENTS
Steve Brusatte would like to thank Richard Green from Quercus Publishing; his advisers Mark Norell, Mike Benton and Paul Sereno; his wife Anne; his parents Jim and Roxanne; and his brothers Mike and Chris.

Created for Quercus by Tall Tree Ltd
Managing Editor: David John
Editor: Patricia Burgess
Designer: Siân Williams

Tall Tree Ltd would like to thank Chris Bernstein for the index.